The
Cheshire
Village Book

THE VILLAGES OF BRITAIN SERIES

Other Counties in this series include:

Avon

Bedfordshire

Berkshire

Buckinghamshire

Cambridgeshire

Cleveland

Cumbria

Cornwall

Derbyshire

Devon

Dorset

Essex

Gloucestershire

Hampshire

Herefordshire

Hertfordshire

Kent

Lancashire

Leicestershire
& Rutland

Lincolnshire

Middlesex

Norfolk

Northamptonshire

Nottinghamshire

Oxfordshire

Powys Montgomeryshire

Shropshire

Somerset

Staffordshire

Suffolk

Surrey

East Sussex

West Sussex

Warwickshire

West Midlands

Wiltshire

Worcestershire

East Yorkshire

North Yorkshire

South & West Yorkshire

Most are published in conjunction with
County Federations of Women's Institutes

The Cheshire Village Book

Compiled by the Cheshire
Federation of Women's Institutes from notes
and illustrations sent by Institutes in the County

Published jointly by
Countryside Books, Newbury
and the CFWI, Chester

First Published 1990
© Cheshire Federation of Women's Institutes 1990
Reprinted 1993

Countryside Books
3 Catherine Road
Newbury, Berkshire

ISBN 1 85306 075 5

Cover Photograph taken from Beeston Castle
by Andy Williams

Produced through MRM Associates Ltd., Reading
Typeset by Acorn Bookwork, Salisbury, Wilts
Printed in England by J.W. Arrowsmith Ltd., Bristol

Welcome to Cheshire

Many people know Cheshire only by the hoary old joke of waiting for a train on Crewe station. Crewe is indeed one of the major junctions of the rail system but there is also a thriving county to explore. From the heights of the Pennines, across the rich agricultural pastures to the sandy shores of the Wirral peninsula there is much to discover here.

Cheshire is now famous for its dairy produce with its well known Cheshire cheese, but in earlier times it had been known as the bread basket of England – hence the three wheatsheaves on our County Shield.

The Romans realised its importance and since that time it has prospered. Deep underground lies its original source of wealth – salt – from which has sprung a successful chemical industry.

Our old silk towns should be visited and our historic villages with their extraordinary number of black and white timbered buildings are waiting to be admired.

Come and spend some time in the county of which we are so proud and learn a little more of the secrets of its charm.

Sylvia Batty
County Chairman

CHESHIRE

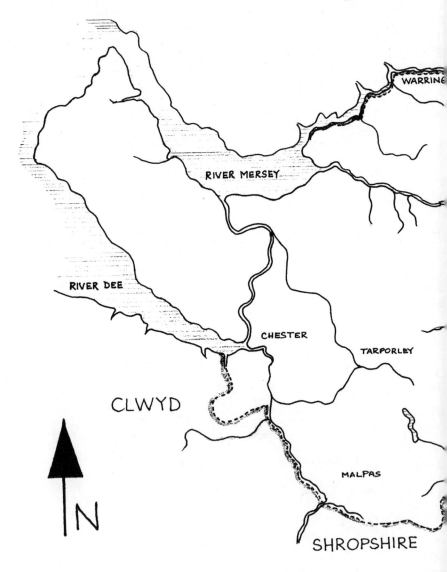

WARRING[TON]

RIVER MERSEY

RIVER DEE

CHESTER

TARPORLEY

CLWYD

MALPAS

N

SHROPSHIRE

Acknowledgements

The Cheshire Federation of Women's Institutes would like to thank all those who have made this book possible. We are most grateful for the hard work and research put in by members and Institutes who provided all the information about and drawings of our villages. We hope they enjoyed the challenge.

Special thanks to the members of the co-ordinating committee, Ann Brooks, Helen Carey and Jackie Woolsey.

Acton 🦌

Throughout the last four centuries Acton has been dominated by its seats of power – Dorfold Hall (1621) and Woodhey, a greater house standing, alas no more, at Burland. All that remains of the latter is a chapel erected in 1700 by Lady Wilbraham. Interesting features of it apart from its elaborate wooden carvings and high-backed pews, are its brickwork passages, 7 ft high. The remaining Dorfold Hall with its iron gates and majestic drive, is a delight to the motorist on the A534 Chester to Nantwich road. The Spanish chestnut tree in its grounds is thought to be the last tree remaining of Delamere Forest in this area – its age reputed to be 1,000 years.

As one approaches Acton village from any one of three directions, the sense of history is enhanced by the rise of the 800 year old tower of St Mary's. It is mother church to five others, including the pretty St Mary's in Nantwich, some two miles distant. Originally established by monks from Combermere Abbey in 1180, it was used as a safe house in the skirmishes with the Welsh. Its font, rescued from a farmyard, is decorated with a man and a hare-like animal, both reputed older than Domesday. Its figures of William Mainwaring, recumbent for 600 years, and Sir Richard Wilbraham in 17th century armour, lie within.

From here the siege of Nantwich was directed. In fact it was used as a garrison by the Royalists and fighting actually took place within the church. Some say that the turning point of the Civil War was the battle fought at Acton and Dorfold, on 25th January 1644. Women took part in the battle and 120 were taken prisoner. As a result of these troubles the vicar, Rev Lowe, is reputed to have buried the altar vessels for safety. His secret went with him to the grave and the vessels are yet undiscovered.

Days of battle are presumably ended and Acton's only apparent activity is that of cars passing through. Do not be deceived however. The parish hall, small and set back amid shrubs, is used by many. Between the church, the parish hall and the school, Acton remains busy – another centre of activity being the Goodwin Hall at Faddiley, with its regular car boot sales and annual events.

Though not on the present site, there has been a school at Acton since 1662. The one class then numbered 80, the vicar being the 'university man' appointed master. A local hero attended Acton school, Wallace Oakes GC, who died of injuries sustained during a railway disaster. Hundreds of lives were saved by his courage.

Acton village has a pub, the Star Inn, and until recently also had a shop and post office. Since it seems set for some small development, perhaps the latter will return to the village in the future.

Acton Bridge

On the face of it, the sleepy little village of Acton Bridge, once named Acton-in-Delamere, has not changed much during the last half century. But 'sleepy' is actually a deceptive adjective. In the late 1980s the villagers were engaged in enlarging and refurbishing the village hall and providing a car park, and in restoring the Methodist chapel, one of the two places of worship in the village, the other being Milton Baptist chapel.

The two waterways (river Weaver and Trent and Mersey Canal) are both used mainly for pleasure these days, as due to diminishing production capacity at ICI Winnington, there has been a reduction in the number of ocean-going vessels moving up and down stream. When the river overflowed during 1946 causing severe flooding, small boats were commandeered to rescue people living on the low-lying roads, ferrying them to the bottom of Acton Hill.

Looking down from the bridges over the canal at weekends, there is great activity in the marina, as boats return from weekly trips and are cleaned and fitted out ready to leave again in a few hours. The Acton Bridge Cruising Club on the river is very busy too, with the renovating and building of boats. Visitors using the waterways can find good eating houses here – The Rheingold, Maypole and Hazel Pear. The new bridge was built in 1932 and was the first swing bridge on a floating pontoon in the country.

Old industries which once thrived in Acton Bridge, such as the zinc factory, the sawmill, the flour mill and the salt-petre works have long since gone, and recently the petrol pumps have been removed from the forecourt of the garage, although the blacksmith's forge founded in 1968 is well patronised by the farming community.

The railway station still serves the village with approximately 350 trains passing through daily. Of these however, only 13 trains in each direction stop at the station.

Although there is now only the post office, which also sells groceries, there were once four shops in Acton Bridge and the Parker family had their own bakehouse, delivering fresh bread by horse and cart.

A beautiful residence along Acton Cliff, The White House, was built by Mr Herberts, living at Weaver Holt, for his son who married the vicar of Weaverham's daughter. Later it became the property of the Whitleys, the brewery family. Then it was sold to the Lyles of Tate & Lyle (sugar manufacturers). During this period the Aga Khan was often to be seen in the village as he was a relative of Mrs Lyle.

Two of the most attractive features of the village are the newly thatched cottage called Pepper Street (once known as Lane End Cottages, until it caught fire in 1953 and was rebuilt as one dwelling), and the renovated next-door barn with its circular windows and magnificent dry-stone walling.

The overall aspect is truly rural; the names of the roads such as Strawberry Lane, Orchard Avenue and Pear Tree Lane trip off the tongue; gardens are delightfully kept and a pleasure to view. Being situated in the centre of Cheshire, farming life is predominant, there being eleven farms intermingling with the cottages, houses and bungalows. Mr Greg, one of the fruit farmers, is the oldest surviving member of the family who owned Styal Mill, which he has lately handed over to the National Trust.

There are 24 public footpaths meandering through the village, enabling ramblers to enjoy the peacefulness of the countryside, and one such walk is along the river over Dutton Locks, passing under the imposing viaduct which carries the railway line. This structure consisting of 20 arches was built by Sir Joseph Locke in 1878.

Adlington 🌿

Travellers passing along the A523 between Macclesfield and Hazel Grove will look in vain for the 'village' of Adlington. Although they may notice the Legh Arms, a garage and the railway station, there is no sign of a village centre. Adlington is, in fact, what the historians call a 'dispersed' village and really consists of a series of mostly small hamlets widely scattered over something like 4,000 acres. Its population is probably round the 1,000 mark.

Centuries ago most of the area was wooded or rough country, although the Domesday Book's reference to Adlington's 21 acres of meadow was the highest such figure in the county. Over the years more and more land has been taken in from the waste and as field names in a map prepared by Adlington WI suggest, cultivation was for long carried

11

out in the old strip field system. Farming was mostly mixed but the coming of the railway in 1845 gave an impetus to dairying and soon saw the transport of large quantities of milk to more industrialised areas.

What may come as a surprise to visitors to the area is the fact that for a period of nearly 200 years coal mining was actively carried on. At first this was on a very small scale, but from the middle of the 18th century the lords of the manor, the Legh family, leased the coal-getting rights to various companies. For about 30 years from 1820 the Leghs themselves carried on the mining, with the opening of the Macclesfield Canal in 1831 giving the opportunity for easier transport and greater production. In its heyday mining employed more than 120 men and boys – more than the number in farming – and many of these workers came to the village from outside the area, attracted by the prospect of better pay. As a result the population grew to 1,159 in 1841 – the highest figure ever recorded. Only one or two women are recorded as having been employed in the mines but there were certainly many children. There was always plenty of other work for women – on the farms and smallholdings, as hand-loom weavers, or, from about the 1830s, in the cotton mills of Bollington.

For well over 600 years, since 1315, the Legh family have been very closely linked with the village and its activities. They owned most of the land and leased out many farms, laying down strict instructions about how the land should be farmed, specifying the amount of manure or marl – a kind of clay which was readily found in the area – that should be applied to the land. There were often restrictions on the quantity of potatoes that could be grown and it was laid down that all manure produced on the farms should be put back on the land.

The Legh records provide an excellent example of the working of the manorial system. The lord of the manor or his steward twice yearly presided over the Court Leet, at which attendance was compulsory for all the tenants on pain of fine. Here complaints about neglected footpaths, trespass, and the poor quality of ale, or failure to grind corn at the lord's mill, were heard by a jury of twelve. Under the manorial law many tenants were called on to keep a musket in good order in readiness for possible war service, and some had to keep spaniels or greyhounds for the lord's use when hunting.

Adlington Hall, home of the Leghs over the centuries, contains some splendid examples of Cheshire half-timbering and a stately Georgian wing built by Charles Legh in 1757. Hall and grounds are regularly open to the public.

Alderley Edge ✄

Alderley Edge is a small village and well-known Cheshire beauty spot, approximately 14 miles south of Manchester and 18 miles north of Crewe. Until the middle of the 19th century, it was called Chorley or Chorleigh, but later the name was changed to Alderley Edge. One notable exception is Chorley Hall (about half a mile from the village).

The village lies under the shadow of Castle Rock, a large projecting rock roughly 650 ft above sea level. Visitors come all year round to wander through the wood and enjoy the fine view of the Cheshire Plain from the Rock.

There are a number of caves, the result of tunnelling underground in search of copper. The entrance to these caves was approximately half a mile from Castle Rock and the sand extracted from the workings formed two large sandhills where years ago the village children could spend the day playing quite safely. Several unsuccessful attempts have been made to work the mines.

Two more caves are situated in an area of the woods known as Stormy Point. The entrance to one (known as the Devil's Grave) is narrow and legend says that if anyone walked round it seven times and repeated the Lord's Prayer backwards, the Devil would appear. The other cave has a large open entrance and again legend says it was once occupied by an army of 40 warriors and 40 white horses, who, should the country be plunged into war, would be there to defend us. Their leader was called the Wizard and a small hotel of that name is still there.

There were three hotels in the village, the Trafford Arms, the Queen's Hotel (now offices) and the Royal Oak, and a small inn originally called the Drum and Monkey. Again, legend decrees, should the country be involved in war – 'the Wizard would bring his army, the Queen's Hotel the Charter sign, the Oak would give the Royal Command and the Drum would beat the time!'

On the western side of the woods stood a beacon, erected before 1577. It was a square building containing an iron vessel used for storing pitch and tar. The beacon collapsed in a gale on Christmas Eve 1931 and has not been rebuilt.

When the railway came to Alderley, Manchester businessmen, chiefly cotton merchants, were persuaded by the railway company to build houses here. A number of very large houses were built, whose owners were rewarded by a silver medallion (worn by the gentlemen on their watch chains) entitling them to free first class travel to and from Manchester for a number of years. These families provided work for the poorer villagers, who were employed as servants, gardeners, coachmen and butlers.

There are three churches – Anglican (St Philip's), Methodist and Roman Catholic, all of which have fine steeples.

The main street, London Road, is part of the A34. It has wide pavements with trees planted at intervals, a big asset at Christmastime when local tradespeople decorate the village with lights.

Years ago the village had its own fire station. The engine was horse-drawn and when fires occurred a 'buzzer' sounded, and men would rush from work to catch the horses grazing in a nearby field. This caused great excitement and people would go to the scene of the fire on their bicycles.

The ambulance station has gone but a cottage hospital was donated by a former resident for the benefit of the people of Alderley. There is a Temperance Hall (village institute), originally a resting post for people travelling by coach. The village has a good county library but has been reduced to a sub post office in a shop.

Aldersey ✤

The village is surrounded by brooks, on the banks of which alders grow. The termination 'ey' in Aldersey is an old Saxon word meaning island, hence Aldersey means an island of alders. The family of Aldersey takes its name from the village, the first of the family being Hugh, who lived here in the 13th century. In 1594 Thomas Aldersey, a citizen and haberdasher of London, founded the Aldersey grammar school in Bunbury.

In one of the meadows there is a brine spring of sufficient strength to leave an occasional incrustation on the banks, but salt has not been extracted there for many years.

The road leading from Aldersey to Chowley is called 'Dog Lane'. Some say that from its many bends it is like a dog's leg – but a general belief is that it is haunted by the Dogs of Odin. Their presence was felt by one Joe Price who, when he was a young man (at the end of the 19th century) was walking down the lane and heard them behind him. He was so 'frit' that he never stopped running until he was safely within his own house. During the Civil War it was the scene of many a combat and a cannonball was found lodged in one of the many very old oak trees that stand nearby.

Aldford 🦋

Aldford, situated some five miles south of Chester, is one of a cluster of villages, including Eccleston and Saighton, which make up the larger part of the Eaton estate, the seat of the Dukes of Westminster. Traditionally the village housed the artisans and skilled workers essential to the life of the estate.

Aldford derives its name from the Roman ford (part of Watling Street) which crosses the river Dee a half a mile from the village. The ford is no longer visible in normal conditions due to the building of the weir in Chester, which raised the level of the river, but when the water is very low one can see the outline of the ford from the Iron Bridge which crosses the Dee at the same point.

Aldford is a compact village, circular in shape, and divided by a central road. Some 78 houses go to make up the village, which is served by a shop-cum-post office, a pub (the Grosvenor Arms) and the church of St John the Baptist. Although there has been a church on the present site for many years, the building in use today celebrated its centenary in 1966, and indeed almost the whole of the village was rebuilt by the second Marquess of Westminster in the mid-Victorian period. The architect responsible for the design of the church, and many of the houses, with their characteristic barley-sugar twist chimney stacks and fine shaped windows was John Douglas (1829–1911) and his strong influence is to be seen in other parts of Chester and its surrounds.

Aldford is also of some historical importance. The site of the 12th century castle, located immediately behind the church, is a most fascinating historical monument, a reminder of our ancestors in the Middle Ages. The village stocks are also still to be seen, though their position in a wall by the roadside is unlikely to have been their original location.

Well into the 20th century, each cottager had one and sometimes two cows. Each cottage, within its outbuildings, had accommodation for the cow, pigs and hens; and with the addition of a large garden, was very nearly self-sufficient. Fields were set aside for the grazing of the cottagers' cows, and for the making of hay. Other land was made available by the Eaton estate for the cultivation of root crops, corn for the animals and potatoes for the family, each plot being marked by boulders.

Harvesting was a communal effort, the hay first and then the corn. No cottager owned a horse and cart, so the local farmer came to the rescue, sometimes lending his 'man' to do the mowing; and to ensure a quick harvest, most neighbours gave a hand. The cottagers' corn was stored in the barn in the centre of the village. How did each man know he was getting his correct amount of grain during the threshing? Quite simple, after he had carted his acre or so of corn, and placed it in the barn, he would cover it with paper on which he had written his name, then his neighbour placed his on top and covered his, and so the process continued until all was safely gathered in.

Since those days most of the small farms have gone. As each tenant farmer died, the farm was not re-let, but absorbed into the Eaton Home Farm complex. Farmhouses and their outbuildings, the old smithy and the school, whose closure in 1982 meant considerable change in the village, all had to have new uses, and Aldford has sucessfully attracted a variety of small businesses which have made sure of continuing activity, while keeping the visual harmony of the village.

Alpraham & Calveley

Alpraham and Calveley are adjoining villages on the main A51 road, about six miles from Nantwich.

There used to be two chapels in Alpraham, the Wesleyan Methodist and the Primitive Methodist, but both have now been demolished and the only relic connected with the Wesleys is at the Moat House Farm. It was here in the 18th century, in the orchard under a pear tree, that the Wesley preachers assembled. The original tree fell during a gale but another one has been planted and this bears a commemorative plaque.

The two public houses remain: the Traveller's Rest with its delightful bowling green and the Tollemache Arms, a charming black and white building named after the Tollemache family, who until the 1950s, owned a lot of property in the neighbourhood.

The Cheshire point-to-point now seems to have found a permanent home at The Rookery Farm.

The Alpraham and Calveley reading room was erected in about 1882 with money raised by public subscription, and serves the purpose of 'village hall'. A playing field stands at the side of the village store, on land acquired from the Tollemache family. There is also a sub post office/shop in the village.

The Shropshire Union Canal borders the village and along the tow path leading back towards Nantwich the ruins of the old brickworks can be seen.

The public house in Calveley is called the Davenport Arms, and is near to the site of the old Calveley station. The United Dairies works has been demolished and the site is in the process of being made into a housing estate.

Calveley now literally looks to the stars because on a concrete slab which was once the floor of a hangar stands a huge radio telescope. In 1941 (during the Second World War) an airfield was built by Peter Lind Ltd. It was planned as a fighter station but was relegated to training. The runways have now been broken up and the buildings are used for light industry.

Calveley Hall, where Squire Davenport was reputed to have entertained John Wesley in 1749, was demolished towards the end of the 18th century. The second Hall was demolished in the 1950s. It was for a time the home of Earl Grosvenor, who became the first Duke of Westminster.

Antrobus ✍

The village lies off the A559 Warrington/Northwich road. People named Antrobus take their name from the village, which is the only one so called in England and appears in the Domesday Book as Enterbus or Entrebus – 'between the thickets'. Foggs Lane is thought to be an old Roman road, although this has not been proved.

In spite of this, Antrobus is of more modern times. The church, the Church of England school and the Methodist chapel were all built in the 19th century, also the majority of the houses. The oldest is of cruck construction, known as Broom Cottage. The newest developments are eight bungalows for the elderly and a new estate of 31 houses and bungalows built on the site of an old orchard.

The earliest place of worship and the most interesting historically is the Friends' Meeting House, Sevenoaks, Frandley. George Fox is reputed to have preached under an oak tree nearby, one of seven, all of which have now died.

Many present day parishioners remember Major Arnold Boyd, the great Cheshire naturalist who lived in the village, well known for his natural history books of the area. Major Boyd also helped to revive the soul caking play which is still performed every year on or near All Souls' Day in nearby inns etc, although in earlier decades they went from house to house performing the old verses. The horse's head used is over 100 years old.

The local pub used to be an old coaching inn, known as the Wheatsheaf, but since the 1970s it has been completely modernised and renamed the Antrobus Arms, where darts and pool teams regularly play neighbouring rivals.

An area of land was set aside in 1854 for 'Allotments for the Labouring Poor', administered by the Parish Council. In the 1980s this land was sold and the money invested by the new Antrobus Relief in Need Charity, using the interest to help present day residents, either individually or in groups.

In days gone by the population consisted mainly of farmers and those connected with agriculture, such as Irishmen who came for seasonal work, wheelwrights, shoemakers and blacksmiths, as well as a mole catcher and a gamekeeper, who always found a fox for the Hunt (but some thought he kept one in a bag for the occasion!). In 1831 the poulation was 481 and in 1989 it was over 1,000. In 1956 there were 44 farms, today many of these are private residences with two or three acres of land used as horse paddocks and the farms that are left, 27 only, are mainly family run.

Friends Meeting House, Antrobus

The names of fields, woods etc are fascinating and intriguing – Grandsire's Green, Cobblers Gorse, Shutterduck Meadow, Hades' Nook, Tinklers Field, The Folly, Newalls Rough, Bang'em Lane (now Occupation Road), Gypsy Field, the Pleasure Ground.

Appleton Thorn

Appleton Thorn, in the Domesday Book as Epletune, is the village central to a wide area known as Appleton. In 1178 the landowner was Adam de Dutton, an ancestor of the Egerton Warburton family of Arley. It was he who set up Appleton Cross, the steps of which still remain, and brought and planted the original thorn tree which gave the village its name.

The tree was said to have been an offshot of the Glastonbury thorn which grew from the staff of Joseph of Arimathea. This is thought to be the only place in England where the 'Bawming of the Thorn' still takes place, always in the middle of June. The tree is decorated with flowers and ribbons and children dance round it in the style of a maypole chanting verses to the tune of *Bonnie Dundee*, each followed by the chorus:

> 'Up with fresh garlands this midsummer morn,
> Up with red ribbons on Appleton Thorn.
> Come lasses and lads to the Thorn Tree today
> To bawm it and shout as ye bawm it "Hurray"!'

The ceremony had not been performed since 1933 until its revival in 1973, apart from an occasion in 1967 when the present tree was planted.

As in most villages the church dominates the scene, St Cross being a towered building of simple design provided by Mr Roland Egerton-Warburton in 1886. The old village school stands close by, now a much used community hall. The new school not far away, which opened on 5th October 1970, now has a much larger intake due to the increase in property building in the village, the most recent of which features large Georgian-style homes.

Much traffic now passes through the village as the road links the M56 and M6 motorways to the large industrial estate established on the site of the war-time naval airfield, then known as HMS Black Cap. Also on this site but within the village, opposite the school, stands the prison, first opened in November 1960 as an open prison for mild offenders and now,

19

following an £8,000,000 rebuilding scheme, known as Thorn Cross Youth Custody Centre. Integration with the village has been good and it is possible to hold events within its walls.

There are thatched cottages in Chapel Lane and Pepper Street and the post office alongside the prison gates has a Dickensian appearance. The 'Lily Pits', a local beauty spot, has been rejuvenated helped by the 'Bird Man' of the village to whom the police and RSPCA turn when in difficulties with animals and birds.

At the present time, but now unhappily in danger from building development, the main local industry surrounding the village is farming. This is mainly dairy, catering for neighbouring industrial and residential markets with milk, potatoes, pigs, poultry and eggs. Crops include grass for silage, kale and turnips for forage, with oats, wheat and barley for bedding and fodder. Soil is sandy marl, usually heavy. One specialist farm (TV Seeds) produces seeds much used in the area and abroad. Nearby is another industry – the Langley London Tile Co producing ceramics.

The Appleton Thorn Potato Exchange was established here in the early 1930s. Farmers brought their produce and merchants came from Wigan and other areas to agree a price. In 1940 this exchange was officially stopped by the Ministry but farmers still met three times a week to agree a price and continued to do so until the 1980s, when it finally ceased. The land opposite the thorn was then sold and the money invested to provide a scholarship for research into potato husbandry.

The Thorn Inn is the village pub, situated at the crossroads by the thorn tree, the cross and the church and is, as ever, a centre of village activity.

Ashley

Ashley is a small village on the north-eastern border of Cheshire, adjoining Greater Manchester. It covers an area of approximately 2,173 acres and is crossed north to south by the Altrincham to Mobberley road and east to west by the Wilmslow to Knutsford road. On the west border is the popular tourist attraction, Tatton Park and on the east border is Manchester airport. In 1971, the M56 motorway cut through Ashley, just north of the village centre.

All essential services for village life are contained in the village centre –

the church, school, pub, post office, cricket club, garage and police house.

The church of St Elizabeth was built in 1880 for £4,000 by Lord Egerton of Tatton, who had bought the Ashley estate in 1841. The first vicar was the Rev Geoffrey Birtwell. In 1986 the parish of Ashley amalgamated with St Peter's in Hale. Each year, a Rose Queen festival and garden party is held in mid-May to boost church funds and is the one event of the year when the whole village takes part.

The pub called the Greyhound, situated at the central crossroads of the village, is a popular place in an attractive country setting. At the end of the 18th century the building was a farmhouse, and on becoming an inn, it was initially called the Orrell Arms, after Robert Orrell of Arden House. After becoming part of the Tatton estate in 1841, the pub was renamed the Greyhound, after Lord Egerton's favourite dog.

Village horizons were greatly widened in 1841 with the coming of the railway and Ashley station. Apart from enabling people to travel, it opened up markets for the sale of farm produce and brought supplies direct to the village. An average of 50 tons of coal a week were used in the furnaces of Tatton estate. Today, although trains stop for passengers, there is no stationmaster and no ticket office. Fares are paid at the destination.

Ashley Smithy Garage is also sited at the crossroads and as its name suggests, was originally the village smithy. Mr William Ellison came to the smithy in 1887 and had a thriving business shoeing the local horses, later turning to farm machinery repairs. After 1957, Mr Ellison's daughter and her husband saw the future lay with the motor industry. A company was formed, a petrol pump installed and the garage progressed to the busy filling station and car showroom it is today, with Mr Ellison's daughter still involved.

There are approximately 115 residences within the village, ten of which are still working farms, equally divided between dairying and arable farming. The oldest house is Ashley Hall, built in 1492 by Hamon de Mascy, which then came into the Dutton family, who took the name Ashley after their village.

Ashley has a very interesting old tithe barn situated at Coppice Farm. It is a cruck barn with heavy, weathered oak boarding which remains in fairly good condition.

Although the land is mostly level, along the border with Greater Manchester runs the river Bollin and the Bollin valley. This area contains some scenic footpaths and popular beauty spots, and is managed by the Bollin Valley Project. At the eastern end of the village at Castle Mill,

21

between 1932 and 1975, was an open air swimming pool which attracted many people from miles around on hot summer days. A large house has been built on the site since the pool was closed.

Ashton

Ashton, including the hamlet of Horton-cum-Peel, lies on the outskirts of Delamere Forest and eight miles from the historic city of Chester.

Ashton brook flows between the village of Ashton and Mouldsworth, and is peaty in colour due to the nature of the land through which it passes. Pentre brook, culverted many years ago, passes close by the medieval kiln unearthed in 1933 in the garden of the house known as the 'Forge'. This site was chosen by the medieval potters as water, clay and timber were near at hand. Jugs and pots now pieced together are stored in the Grosvenor Museum, Chester and the British Museum, London.

Agriculture has been the main occupation for many years, and three farms are still within the compass of the village. There are three conservation areas, two of which contain a Grade II listed building, namely Ashton Hall and April Cottage. In Horton-cum-Peel stands Peel Hall. Built in 1637, it is the third to have stood on the site. Originally it may be presumed to have been moated and fortified against incursion from the Welsh.

In the 1840s the village was given a church and school by its benefactor William Atkinson, residing at that time at Ashton Hayes. William Atkinson was a Yorkshireman, born in Knaresborough, and a textile manufacturer. On leaving Ashton he went to live in Southport, Lancashire, and donated and built Southport's free library and art gallery.

There was in 1845 a Wesleyan chapel, now a house, and in 1846 a Primitive Methodist chapel was built. A service is still held there each Sunday.

Robert Charlton Parr, an incumbent of Ashton Hayes, paid for a water supply to be brought to the village at the beginning of the 20th century.

In the past there used to be a baker, pie maker, tailor and saddler, and blacksmith. Times change, but Ashton today is alive and well. The parish room, owned by the Parish Council, is in the West End conservation area, and the old school is now the village hall. There are about twelve organisations, well supported in the village, and involving people of all ages. A private nursery has been opened, and attracts customers from surrounding villages and also provides employment. There is one general shop, a post office, and an attractive country pub, the Golden Lion.

Astbury 🐿

The village of Astbury lies two and a half miles south-west of the Cheshire town of Congleton. Evidence of a Roman settlement lies in the discovery over 200 years ago of the remains of a Roman camp, and the even earlier history of the village can be traced back to the Bronze Age, strikingly illustrated by the site of a cremation and burial ground. A further remarkable discovery was that of a dug-out canoe found in the bed of a stream in the village in the 1920s.

The triangular village green, daffodil-covered in spring, and surrounded by picturesque cottages, is crowned by the ancient parish church of St Mary and provides one of the most photographed scenes in Cheshire. A fine Queen Anne rectory, village hall, the Church of England school for 100 children, built in 1843, with a village store, post office and inn and small groups of houses and farms complete the village scene.

The parish of Astbury lies on the edge of the Cheshire Plain, rising from the village through farmland and woodland to the moorland ridge recognised as an extremity of the Pennine range, leading to Mow Cop, the 'Cradle of Methodism' and the boundary with Staffordshire. The 1,000 ft high ridge commands admired views westwards over the Cheshire Plain to the distant Welsh hills and eastwards to the Staffordshire and Derbyshire moors.

Astbury's Gothic church, with its unusual feature of a detached tower and steeple, dates back to the 14th century. Its origins lie in the original church mentioned in the Domesday Book. A further link in the history of the village is provided by the 1,000 year old yew tree in the churchyard, its leafy branches spreading above the shell of its hollow trunk.

Astbury is a farming parish of some 500 souls but in common with modern trends only a small number are now engaged in agriculture. With a long tradition of dairy farming, cattle breeding has gained increasing importance in recent years and the standard achieved is reflected in the successful prize-winning herd at Glebe Farm in the village.

The parish has never lacked 'characters', amongst them a past resident who claimed to have the longest beard which, at a length of 11 ft, he is reputed to have hung over an apple bough to dry after washing! Not only human but animal records emerge, amongst them one from the year 1774 of what is claimed to be the heaviest pig ever recorded. Clearly an imposing animal, it is recorded as standing 4 ft 8 inches high, 9 ft 8 inches in length and weighing-in at 12 cwt.

Some ancient customs with origins in pagan times are happily still observed, including the May Day festival and a Wakes at harvest time. Sadly other customs which long survived have lapsed in recent years, amongst them bell-ringing linked to Shrove Tuesday celebrations, rush-bearing ceremonies and the once nightly curfew.

Aston 🐝

The village of Aston, on the outskirts of Nantwich, has seen many changes, but it is still dominated by farming and the mill. Aston House Farm, built in 1667, is one of the oldest farmhouses in the area and is owned by Mr Fred Pass, a member of the largest family in the village. Yew Tree House, built in 1645, is even older.

The focal point of the village is the Methodist chapel built in 1865, now officially known as St Andrew's. This has been renovated into a modern chapel with a community room upstairs. The cemetery opposite, opened in 1921 by Mr Geof Pass, the grandfather of the present Pass family, has many an interesting secret to hide, being, along with the village ford, the local courting spot in the village!

The Bhurtpore Inn, another meeting place also recently modernised, was named after one of the battles in which Field Viscount Combermere fought in India. It was the regular inn for the local farm workers, but now attracts people from far and wide.

The Sumner family, whose direct descendants still live locally, had a great influence on the village. The mill built in the 19th century and owned by the Sumner family for many years is now part of the Dalgetty group and provides much employment in the area. Their family home is now the offices of the mill. They owned the cricket club, which is still thriving after 80 years, but the tennis club with its snooker room has now gone, as have many other amenities in the village.

The first shop, again owned by the Sumners, was in the present mill yard for many years. Later the shop was housed in a hut at The Croft's before its closure in the 1970s. There was quite naturally a bakehouse at the mill. Job Stokes, the local baker for many years was also the milkman. Eventually the business moved to Crewe, but Aston still has a bread delivery round. Mr Walter Hockenhull was the local butcher, but on the site of his shop is a bungalow. Another loss! The local coal merchant's, owned by Mr Borton and his family, ironically burned down.

In the days of the horse and cart Aston had a saddler's shop opposite the chapel and a blacksmith's shop in Sandy Lane. The blacksmith was kept busy in the First World War shoeing horses for the Yeomanry. The family from Highfield House supplied the horses, and incidentally trained a Grand National winner – *Tipperary Tim*.

Huntbach's of Hanley built the four workhouses in Sheppenhall Lane and ran the village bus to Hanley, so people could shop in their Emporium.

Mr Dodd, the son of the ex-postmaster, who received a long service medal from the Post Office, still lives in the village. He tells a humorous tale about Billy Lumbas, a local character who never left his house, which was full of cobwebs and smoke and who shot at anyone who approached. Once during an election, which was the event of the year (no television then!), he erected boards around his property covered in Conservative posters. Mr Dodd's father and a friend re-pasted them with Liberal posters. While they were at the Bhurtpore the next day, a holiday, he shot at them! On this same day Nantwich Town Band, followed by a Mrs Cook from the Salamanca Inn of the neighbouring village, played a death march through the village because the Liberals had lost. Mr Dodd threw an old tin bath over the band leader's head and Mrs Cook, in her pony and trap, had to go home as she was so upset!

The village has grown to three times its size since the 1940s. At least 50 new houses were built on Sheppenhall Grove and many houses and bungalows have been built in Wrenbury Road between the pub and the chapel. Aston now has many commuters to Crewe and Nantwich and even further afield. The village may not have any shops now, but it has a garage, a hairdressing salon, a pottery and many social activities.

Aston juxta Mondrum 🌿

Aston juxta Mondrum is a scattered hamlet consisting of just over 1,200 acres, mostly dairy farming. The name derives from the Old English East-tun, and the ancient forest of Mondrum. The centre of Cheshire at the time of the Domesday Book was covered by the forests of Mara (Delamere) and Mondrum and there were few settlements.

In April 1913 King George V and Queen Mary visited Worleston Dairy Institute, which was situated in Aston Juxta Mondrum. It is now Aston Hall Farm. The Dairy Institute closed in 1926, being transferred to the Cheshire College of Agriculture at Reaseheath.

Perhaps the oldest building is Brayne Hall (Brayne's Weir), now a farm. There is evidence of a 13th century mill there, on the river Weaver. It was the seat of the Brayne family from the time of King John until the beginning of the 19th century.

The church and school, although situated in Aston juxta Mondrum, are both referred to as Worleston church and school. Indeed the parish is St Oswald's Worleston.

The main sewage treatment works for the borough of Crewe and Nantwich is situated in Aston juxta Mondrum. Ironically all the houses in Aston juxta Mondrum are on septic tank sewerage!

Farming still dominates as the source of employment within the hamlet but it is rapidly becoming a dormitory village.

The Shropshire Union Canal crosses the hamlet, and is now very busy with holiday cruisers. The Crewe–Chester–Holyhead railway line also crosses the hamlet, but unfortunately there is now no station.

Audlem

Audlem, the most southerly township in Cheshire, is noted in the Domesday Book as Aldelime, deriving from Alda, a personal name, and lyme, a forest. The parish includes the ancient coaching and market town of Audlem and also the townships of Buerton and Hankelow.

Audlem has long since ceased to function as a market town and today, although still in the centre of a thriving farming area, it is home to a growing number of commuters.

The Shropshire Union Canal, once used to carry the local cheese to Liverpool and Birmingham, now carries upwards of 60,000 visitors through the village each summer and the old canal warehouse on the wharf is now a public house catering for the needs of those who have worked through the 15 locks which bring the canal from Shropshire down to the Cheshire Plain! The old mill, also on the wharf, is now a gift shop, but great care has been taken to retain the appearance of the building in its working life. The Bridge Inn had stabling for the canal horses in the 'Shroppie's' heyday and Mr Hopkins, the landlord, who died in 1988, told of how his wife used to take the horses' collars as surety for the stabling fee, as it was not unknown for their owners to slip off without paying.

The church of St James the Great was built in 1278 and dominates the centre of Audlem from its position on a large mound. The old butter cross stands below by the church steps and beside it is the bear stone, a large granite boulder which still shows where the ring was attached to which bears were tied for baiting at the local Wakes.

The free grammar school, now an old people's home, was built in 1655 with money raised locally, to teach classics and English grammar to boys. It ended its educational life as a secondary modern school in the late 1960s. Geoffrey Whitney, an Elizabethan poet and author of *Choice of Emblemes*, was born at nearby Coole Pilate. One of his emblems is dedicated 'to the youth at the school of Audlem in England'. The school he refers to pre-dated the grammar school.

In the centre of the square in Audlem is an ornamental lamp erected by the people of the town in memory of Richard Baker Bellyse, who served the inhabitants as surgeon for 40 years until his death in 1877. Dr Bellyse was the grandson of one of Audlem's 'characters', also Dr Bellyse, born in 1738 and king of Cheshire's cock-fighting fraternity. He would have a hundred cocks ready for Chester Mains, which were fought in a pit at Soutars Lane.

Hankelow, a mile from Audlem on the road to Nantwich, has lost both school and post office in recent years but it is nevertheless a lively community, keeping the green with its pond and ducks as an attractive centrepiece. Near the green is the Ball Farm built in 1510, once owned by Richard Hassall who was Justice of Chester in 1540.

Hankelow mill stands in a very quiet and beautiful part of the Weaver valley where there has been a mill for over 300 years. It was said that a widow's curse hung over the mill and certainly in the 19th century there were three fires and a wall fell in. The mill is now a private house.

Barnston ❧

Barnston appears in the Domesday Book as Bernestone, then held by William Fitz-Nigel, second Baron of Halton.

Barnston used to be part of the parish of Woodchurch. There is a board in Woodchurch church recording that 'James Goodyker of Barnston in the parish of Woodchurch died in the Year of our Lord 1525, left 20 Marks to buy 20 Yoke of Bullocks, which were afterwards, by order of the Commissioners of Pious Uses, converted into Cows and given to the poor of the said Parish'.

Barnston's Christ church is of recent origin, 1871. The first person to be buried in the churchyard was a small girl called Amy Pickering Thomas who had watched the consecration of the churchyard from her bedroom window at Bank House Farm. She died four weeks later at the age of two years and eight months.

The buildings in the village which surround the now enclosed green are of the 18th and 19th centuries. A cobbled lane leads from the green to the rear of the churchyard and some of the cottages there are much older. Behind the church are earthworks which are the remains of the earlier village.

In Barnston Dale is a very ancient watercourse, the Ayne, which eventually joins the Fender. There is said to have been a watermill here. A Richard of Barnston, miller, is recorded in 1376. There is also a well which was in use until just before the First World War.

On the excavated sandstone at the side of the road as it drops into the Dale there is a mark in the form of an arrow-head which records the height of the flood on 19th September 1875. It was Harvest Festival and Evensong was in progress when a violent thunderstorm occurred. The wooden bridge in the Dale was swept away and the congregation had to take the long way home. At Heswall church the organist was killed by lightning.

The public house, the Fox and Hounds which dates from the 16th century is in the Dale. Its previous names have been The Flag, The Hen and Chickens and The Black Horse. Further down the road at the bottom of the Dale are two cottages, one of which was previously occupied by a wheelwright.

By the bus stop in the village there used to be a granite boulder (probably of glacial origin) known as the 'Barn Stone'. It was wrongly thought by some people that it was from this stone that the village derived its name. It was removed in 1948 as it was said to be an obstruction but was returned by public demand to a safer position outside Beech Farm.

Part of Bank Farm was a tollgate cottage with gates onto a turnpike road. Houses in Storeton Lane preserve the names of the fields in which they were built – The Longcroft, The Woodcroft and The Aynecroft.

Today the land use is predominantly agricultural with five farms, four of which are owned by the Leverhulme estate, but the population is predominantly composed of urban commuters.

Barrow 🦔

The parish consists of Great and Little Barrow with the hamlets of Broomhill, Stamford Bridge and the areas of Long Green and Hollowmore Heath, and lies between two main highways about four miles from the centre of Chester city. Although there has been some new building and much refurbishment since the 1950s, Barrow has mercifully escaped the large-scale development of many local villages and still retains its rural peaceful air. In former times most of the population were engaged in agriculture, but though there are more than 15 working farms in the parish and some light industry, many of the occupants now travel to work in Chester or the industrial areas of Merseyside. In the 1981 census the population was around 900 with 309 households.

The village lies on and around a low sandstone hill lying north to south. Many parts of the parish have magnificent views over the surrounding countryside – particularly towards Helsby Hill in the east and Beeston and Peckforton in the south-east. The bedrock gives rise to the most typical feature of Barrow – the lanes cut through the rock and the many sandstone walls. Many of the older properties have foundations (and cellars) of sandstone, though the typical building material is brick.

Stamford Bridge (formerly Stone Ford) was an important ford on the river Gowy in prehistoric times and the Romans used this crossing when they constructed Watling Street – the route of which still forms the southern boundary of the village.

By 1291 there was a church at Barrow and there is a complete list of rectors from 1313. The position of the church, on the southernmost part of Barrow Hill, gives it an attractive site. The church was extensively remodelled and refurbished in the 1880s and today contains many items of the Victorian era.

There are many villagers who talk of life in the 1930s when a trip to Chester was quite an expedition and the village fetes and Sunday school outings were special times. Shopping for most items was done in the village shops – there were two or three in the village as well as those at Broomhill and Little Barrow. Nowadays there is just one general store and post office in the whole village.

Barrow has always been a farming community, formerly famous for its milk and potatoes, much of the milk being taken to Manchester on the 'Milk Train' from Barrow station, closed since 1953. Nowadays there are fewer herds and although much of the land is used for arable crops, a

Barrow village centre

recent feature has been the number of nurseries becoming established in the parish.

Many of the older houses in the village were or still are farms. Most date from the 17th and 18th centuries and several houses contain beams which are said to have come from ships broken up in the Dee shipbreakers' yards. One notable house is the Old Rectory. The present house dates from about 1744 though it has been altered over the years. One rector in Victorian times had twelve children and not surprisingly decided to add an extra three bedrooms.

Barrowmore Hall was built in 1879/81 for Hugh Lyle Smyth of Liverpool. It was an impressive residence designed by John Douglas, the noted Chester church architect, with landscaped gardens containing specimen and unusual trees which still thrive. In 1920 it became the East Lancashire Tuberculosis Colony, which developed into Barrowmore Village Settlement – providing work, homes, rehabilitation and training for disabled people. The sanatorium based in the former Barrowmore Hall was completely destroyed by a landmine in 1940 with the deaths of 32 patients and staff. In 1947 the NHS acquired the hospital premises and it became Barrowmore Hospital, which only closed in the last few years. The Village Settlement continues to be a thriving community and many of the redundant hospital buildings are now let to small industrial and business users.

Barthomley ૠ

Little is known of Barthomley before late Saxon and early Norman times. Formerly the church was the centre of a parish of considerable area and included Barthomley, Balterley, Crewe (Crewe Green), Alsager and Haslington. Now only the two former 'townships' remain.

Older residents can recall some customs of the past. For instance, from Michaelmas to Lady Day the curfew was rung at eight o'clock and the 'Pancake Bell' on Shrove Tuesday, which was significantly known locally as 'Guttit' Tuesday (Good Tide Tuesday). Also, daily at one o'clock a bell was rung to summon the farm workers back to their work. This custom ended at the beginning of the Second World War.

Christmas plays were performed until about the middle of the 19th century. These usually took place in farmhouse kitchens and the players were rewarded with ale and good food. Another custom was for the cottage women to go round begging corn. Farmers usually gave a quart of wheat to each woman and from this was made the Christmas 'batch'.

'The Old Rectory' as it is known today, was once 'The Hall'. It was originally a large three-storeyed house built in Georgian style. Some years ago the top storey was removed, making it more manageable. Doing this ended the traditional ghost story of the spirit of Randle Crewe, which at the witching hour of night visited the top storey, walking the passages clanking chains.

There is a legend that the last wolf killed in England was actually caught in a wood in Barthomley, hence 'Wulvarn', the name of the brook running through the village.

The church, St Bertoline's, has been called the 'Church of the Massacre', in consequence of a tragic occurrence in the Civil War. A number of villagers led, it has been said, by the son of the rector, who had fired on the Royalist army advancing from Nantwich, escaped to the church tower for refuge. They were smoked out and twelve of them massacred. It may be a significant fact that the parish register of this date has been mutilated.

The attractive White Lion Inn near the church must surely be one of the most quaint in Cheshire. It is a black and white thatched building dating from the 16th century. According to old records, it was previously the home of the parish clerk and was not used as an inn until the latter part of the 19th century. Prior to this the village inn was the Punchbowl, sometimes known as the 'Steps'. According to old prints it was built into the church wall. It was taken down in 1867 and the site absorbed into the churchyard, and no traces now remain.

On entering the village from the Crewe road, there is a row of three black and white thatched cottages, known as Fir Tree Cottages. They were originally one house, a longhouse of the Welsh type to which a gable end was added.

Old Hall Farm house, nearby, is a typical Cheshire magpie farmhouse dating from the 17th century. Now there is little of the original fabric remaining. Two other half-timbered farm houses are equally picturesque. These are Cherry Tree and Mill Farm. Both are similar in design, dating from about 1600. Although they have been modernised internally, in outward appearance they still retain some of the original features.

Farms in the parish are mainly part of an estate once owned by Lord Crewe and acquired by the Duchy of Lancaster in 1937. During the past 20 years smaller farms have been amalgamated with larger ones and farmhouses and buildings sold. According to their years of tenancy, one or two tenants and their wives are invited to a garden party at Buckingham Palace where they are presented to the Queen. A truly memorable occasion.

Beeston 🦋

The village of Beeston is dominated by the castle, which is situated on a pyramid-shaped crag, with magnificent views of the surrounding countryside. It was originally occupied by the Romans and in the 13th century it became a key point among the border strongholds.

The castle has a 360 ft deep well. It was in this well that Richard II's treasure, valued at 20,000 marks, is reputed to have been stored, before it was surrendered to Henry Bolinbroke. Later, during the Civil War, the castle was used for storing arms and for safe keeping of the local gentry's valuables.

In 1959 the castle was taken over by the Ministry of Works, now the Department of the Environment, and some restoration has been carried out. It is a popular place for families to visit and the Bunbury church fête is held there every August Bank Holiday.

The village itself has some 300 residents and it is bordered on one side by the main A49 road from Warrington to Whitchurch. Apart from some private houses and many cottages, the land which comprises seven farms is owned by the Tollemache family. Interesting places include Beeston Towers, a pseudo-Tudor mansion, the Wild Boar Hotel, the Beeston Castle Hotel, the two chapels (no churches), the Image House, the railway and the Roman bath.

Dr Barbara Moore, a Russian lady married to a Londoner, stayed the night at Beeston Towers in 1959, in the course of her walk from John o' Groats to Lands End, and almost a century earlier two brothers, Robert and John Naylor who lived at Beeston Towers were probably the first to do the same walk.

The Image House is an old cottage, so named because of the images of faces on the front of the cottage. It has a legend of having been built in a night in the days when if a man could 'fashion a dwelling and have smoke coming out of the chimney by the morning', he could call it his own.

Beeston station was used regularly by the local residents until it was closed in the 1970s. The land was originally sold to the railway by the then Lord Tollemache and the trains only stopped there by request.

Present day interest in the village is maintained by a thriving cattle market held each Wednesday and Friday and a lively and colourful general market every Bank Holiday Monday to which people travel from miles around.

The first Outdoor Education Centre in Cheshire was opened at Beeston, close to the castle, in 1970.

Blakenhall 🌿

The village of Blakenhall is situated on the Cheshire/Staffordshire border and is mentioned in the Domesday Book. It was ravaged during the Civil War, when troops were quartered in the area. Until 1917 Blakenhall was part of the Doddington estate.

Nathaniel Turner, the famous missionary, had family connections with Blakenhall. One of his most successful missions was to the island of Tonga where he converted the entire population to Methodism, including the Royal Family.

There is evidence that a school existed in the late 19th century. Blakenhall appears to have been an important centre in the area in previous centuries, as manorial courts were held here.

33

On the fringe of Blakenhall lies Doddington Old Mill which was active until 1925. The millstone was French Bun from the banks of the Seine. The roof tiles were hand made at Madeley Heath. The same site was used as a furnace by Sir Thomas Delves, where the hammers and anvils were cast, and in 1667 the forge's output of pig iron was 500 tons. By 1892 it was a coin mill and the occupant was Joseph Edwards.

Bollington 🦜

The original settlement of Bollington comprised Lowerhouse, Bollington Cross and Kerridge to the east, with its quarries and stonemasons, and there is evidence of a pre-industrial, working community. It was not until the opening of the Lowerhouse Mill by Samuel Greg, son of the owner of the now well-known Quarry Bank Mill at Styal, that the development of Bollington started along the narrow valley to the north-east.

The opening of the canal in 1831, and the coming of the railway in 1870 made it possible for an increase in every aspect of the trade development, and the hamlets of Bollington Cross, Lowerhouse and Kerridge joined into the industrial town which is still called a village to this day. In 1848 Slaters' Lancashire and Cheshire Directory recorded Bollington as 'A thriving village with some collieries and extensive cotton factories.' In the first half of the 19th century the population increased from 1,200 to just over 4,600.

Meanwhile Kerridge continued with its quarrying, as it is still doing with some distinction. The cathedral at Coventry is paved with Kerridge stone.

The damp climate and soft water suited the spinning of the finest quality Egyptian cotton, and for many years the best Liberty cottons were woven in Bollington.

This prosperity continued happily, helped by the fact that for some reason Bollington avoided the influx of the unfortunate inmates of workhouses from the south, and the mill workers were local folk. World conditions in the years following the Second World War have changed things to a great extent, and the splendid mills are either closed or divided into premises for new concerns.

The interest in vernacular architecture and the fashion of gentrifying old cottages, combined with the ease of transport nowadays has brought a new era to Bollington.

Leisure activities of all kinds are organised by an energetic group of the

Groundwork Trust, and the locality is becoming almost a tourist area.

Situated at the foothills of the adjacent Peak District, and with the good fortune to have beautiful views from almost every dwelling and street corner, Bollington has many attractions. The stone cottages are built to withstand the climate – fierce winds sweeping over the Derbyshire Peaks and early snow on the heights of Kerridge.

Bosley 🐝

Mentioned in the Domesday Book as Boselega, Bosley is a small but somewhat scattered village with a population of approximately 350, nestling at the foot of the Pennines and five miles south of Macclesfield. Lying on the verge of the county and separated from Staffordshire by the river Dane, it is mostly a sheep and dairy farming district. The Cloud, which is actually in Staffordshire, dominates the village and is the penultimate peak of the Pennine chain.

Bosley Works, which is a large sprawling establishment at the foot of the Cloud, was originally built on the orders of Charles Roe as a copper rolling and hammering works, together with 19 cottages for the workers. With the help of James Brindley, he harnessed the power of the river Dane. The works were later converted into two cotton mills and around 1860 they were occupied by three corn millers and a silk throwster, but from the early 1920s to the present time it has been and still is a very busy wood flour treatment works employing around 120 people.

The church of St Mary is a small edifice with nave and chancel and is built of brick, except the tower which is of stone, low and embattled, and which belonged to a former church built around 1300. This was destroyed by fire and was rebuilt in 1777. The tower contains six bells, the first having been installed in 1756 before the fire. When the church was rebuilt the font went missing and was not seen again for 70 years, when it turned up in a local farmyard where it had been used as a pig trough. It was returned to its rightful place in 1848.

The Methodist church in Tunstall Road was built in 1885 and replaced the Wesleyan chapel which had stood at Bosley Works since 1832.

Higher up from the chapel is Key Green Farm where recent alterations uncovered old beams, wattle walls and a fireplace with the date 1610 and the initials RB and IB engraved in the sandstone. These are reputed to be the initials of members of the Broster family, who originally came to Bosley after crossing from France with William the Conqueror. Their name in those days was Brostirre, and descendants of the family still reside elsewhere in the village.

Bosley reservoir, built by Messrs Tredwell in 1832, is a fine stretch of water covering upwards of 120 acres. It supports abundant wildlife and was built as a feeder to the Macclesfield Canal, which was engineered by Thomas Telford and which opened in 1831. Canal users are only too familiar with the twelve locks which have to be traversed on this stretch of the canal.

Unfortunately the Bosley Sports are no longer held, the last sports day being in August 1982, but the tug-of-war team is still going strong having had recent successes both at home and abroad. The village also still holds its annual Rose Queen festival, usually on the third Saturday in June when all the villagers turn out together with neighbouring Rose Queens, to give their support, a custom which has been maintained since the 1950s.

Bostock 🌿

The village of Bostock, present population approximately 110, is situated on the Middlewich/Northwich road and villagers have always claimed Bostock to be the centre of the county. There has been an oak tree on the village green for many generations to mark the exact spot – the present tree was planted by Canon Thomas France-Hayhurst and Col C. H. France-Hayhurst in 1887, the Golden Jubilee year of Queen Victoria's reign.

The village has a long history. The Domesday Book records Bostock as being held by Osmer, a Saxon, whose family later took the name of Bostock and lived here for generations. The present Hall was built in 1775, and Thomas Hayhurst, later known as France-Hayhurst, bought the Hall and estate. The stone used to build the wall surrounding the hall came from the old Danebridge church, Northwich, which was demolished because of structural damage due to subsidence.

Bostock parish consists of estate farms and cottages for the estate workers. These buildings are constructed of red brick and have attractive black and white gables. The distinctive red bricks were made from clay extracted on the site and fired in a kiln situated in what is still known as Brick Kiln Lane.

Records show that in 1824 there were five cottages belonging to the overseer of the poor, housing families dependent upon parish relief.

In 1905 the estate laundry was built on the village green, in which was done the washing from the Hall. Reading rooms for the estate workers were housed in a pleasant building facing the green. Times change, and the laundry is now the village hall, frequently used by the community. The reading rooms became a social club for the estate employees and in recent years membership has been extended to include people living outside the village.

Bostock is a small but active community. In the early part of the 20th century land was given to the villagers by Col W. H. France-Hayhurst to provide a bowling green, tennis courts and sports pavilion with a grass play area, and these facilities are still well used.

There is no church at Bostock but until the 1920s the rector of Davenham held services in the village reading rooms. There is a public footpath across the fields from Bostock to Davenham church – no doubt used by countless churchgoers over the centuries. There are no shops in Bostock, so the villagers have to travel to the adjoining villages to do their shopping. However, facing the village green is the attractive work-shop of the village 'blacksmith', now known as an agricultural engineer.

The principal occupation of the villagers today is still farming, and the estate of approximately 2,000 acres is still in the ownership of the France-Hayhurst family. Since 1976 the village has been designated a conservation area – even the two mile posts are listed as protected 'buildings'.

Brereton ✿

The village which centres around Brereton Hall and the church of St Oswald, on the banks of the river Croco, lies in a fertile agricultural area, with natural resources which have greatly influenced its development. Although the finding of a box of Roman coins near Brindley Moors Farm in 1820, and the Anglo-Saxon derivation of the actual name, suggests that a settlement existed prior to the Norman Conquest, no recorded mention exists of the 'manor of Bretune' until the Domesday Book.

The existing Hall, a Grade I listed building which is approached through the lodge gates built in 1800, was constructed during the reign of Elizabeth I by Sir William Brereton. The Hall was eventually sold in the 1940s and converted into a day and boarding school for girls.

The adjacent church dedicated to St Oswald dates from the 15th century and has a square tower with five bells, rung from the ground floor. It is believed that one of the Breretons who had fought in the Crusades pledged to build the church in gratitude for a safe return.

Evidence of the village's continued importance to travellers is the Bear's Head, a black and white 'magpie' coaching inn, dated 1615. It carries as its sign the head of a muzzled bear, which was the traditional emblem of the Brereton family. Legend has it that Sir William was interrupted, while dining, by his valet, and in his anger pursued and subsequently murdered him. In remorse Sir William travelled to London to crave pardon from the King. He was detained in the Tower of London, his life being spared on condition that he designed an effective muzzle for a bear! When confronted by the bear, the creature was successfully muzzled, Sir William was duly pardoned and the muzzled bear's head became the family emblem.

Across the years the Bear's Head has been the focal point of village social life. Prior to the sale of the estate it was the meeting place for tenant farmers to pay their rents on Lady Day and Michaelmas, or engage in a game of bowls. Demand now dictates the need for motel accommodation, which the Bear's Head provides, and the village school, founded in the early 19th century has increasingly become the venue for village activities.

Leisure provisions have become increasingly important to Brereton. Packhorse days are long past but equestrian pursuits are extremely popular and the annual gymkhana at Brown Edge provides competition and stimulation for participants. Where water once provided power for Brereton mill and for agriculture, it is now proving to be a leisure attraction. An area of estate land which was unproductive and remained as heath and woodland, was transformed with the discovery of pure silica sand in 1959. The topsoil removed, the quarrying proceeded for more than ten years providing sand for industry, glassmaking and cosmetics. Then after it had lain dormant until 1981, the Borough Council purchased the land and the Country Park was created.

Bridgemere ❦

In medieval times Bridgemere boasted a bloomery or iron foundry. Included in this district are the hamlets of Doddington and Hunsterson. There is no village in the accepted sense but a scattering of farms, houses and cottages and typical Cheshire scenery of open fields, woods and copses.

Doddington Castle, near Bridgemere

On the Doddington estate in the midst of farmland stands a red sandstone castle, the remains of the crenellated manor house built in 1364 by Sir John Delves. The Delves family, or as it later became Delves Broughton, has retained some of the estate and lived here continuously ever since.

A short drive, known as Wilbraham's Walk, through the main lodge gates passing one side of the lake, brings one to Doddington Hall. This house, built between 1777 and 1797 to the design of Samuel Wyatt, in the English Renaissance style, is of grey Portland stone. A magnificent sweep of stone steps, reputed to be the work of Adam, leads to the main entrance. After many years as a girls boarding school, the Hall sadly stands empty, but the lake of 52 acres is rented by the Nantwich and Borders Counties Yacht Club and the pool is a rich source of fish for local anglers.

During the 18th century the banqueting hall was built on an island in the middle of the lake in keeping with the architecture of the Hall. In 1813 it was pulled down and the island submerged.

Some of the stones were used in the building of St John's church, Doddington – a chapel of ease – in 1837. The church, standing in park land, was built by General Sir John Delves Broughton, who is interred in the vault.

A tragic murder took place in the Chapel Field, Hunsterson on the night of 28th June 1835, when an elderly married man, Thomas Baggu-ley, strangled 15 year old Mary Malpas, throwing her body into Chapel Pool. Later he committed suicide in the stables of Doddington Cottage, where he had been employed. There are those who believe he haunts the stables still. A stone over Mary's grave was raised by public subscription and on it was engraved a dramatic verse describing the murder:

> Lone was the place and dark the midnight hour
> Which gave sweet Mary to the ruffian's power
> Steadfast in faith and strong in virtue's might
> She fell a martyr on that awful night
> Now safe from sin and harm she rests secure
> Among the blessed who in heaven are pure.

A few hundred yards from the school stands Bridgemere Hall and farm, which until 1989 had been in the Noden family for over 130 years. In 1972 Joe Noden, who had always had an interest in waterfowl and conservation, landscaped 30 acres and developed what has become known as Bridgemere Wildlife Park.

Bridgemere Garden World was created in 1961, when John Ravenscroft with two assistants began what has become a 25 acre display of fascinating plants and gardens. Indoors is Europe's largest collection of house plants, a restaurant and well stocked shop. Over 140 people, many local, are employed in the growing areas and the centre itself.

Brimstage 🦎

Brimstage's village hall is known locally as 'The Red Cat', because it was built on the original pub site of that name. This was a stopping place on the way to Chester from the priory of St Mary, Tranmere, where the monks ferried folk across the Mersey.

Brimstage is really a hamlet as it has neither church, school nor public house. Nearby Brimstage Hall was built in the 14th century, complete with crypt, priest's hole and watch tower. This latter was used as a 'lookout'. The old barn buildings surrounding the original cobbled yard have been converted to various small but thriving businesses – a wrought iron expert, a delicatessen, an Egyptian market, an art gallery, and Voirey Embroidery.

Bromborough 🦎

As you pass along the busy A41 or stop at Bromborough railway station, you might not be aware that the village of Bromborough has a focal centre and connections with the Ice Age. Indeed, the oldest object in the village is a large granite stone at the entrance to the church car park, known as the 'Big Stone'. The stone is totally alien in nature to this sandstone area and is thought to have been brought down the Dibbin gorge by a glacier during the Ice Age.

There has been a religious settlement here since Saxon times, when King Alfred's daughter Ethelfleda had a monastery built here and had it defended.

Around the outskirts of the area winds the Dibbin valley. It is a protected, ancient woodland laid out as a nature trail. Along the path through the forest a petrifying well can be found, as well as one of the springs, St Chad's. Most of this area was a favourite Royal hunting ground and the local crest depicts the Wirral horn, a hunting horn.

Bromborough has earned its living in many ways, from quarrying and the shipment of stone to seafaring and business enterprises too numerous to mention. Alongside these there has always been a rural community.

In the centre of the village stands a large sandstone cross, situated at the head of a road called 'The Rake' (a Norse word). It was the centre point for the market and the striking of bargains. This road is thought to have been a very ancient link with outlying villages.

When Edward I stayed at the now non-existent courthouse on his way to supervise the building of Flint castle, he rewarded the villagers by granting them a market charter. They have revived this tradition and hold a three day Victorian fair on St Barnabas' Eve on 9th June.

The present day church is a lovely 19th century building in sandstone, with fine vaults and a collection of tapestry kneelers, each one in its owner's place and depicting personal or historical connections with the church.

In front of the church stands the old schoolhouse, where you can always have a coffee and gossip. On the edge of the village stands Stanhope House, a lovely Tudor building, which has carved panels from Chillingham Castle in Northumberland.

The compact shopping area is bordered by pleasant tree-lined roads, progressing to a more rural scene and culminating in a beautiful spot called Raby Mere, which is attractive in every season.

The work today is a mix of technology, business and the traditional light industries. Because of the proximity to the sea, there are many seafaring families and consequently some of the present villagers work great distances away.

Broxton & Bickerton 🌿

The Sandstone Trail winds its way across the Broxton and Bickerton hills, and walkers can look down into the villages and away across the Cheshire Plain.

The Maiden Castle site is visible, a stronghold of another era on the Broxton hill, while King James' Parlour, the cave reputed to have sheltered the monarch and his horse, is in the woods by the rebuilt Broxton Hall.

Many cottages have been modernised, and new dwellings erected in both villages. One bungalow is to be featured in the new Domesday Book as an example of 1980s architecture. Farmhouses and their buildings have been converted into private dwellings, the farmlands divided between neighbouring farms.

Friesian Holstein cattle are the predominant breed in this dairy farming area, this industry gives work to many and attendant skills are put to good use. Several racing and breeding stables and other equine interests flourish around the foot of the hills.

The second Methodist chapel, erected in 1913, stands at the head of the Brown Knowl village, a fitting memorial to John Wedgwood of Potteries fame, who brought Methodism to the area in 1822, and was finally laid to rest there as was his wish.

Holy Trinity church, Bickerton, nestles between the two hills, set within its own walled churchyard and adjacent to the lovely vicarage, making it a focal point for the village since 1840. The Church of England primary school was built in 1844.

The copper mine chimney stands tall against the hillside, a reminder of activities in bygone days; the tools and mining equipment on display in the Copper Mine public house are fascinating to see.

Rawhead, the highest point on Bickerton hill, is the scene of game shoots, the pheasants roaming and nesting on the rocky terrain, with trees, bracken and gorse giving ideal cover for the birds. The Bickerton Poacher public house is a venue for the walkers, providing refreshment and entertainment, the indoor well reminding them of the abundance of water in the area.

Millions of gallons from Lake Vynwy are tested and boosted on their way to Liverpool at the Bickerton pumping station: the two other pumps draw water from underground sources, pipe it onto the hill top, from where the natural flow takes the water into Staffordshire.

Buerton 🌿

In the 1851 Gazeteer of Cheshire, Buerton is described as a small village and township in the Nantwich Hundred. It has changed little since and forms the south-eastern boundary of the county, bordering Shropshire and Staffordshire.

Although the village is geographically extensive, the centre is really a small hamlet straddling the A525 Woore to Whitchurch road.

It now has only one place of worship, an Independent chapel built in 1885, on land begged from a local landowner as a result of a dream!

At the centre of the village stands the school. It has a rather ecclesiastical appearance, which is not surprising since it was originally a Band of Hope lecture hall. It still has its original windows but some of the amber glass was removed to improve the natural lighting for the pupils. The village war memorial is situated on the front of the school, where can also be seen a 'Bench' mark. Two old oak trees in the playing fields are the subject of a preservation order.

Opposite to the school is a house which for many years was the village shop, but further back in time was an inn called the Coach and Horses. Nearby stands Buerton Old House, probably more than 300 years old and now authentically restored by its present owner; its distance back from the road suggests that it was a landowner's house and that its first owner, John Twemlow, was a man of substance.

Buerton House, another medieval building cloaked in Edwardian brickwork, was originally known as Tythe Barn Farm and portions of the long timbered barn still survive.

On high ground by Hankelow Lane stands the large brick tower of Buerton windmill. The wheels are of the 'clasp arm' type invented early in the 13th century and the mill bears the date 1779. Although it is a listed building, it is now in a dilapidated condition. It was last used in 1880 and was then virtually intact. It has been adopted by the pupils of the school as their emblem.

In the past, Buerton gained notoriety for encouraging cockfighting, but for many years now it has been well known for the farmhouse cheese still produced here. With the addition of some new houses, it has become a pleasant hamlet in which to live and work.

Bunbury 🐝

The old Saxon settlement surrounded an early church of the 8th century, dedicated to St Boniface. Sir Hugh de Calveley, renowned for his fighting in France and Spain, instigated the 14th century re-modelling of the church and established it as a collegiate church.

Sir Ralph Egerton was Standard Bearer to Henry VIII and in 1527, he built a chantry chapel onto the south chancel of the church; also a chantry house nearby, for two priests who were to pray for his soul. The box-framed chantry house, now beautifully restored and privately owned, played an important part in the life of the village for over 300 years.

Following the suppression of chantries by Henry VIII, it came into the

Cottage at Bunbury

possession of Thomas Aldersey, a wealthy merchant from Spurstow, who in 1594, obtained letters patent from Queen Elizabeth to establish a free grammar school for boys in the field next to the house, which then became a home for the headmaster, and also boarders.

Before he died, Thomas vested the school and house in the Worshipful Company of Haberdashers of which he was a member. In 1874, the school was demolished and a new one was built, but to this day, although now County Council-maintained and a mixed primary school, it is still owned by the Haberdashers' Company. On Deputation Day, the Master, wearing his robes, and accompanied by other members of the Haberdashers, visits the school, to be presented with a bottle of port and anchovies, by two pupils each wearing the silver badge of the Company.

Only a few black and white houses remain. Because the village lay in the flight path of German bombers turned back by the barrage around Crewe, it was bombed several times. In 1940, a row of cottages was demolished and the church severely damaged by a landmine. Its roof, windows and half of one side were blown out.

A small timber-framed building opposite the church served as a

45

meeting place for a group of Puritans, which later became the first Methodist Society in Cheshire.

In the village centre is the red brick cottage, Brantwood, c 1831, once the old lock-up. The cell now forms the entrance hall.

Bunbury 'Wakes' originated centuries ago from the patronal festival of St Boniface. An old handbill of June 1808, states: 'Wanted, a person to conduct performances at Bunbury Wake, on 20th, 21st and 22nd instant. It is necessary that he should have a complete knowledge of pony and donkey racing: wheelbarrow, bag, cock and pigeon racing; archery, single-stick, quoits, cricket, football, cocking, wrestling, bull and badger baiting, dog fighting, goose riding, bumble puppy etc.' What could the 'etc' have been?

There are about 1,400 residents today, in contrast to 884 in 1881, when the village was entirely self-supporting and agriculture was more labour intensive. All the trades and professions were well represented, including two surgeons, a vet, a registrar of births and deaths for Bunbury district, a relieving officer, a cooper and coffin maker and various shopkeepers. In the 1920s there were 14 shops, two banks, a doctor and a visiting dentist. Today, only eight shops remain and the last bank has now closed down, but there is a splendid medical centre and pharmacy, with three local doctors.

Burleydam 🐚

The village, which was originally called Burledam, is situated on the Cheshire/Shropshire border, and it has been said that the real Burleydam consists of one house near the centre of the village. This stands between two brooks, the Burley and the Walkmill, both of which eventually join the river Weaver.

The church was built in 1769 by Sir Lynch Cotton and until 1869 it was the private chapel of Combermere Abbey. It then became the parish church. The Rev Thomas Meredyth was appointed the first vicar, having previously been private chaplain to Lord Combermere. The beautiful stained glass windows include an exquisite children's window in the children's corner, presented by Lady Crossley.

The school and the post office have now sadly closed, but it is well remembered that the doctor, who came from Wrenbury, would hold a surgery in the back room of the post office shop at Burleydam on Tuesdays and Fridays. The postman who travelled from Whitchurch on horseback would put his horse up at the Combermere Arms and stay there himself all day until it was time to return to Whitchurch with the evening post.

Combermere Abbey stands on the site of an old monastery, originally founded by Baron Hugh de Malbanc, of Nantwich, in 1133. It has been said that after the Dissolution of the Monasteries, the abbey bells were removed and taken to Wrenbury and are still there. Another version of the story is that the bells were thrown into the mere, a lake covering 132 acres and the largest in any private park in England.

The Combermere Arms is 450 years old and has solid oak doors and beautiful panelling. This well known hostelry is said to have been haunted by a ghost, but two clergymen persuaded it to enter into a bottle, which is buried under the entrance step. If this is ever broken the spirit will be released!

Burleydam Races were an annual event during the 19th century, comprising a varied three-day programme. The rules stated 'All disputes to be settled by the Stewards, whose decisions will be final'. The Race Ball was held on the third night at the Combermere Arms as a conclusion to the racing festivities, dancing starting at 8 pm.

With excellent agricultural land, dairy farming is an important occupation in the area and there is also Burleydam Nurseries, situated in the village, where many fine chrysanthemums are grown. A pleasing sight in the spring is provided by 'a host of golden daffodils' planted by the Women's Institute.

Burton-in-Wirral

Burton, a tun or settlement near a defended place (probably the Iron Age promontory fort just outside the village), is considered to be one of the most picturesque villages in Wirral. Certainly it is one of the friendliest and a joy to live in.

The Domesday Book says 'there is a priest', but does not mention a church, which is not unusual. The church, dedicated to St Nicholas (the patron saint of sailors, because Burton was the port of Chester from about 1200 to 1500) was rebuilt in 1721 after the medieval church had fallen into disrepair. There was a Norman church and it is thought that there was an even earlier one, but it is not possible to be certain.

Thomas Wilson was born in the village in 1663. He later became the Bishop of Sodor and Man and founded a school in 1724 'for the free education of Burton boys and girls and four from Puddington' (the next village about a mile away, in the same parish and sharing the same church).

For about 750 years Burton had an absentee landlord, who was the Bishop of Coventry and Lichfield, but in 1806 Richard Congreve became the first resident lord of the manor. In 1902 the estate passed to new owners and Henry Neville Gladstone became the new lord of the manor. He was the third son of the Prime Minister and he laid a sewer down the village street and later presented us with our village hall, known to this day as the 'GVH' (Gladstone Village Hall). In 1924 the manor estate of Burton was sold, not to a new lord of the manor, as believed by Mr Gladstone, but to a firm of estate agents, who sold off the land piecemeal as 'prime building land', thus ending forever a village way of life that began over a thousand years ago.

For about 500 years before this, the village had seen little change. The population and number of houses had hardly altered and almost every inhabitant had been connected in some way with the seven village farms. Now, there are only two working farms and the population has increased by almost 400% with a similar increase in the number of houses. Of course, the land is still there, but with modern farming techniques the small medieval farms have been swallowed up by larger farms, the hedges and boundaries grubbed up and little now remains of the 18th century landscape. Several residents earn their living by horticulture now, rather than agriculture.

The Gladstone manor house is now a residential college of adult education, where day, weekend or week-long courses are held. This gracious house is not an old building, having been built in 1806 and extensively altered in the early 1900s, but there are several picturesque cottages 500 years old or so, which help to make Burton so attractive and photogenic. This old world charm and feeling of tranquillity has been preserved, now that the village has been declared a conservation area. Just outside the village on Burton Hill are the remains of an old peg-mill built by the Massey family in 1629 and on the edge of the marsh on the Dee estuary are the even older remains of an ancient 'hospice', mentioned in a deed of 1293.

Burtonwood 🌿

Burtonwood is situated near the M6 and M62 between St Helens and Warrington. It is a village with tree-lined roads, the trees having been supplied by T. Forshaw of Burtonwood Brewery fame and planted by the schoolchildren.

Although a small community depending on agriculture, the village had its own blacksmith and wheelwright's shop for centuries. The trade register shows that watchmaking, machinery and claypiping also played an important part.

In 1867 James Forshaw purchased the land on which the Burtonwood Brewery now stands, the trade then supplying free houses, farmers, and private landowners with small 4½ gallon casks known as 'Tommy Thumpers', delivered by their own horse and dray. The site was chosen because of its adequate supply of spring water. In 1880 James Forshaw died and the business was passed to Richard Forshaw and his aunt. Richard married in 1887 and was survived by four children. During the miners' strike of 1893, Richard provided free bread and potatoes to hungry families. After the death of his father in 1930, Tom Forshaw continued the family business, gaining respect and admiration from employees and locals, being a knowledgeable farmer as well as a brewer. There was a Royal visit by Princess Margaret in 1987 to officially open the new kegging plant, marking the half stage of a £6 million expansion, including a new brewhouse.

Bradley Old Hall is one of the oldest buildings in Burtonwood, the original Hall having been built in the 14th century. Now a farmhouse, built in the 17th century from the remains of the Old Hall, the only access is through the archway, crossing the moat which surrounds the house. The arch is a striking feature with remains of a small chapel still to be seen.

The legends of secret passages and ghosts at the Hall are well known locally, enhanced by the Oaken Bed in the King's Room, a 7 ft long four-poster with measurements roughly carved in Roman figures. It is said that Richard, Duke of Gloucester, slept in it on his way to repel the Scots in Lancashire. Today, a pleasant corner of Burtonwood, the farm still survives the bustle of modern living, with rolling fields and traditional hedges all around.

Coal mining played a great part in the lives of the families in the village from as far back as the 17th century, and in records dating back to 1697 in the chapel register, a Moses Shaw was buried and described as a 'collier kild in pit'. Many of the collieries functioned until 1984, but then began to close down and only two local pits remain open locally. The head gears are gone, with the coal tips now being landscaped.

Connections with America were formed when the local airfield was taken over by the American Air Force in 1942. The base is now used as a vast store house, being the largest depot in Europe, and still retains an active and thriving community, but now where the mighty bombers rolled down the runways, a new housing estate thrives and the M62 runs through it.

Burwardsley ❧

Burwardsley is a sandstone hamlet nestling on the west side of the Peckforton Hills, 300 to 400 ft above sea level, in south-west Cheshire. There are magnificent views to the Welsh hills to the west and over the Cheshire Plain to Frodsham and Helsby to the east. On a clear day it is possible to see Liverpool Cathedral, some 25 miles away.

It is a rural community and most of the farms and houses are owned by the nearby Bolesworth Estate Company, belonging to and administered by the Barbour family, who were originally in the cotton industry in Manchester. The number of inhabitants on the electoral register is in the region of 190. Their everyday needs are supplied by the one and only local shop and post office: this property also belongs to the Bolesworth Estate Co. The population is a mixed one – the older inhabitants being members of families who have lived here for generations.

Many walkers join the Sandstone Trail in Upper Burwardsley: this is a walk of some 30 miles from Beacon Hill, Frodsham, south to Grindley Brook locks on the Shropshire border. Refreshment is available at the beautifully situated local hostelry, the Pheasant Inn, originally the Carden Arms, built in the 17th century. The more recent craft centre known as Cheshire Workshops produces hand-carved candles which are sent all over the world.

An attractive landmark of the area is a house set against the hillside one mile south-west of the village, with its gable end connected by a Gothic arcade to a barn which has a large cross-shaped arrow slit. It has now been derelict for many years.

The main building of interest is St John's church. The discovery of a parcel of old documents in a wooden shed in the churchyard enabled a local schoolmaster, Frank Whitworth, to research the church's history in 1983. There was a chapel in Burwardsley before the Reformation. In 1730 a church was built on the present site, but it was not consecrated until 1735 when it was dedicated to St John the Divine. The reason for this long delay was a dispute concerning an attempt to separate Burwardsley from the Bunbury chapelries. As a chapelry of Bunbury, tithes were paid to the patrons, the Worshipful Company of Haberdashers. A large tithe map of Burwardsley shows the various properties, each with a number. It would appear that tithes could be paid in kind at the rate of wheat 7s 9½d a bushel, barley 3s 11½d and oats 2s 9d.

Byley-cum-Yatehouse 🌿

Byley was first known as Biurley, named after Warren de Biurley who once owned an estate at Ravenscroft. The village lies three miles north of Middlewich and six miles south of Knutsford. It is bordered to the south by the river Dane and to the west by the Trent and Mersey Canal. It is a scattered area taking in the hamlets of Croxton, Ravenscroft, Yatehouse, Sublach and Leese and has a population of about 350.

Byley is mainly an agricultural village – at one time the menfolk were mainly employed on the farms but as farming became more mechanised less farm hands were required and today the majority seek employment in Northwich, Middlewich, Holmes Chapel or at nearby Cranage Hall hospital.

In the reign of Edward III the monks of Birkenhead owned an estate in the area and claimed manorial rights to use some of the houses as religious houses. With the Dissolution of the Monasteries the land was purchased from the Crown by Sir Geoffrey Shakerley. In 1846 Sir Walter Shakerley, a descendant of Sir Geoffrey, gave a plot of land to the village for the purpose of building a church; in 1847 the church was dedicated as St John the Evangelist, Byley-cum-Leese. In 1932 a church hall was built on land adjoining the church. It still stands today and is the centre for all village activities. The village school was built in 1874 and remains very much in use.

Ravenscroft Hall was built in 1837. The last family to live there were the Kays, but after the death of John Kay, who had no descendants, it was sold and became a girls boarding school. Cranage Hall was once owned by the Carver family, but it is now a hospital for the mentally handicapped.

In the centre of the village on the main road stands the smithy. It was started over 200 years ago by Daniel Clark and is entering its seventh generation of family blacksmiths. Horse-shoeing was once the bread and butter of the blacksmith but since the coming of the tractor he has had to adopt new ways. Walking into the smithy is like turning the clock back 100 years. The small workshop is crammed with scores of hand-made tools and a giant pair of bellows are a reminder of how the forge was pumped by hand. Today the family earn their living with welding, wrought iron work and repairing agricultural machinery. The post office and garage are situated opposite, but the Victorian pillar box remains attached to the smithy.

In 1939 the Ministry of Defence commandeered three farms, demolished the houses and buildings and built an airfield. Cranage airfield was used for the training of air crew and later used for night fighter Squadron 96. Several airmen lost their lives while flying from the base and their bodies rest in the churchyard. Wellington bombers were assembled in hangars built adjacent to the airfield – the hangars still remain and are used by light industries, which brings more traffic to once quiet roads.

Legend has it that a villager, Billy Henshaw, was driving his trap along a lane when the wheel came off and he was flung over the hedge into a pit; it is said that at midnight if one passes the pit, his ghost will appear!

Capenhurst

Capenhurst is situated about six miles from Chester, and in the Domesday Book is mentioned as Capeles. At the time of the Domesday survey Capenhurst was owned by William FitzNigel of Halton.

In 1790 Richard Richardson purchased the manor and in 1792 built the new Hall. The old Hall, a lath and plaster building, was demolished but its site can still be traced near Dunkirk Lane and is marked 'Moat' on present day maps. The Richardson family remained squires of the manor until 1945, when the estate was sold by auction. Unfortunately the new Hall having also fallen into ruin, it has now been demolished.

The church of the Holy Trinity, which is built of red sandstone believed to have been quarried in nearby Ledsham, was erected in 1858 by the Rev R. Richardson and is well worth a visit.

Over 40 men from Capenhurst and Ledsham served in the First World War and several were killed in action or died of wounds. In 1919–1920, as memorials to those who had given their lives for their country, six new bells were inserted in the tower in place of the previous four.

In the first hundred years of the church's history the names of Richardson and Maddock appear as churchwardens – one or other or both being in office. Indeed at one time there was a family of five Maddock brothers living in the village, whose ages ranged from 86 to 94, who were all, despite their ages, perfectly competent to manage their businesses.

The Capenhurst pinfold or pound is a square sandstone enclosure, believed to be the only one in Wirral. Animals were impounded for debts and kept at the owner's expense until redeemed. The owner had the right of rescue when the cattle were being driven to the pinfold by aggrieved person. This custom dates to before the Norman Conquest.

In 1940 HM Government invaded this quiet little country village. The peace of the village was shattered by the incursion of contractor's men from Merseyside. The result of their work was the wartime factory, which became a branch of the United Kingdom Atomic Energy Research Authority. Now, with farmers and their labourers, mixed technicians, scientists and physicists, and with this new company came many new customs and ideas.

Capenhurst had been previously known as a dairy farming village, but it now had a new, and at the time rather frightening, project in its midst. Its new inhabitants, housed in specially built houses, joined in the village activities, but are frequently transferred to other places, so that the population in the village is frequently changing. The factory is now in the hands of British Nuclear Fuels Limited, who have a great interest in the village, helping in many ways, especially financially.

Capesthorne & Siddington

Siddington is situated centrally five miles from Congleton, Holmes Chapel, Alderley Edge and Macclesfield. It is made up of widely scattered farms and cottages.

Redesmere Lake attracts both bird life and tourists and also yachtsmen to the sailing club. An unusual feature is the floating island which, to stop it straying, is now anchored to the eastern edge of the lake.

Capesthorne is mentioned in the Domesday Book. The Hall has been owned by the Bromley-Davenport family since 1748. It is open to the public during the summer months.

The 15th century All Saints' church is situated off the Pexhill road near the crossroads on the A34. It was built of a timber frame-work with wattle and daub filling. The weight of the heavy Kerridge flagstone roof caused the nave walls to bulge, so, in about 1815, they were strengthened by local red bricks, some being painted black and white to resemble the original timbers which remain underneath.

Following the closure of the school in July 1969, the building became the village hall. The village shop and post office occupies one room of a former smallholding.

Village life revolves around the church, Women's Institute and the new bowling green recently opened behind the village hall. It has a magnificent view as far as the Derbyshire hills.

The Methodist chapel was founded in 1865, sold in 1980, then demolished. The site is now an attractive garden.

The old corn mill is currently a wholesale and retail clothing warehouse. Beneath the spreading chestnut tree the village smithy still stands. Although no longer a farrier, Aubrey Davenport remains in demand for mending farm machinery and making decorative wrought iron work.

Although many of the old thatched cottages have been modernised, they have been rethatched to retain their character.

Near the village pump are the five plaques which have been awarded to Siddington in Cheshire's Best Kept Village competition.

Cheadle 🌾

There are people who think that Cheadle is not a village at all, but merely a suburb, and certainly there are signs that Manchester or Stockport might engulf us. But those who live here know that it is still a village, with its own centre, and a high street down which one cannot walk without meeting friends.

One of the surviving remnants of early Cheadle is the Saxon cross, now standing in the parish church, which dates from the 11th century. The parish church of St Mary itself dates from 1520, and is as much part of village life now as it ever was, sometimes with an overflowing congregation.

Several of the leading Manchester industrialists in Victorian times built homes for themselves in what was then a quiet country district. One of the most notable was the Watts family, who built Abney Hall, and in the summer used to transport the whole family and staff to a holiday home in Wales, taking a special train for this venture, from Cheadle Bottom Line.

The last James Watt to live at Abney married Agatha Christie's sister, and several of the Christie books have references to places around Cheadle – notably the *Christmas Pudding Mystery*.

The high street has changed, of course. Many of the old shops have gone, including the saddler's, where a small girl could take her satchel to be mended, to be met by an incredibly old man, who would mutter over it, and say 'I'll 'ave to ask me Dad'. We still have Mrs Robertson though, sitting in her wheelchair at the back of her well-stocked draper's shop, knowing where all the stock is and always ready for a chin-wag. She can tell of the old days when the shop used to be a tailor's, with men sewing away, sitting cross-legged in the window.

It is a great pity that the old rectory, stone-built in perhaps the 12th century, was pulled down just before the Second World War. The post office has been built on the site.

Near there used to stand a pretty little mews, reached by an archway leading to a cobbled yard with a handful of cottages, bright outside with marigolds and stocks, and bright within with shining brass and sparkling grate, but no doubt damp and inconvenient.

The old toll road from Congleton to Manchester came through Cheadle, so it has been on a main route for many years, but it is now bypassed on the north by the M56, and on the west by the A34, so only lorries and cars which are actually coming here now fill up the high street. There is a certain amount of industry, not everyone needs to go into nearby towns to find work. Cheadle is not a holiday centre and nobody would call it picturesque, except for odd corners, but it is a good place to live, friendly and prosperous with plenty going on.

Chelford 🌿

Although typically rural and with several historical buildings, Chelford has certainly not stood still, either in time or location. Initially the village grew around the church, Abbey Farm, the manor house, the post office, smithy, school and the two public houses, the Cat and Lion and the Archer or Robin Hood Inn.

Chelford derives its name from Chellers Ford, where the stream crossed the road near the church.

Until 1774 the church was probably a wattle and daub building. In 1776 the present church of St John Evangelist was consecrated. Church registers date back to 1674. The name Abbey Farm witnesses that the parish church was served by the monks of the Abbey of St Werburgh at Chester prior to the Dissolution of the Monasteries. There are the usual rumours about secret passages linking the church, Abbey Farm and the manor house, although these have never been proved.

The manor house is a fine building with its early Tudor black and white timber and plaster work but has many later additions. It boasts craftsmanship from Tudor, Stuart, Georgian and Victorian times.

When the railway arrived in 1842 the heart of the village was moved to a new location half a mile to the west. This new centre had a cattle market, village hall, and two public houses – the Dixon Arms and the Egerton Arms. The move occurred principally because the landowner of the Astle estate did not wish the line to cross his land. Chelford had a station at a very early date and up to the First World War the approach to the station was crowded in the early morning with horses and milk floats waiting to catch the special milk train. From 1905 it was also used as a collection and distribution point for the Royal Mail.

At Christmas 1894 a tragic and fatal accident occurred when a wagon being shunted was in collision with an express train, resulting in 14 deaths. There is a marble cross in the churchyard which commemorates this event.

The Dixon Arms Hotel, until the railway came, was a bustling and thriving coaching house, with stabling for around 30 horses.

The famous cattle market in Chelford was started by John Braggins in 1911 and joined by Frank Marshall in 1917 at the age of 14. It is a thriving and interesting market and one of international fame. Farmers, sellers and buyers come in from as far south as Cornwall to the north of Scotland and also from France and Holland.

The post-war years have seen many changes in the village and its surroundings, with the reduction in the number of small farms resulting in larger units worked by fewer people. The sand quarry which provides much of the raw material for Pilkington Glass, is still very active today. The road running through the centre of the village has become busier and busier with the advent of cheaper transport and is one of the main link routes for the M6 motorway.

Since the 1970s, Chelford has expanded even further to the west with the construction of an attractive 400 house development. This housing estate has brought people from varying walks of life into the village, which although still basically rural, has fast road and rail links to major cities, and is a haven for many business commuters.

Childer Thornton 🦢

Childer Thornton straddles the main Chester to Birkenhead road and covers approximately 700 acres. Many large houses are scattered over its area, with the village centre still being compact and housing a closely knit community.

As long ago as 1220 Thorintone was mentioned in records, and this later became known as Childer Thornton when it was under the control of the Benedictine monks whose manor house was situated in the neighbouring village of Little Sutton. Also in Little Sutton, but only by 20 yards, is the church of St Paul attended by local residents. St Mary of the Angels is the Roman Catholic church in the area.

The Old School was built in 1640 and was superseded by a new building on the opposite side of the main road in 1913. Since then the old building has had many uses in village life and is now a picturesque residence.

Housing changes have taken place within the village, these mainly being the building of council houses and flats in the 1960s to house Childer Thornton families. A small development of private bungalows has also taken place and the newcomers welcomed into the community.

Although several years ago all general shopping was catered for in the four village shops, plus a post office, today only the post office remains and needs are now met through a journey into neighbouring villages along the busy main road or down a leafy lane, which can be a pleasant outing in summer but in the winter snow and ice make travel more difficult.

The summer fetes were originated by the WI, who also presented to Childer Thornton in 1951 a seat to commemorate the festival of Britain. It still stands in a garden laid out near one of the old cottages on the A41 road.

There are two public houses in the village, the Halfway House, so named from the days when it was a stop on the main stagecoach route, and the White Lion dated 1724.

Cholmondeley 🦢

Cholmondeley is situated in South Cheshire on the A49, halfway between Whitchurch and Tarporley, covering an approximate area of two square miles.

It is part of the estate owned by the sixth Marquess of Cholmondeley and is a particularly pretty area. The road through the woods, flanked by rhododendrons, is a well known beauty spot for picnickers.

Most of the history of Cholmondeley is centred around the park and the ancient chapel owned by the Cholmondeley family.

It is said that there are 24 ways of spelling Cholmondeley. It is of Saxon derivation, and was originally Calmunds Lea, ie a pasture meadow.

The younger sons of the Marcher Barons of Malpas settled here in 1200. Parts of the old house still stand. The family moved to the present castle in 1804.

The Old Hall suffered greatly during the Civil Wars and was almost destroyed in 1644. Many battles took place nearby and it is thought that the dead soldiers were buried in the area that is known as the Walnut Tree Bank by the chapel. There are some cannonballs at the castle, which were picked up in the park.

The Earl of Leinster who was there at the time, took many of his treasures and money packed in firkins to bury them at Bickley Hall. He died in 1659 and because of a dispute as to where he should be buried, his body lay in the Hall for a year. The treasures were found but not the money. Some years ago some men out rabbiting unearthed some of the very old coins. The part where the money was buried is called the Money Pit.

The chapel is of great interest, it is 13th century and permission to hold services there was given in 1323. Each marquess in turn has added to the chapel, which is now a cruciform shape and has a very beautiful screen and lovely east window of Flemish glass. The members of the family were buried at Malpas until the present burial ground was consecrated in 1920.

Cholmondeley played an active part in the two world wars. During the First World War, the dower house, Higgensfield, was opened as a hospital. Then during the Second World War the castle was a naval hospital for shell-shocked sailors. Czech soldiers camped in the park and aroused a great deal of interest. It was an inspiring sight when General Benes came to inspect them. A memorial stone stands in the park, carved by a young soldier, aged 18, Frank Belski, who today is one of our leading sculptors.

There is a flourishing cricket club here, which celebrated its centenary in 1987. The pitch is in the park, making a wonderful setting.

The local school which functioned for over a century was closed a few years ago and is now a flourishing pub, the Cholmondeley Arms. This is a great asset to the district. The school was at one time renowned for italic writing and many pupils won medals in competitions.

The village is very fortunate to have an excellent local store and post office. They specialise in cheese and customers come from miles around to purchase it.

There are several attractive farms on the estate and some good black and white houses. The Marquess and Marchioness of Cholmondeley are in residence here, and they take a great interest in local affairs.

Chorlton & Cuddington

Chorlton and Cuddington are two parishes just outside Malpas in the south-east corner of Cheshire. Both are very rural and Cuddington particularly has a very scattered population.

In 1870 Roman remains were found at Chorlton Old Hall and there may have been a Roman camp there.

At the 1801 census, 94 people lived in Chorlton and 224 in Cuddington, or Kydington as it used sometimes to be called. By the 1830s there were 155 people in Chorlton and 260 in Cuddington but from then on the population has gradually fallen to about 200 altogether.

A free school was built in Chorlton in the 1850s by Mrs Clutton, wife of the lord of the manor. In 1860 there were 32 children on roll, 10 of whom were being educated at Mrs Clutton's expense. However, none of the present residents remembers the school so it must have been closed by or soon after 1900.

Neither Chorlton nor Cuddington has a church, but in about 1908 a non-conformist chapel was built in Chorlton Lane. Sadly it closed in 1977.

Cuddington mill, now a private house, ground wheat, maize and barley etc for the local farmers for generations. The mill, the Black Lion pub (now a house), and the land round both, belonged to one farmer and when he died in about 1930, both the mill and the pub ceased trading.

There was a tannery in Cuddington at Brookside Farm, but not within living memory. The older residents of Chorlton can, however, remember the saw-pit at the house now called Post Office Farm.

Before the Second World War the farmers all had shorthorn cattle and made their own cheese. The whey was used to fatten the pigs and it was piped to their sties close to the back doors of the farms. Forty cows were considered a good herd and would be enough to give the farmer and his family a good living and pay the wages of the farm workers and the maids who worked in the house and dairy.

Both parishes have always had quite a number of trades and businesses centred in them. Chorlton has long had a post office and grocer's and in 1934 Mr Passey took over and made it also a bakery. He and his family built up the business and ran four vans delivering to shops and houses over a very wide area. Gladdy's was the baker's and grocer's at Cuddington and both families are remembered with great affection even now. There were also blacksmiths, wheelwrights, a joiner, a builder and a cattle dealer/wholesale butcher and slaughterer. In 1874 the firm of G & H Clutton were threshing-machine proprietors and between the wars Mr Stevenson of Cuddington still had several threshing machines as well as machine-driven ploughs, all of which were hired out and brought to the local farms in much the same way as big machinery is hired out nowadays.

At the present time there are still plenty of businesses being run in the two parishes. The shops are both closed and the post office is run twice a week in the WI hut, but there are still cattle dealers and a builder. There are now two plumbers, a motor mechanic, a hairdresser, a carpet fitter, a stockbroker and a poultry processing firm.

Christleton

The village of Christleton lies a little over two miles south-east of the city of Chester. The name means 'Christ's little town', which suggests an early Christian settlement.

The village featured largely in the Civil War, the battle of Rowton Moor being fought here in 1645, when the Parliamentarians' headquarters for the attack on Royalist Chester were at the Old Hall. The Royalists burned down the village and the only buildings which survived were the Old Hall, the church, the manor house, and part of the Glass House. The Trooper Inn takes its name from the troopers of that war. The house known as The Old Farm was built immediately after the Civil War and bears the date 1653.

The Glass House was an inn for many years. It is here that the Beating of the Bounds begins and ends when this ancient ceremony takes place every ten years on Rogation Sunday. As the house is half in Christleton and half in Boughton, the rector and a host of parishioners, and their

The Pump and Pumphouse, Christleton

dogs, troop through the lovely home of Mr and Mrs Hellicar at the start of a 14 mile perambulation of the parish boundary, pausing in each of the five little townships which make up the parish of Christleton to pray for the farms, their workers, animals and crops.

The church of St James is the fourth to stand on its present site and, with the exception of the 15th century tower, was built in 1877 under Canon Lionel Garnett, who was rector from 1869 to 1911. It was he too who started the Flower Service, which is held on the nearest Sunday to St James's Day. In his time, there were great jollifications at St James's tide, with merry-go-rounds, coconut shies and other stalls by the village green and, on the great day itself, a procession through the village led by the church choir with the children carrying flowers and all singing hymns.

Some of the large houses are no longer private residences. Two have become well known hotels, Christleton Green is a home for the elderly and Christleton Hall is a college of law with students of various nationalities. There are also two modern schools, the old ones having been converted – one into the parish hall and the other into dwellinghouses.

The village blacksmith is still to be seen working at his craft.

The Shropshire Union Canal passes through Christleton and cargo-carrying narrow boats used to stop overnight, their horses being stabled at the Trooper. Now, in the summer, the boats come smartly decked out for holidays afloat.

'The Pit', overlooked by the picturesque black and white Dixon houses, was always a popular spot for feeding the ducks and, in the old hard winters, for skating. It was originally dug out as a marl pit and its marl was used to make the bricks for local buldings. Newcomers to the village soon learn not to call it 'the pond'.

The Roman bridges are not really Roman at all, but three pretty little medieval packhorse bridges. This is a favourite beauty spot with views of Beeston and Peckforton castles, the little river Gowy where children paddle and young people water their ponies, and the Hockenhull Platts nature reserve.

Despite its proximity to Chester, Christleton has remained a real village. It has won the award for the Best Kept Village three times. It is also a very active village, with good facilities for all kinds of sport and various clubs.

Church Minshull ❧

A picturesque, typically 17th century black and white Cheshire village, which may have evolved from the crossing of the river Weaver by a spur of the Roman road from Nantwich to Middlewich.

There have been three churches on the same site. The earlier ones suffered from neglect and decay and were demolished, and the present building, St Bartholomew's, completed in 1702, was partly financed by a local rate of 40 shillings in the pound and an appeal for Queen Anne's Bounty. The date is picked out in blue bricks on the tower, the other bricks having been made from local clay dug from farm marl pits as required. A new three-arched bridge was built near the Weaver in 1698 to bring stone for the church building from quarries near Macclesfield, as the old bridge was not strong enough, and the river had to be diverted through it. Even this is now suffering from increasingly heavy traffic.

It is said that Field Marshall George Wade, Commander of the King's Army during the 1745 Jacobite rebellion, and his brother Richard are buried in the family vault, first used in 1597, which lies at the foot of the church tower. They were both born at Wades Green Hall, just outside the village, a 17th century, half-timbered manor on even older, moated foundations.

Of the buildings clustered around the central road junction one of the oldest is Church Farm, which has a traditional magpie porch jutting out on pillars, and was the home of Elizabeth Minshull before she became the third wife of John Milton, the poet, in 1660. Until 1984 the farm supplied the village with its own milk from cows that twice daily walked down the main street.

The smithy was the home from 1817 to 1975 of Egerton Brothers, with members of the family engaged in many related trades including wheelwright, signwriters and undertaker. Miss H. Egerton used to run the local telephone exchange from the house.

Next door at Old House the front rooms were used as a shop and post office by the redoubtable Miss Brereton before the First World War. The shop and post office are now to be found behind the pub, The Badger.

The surviving mill, on one of two ancient sites, ground corn and provided electricity for the whole community until approximately 1960. Church Minshull was one of the last places to join the National Grid. Miss Billenge, the miller, in her later years a very eccentric character, kept the wheels turning although the lights often flickered if too much power was required all at once.

The canal which flows round the southern and eastern boundaries of the village is a branch of the Shropshire Union, and was once extensively used for transporting coal and salt. The Wharf House, with distinctive Dutch gables designed by Thomas Telford, was the loading point for a salt-packing business down in the village, but now only private boats go by.

Although the centre has remained largely unspoilt there has been some recent building on the outskirts, but not enough to affect the local community feeling. Even though the last working farm in the village was sold for redevelopment in 1989 and most of the residents now work elsewhere, there is still a rural atmosphere and cows graze peacefully opposite the church.

Churton 🦡

Situated some seven miles south of Chester this village of about 120 dwellings has changed from a farming community to one where many of its newer residents are commuters.

The architecture ranges from tiny black and white 17th century cottages which have been reconstructed into large modern homes, to a modern-style bungalow. There are two rows of tall Victorian terraced houses, as well as much larger Victorian villas, a cul-de-sac of 1970s mock-Georgian houses, a row of old people's bungalows and a road of post-war development. One of the older houses, dated 1650, has an exposed gable-end cruck frame but only one house, Quarry cottage, is as yet unmodernised. In the same family for over 200 years, this old coaching inn still retains its large black-leaded fire-grate, and has only a cold water tap.

There are two major agricultural landowners, one of them being the Grosvenor estates for the Duke of Westminster. In the 19th century the population of the northern part of the village doubled to nearly 300 as craftsmen and labourers were employed on the restoration of the old Eaton Hall, the family seat. In Stannage Lane opposite to the Old Post Office, which is the only remaining thatched cottage, was a row of thatched cottages for some of these migrant workers. Once called Newtown, the cottages have completely disappeared.

In 1841 there were 75 households and some 90 men and women worked on the land. The 15 farmers and smallholders of the past have been reduced today to a farmer who rears sheep for wool and one tenant farmer with a large milking herd who employs only four people at Churton Hall Farm. This is a Grade II listed Elizabethan manor house.

Opposite the farm, in Pump Lane is an old water pump, one of several, which worked until the 1930s and used to supply domestic water. When piped water was installed it was at first considered too hard for drinking. Behind the pump, now storing agricultural machinery, is an old smithy where the workhorses, in the days before tractors, were shod.

Churton at one time had three blacksmiths, three wheelwrights, four shoemakers, two coopers, two weavers, shopkeepers, a tailor and a publican. Near the smithy is Stud Farm, where the Dukes of Westminster bred shire horses. The house is now a private residence but the land is still farmed as part of the Grosvenor estate.

Four shops including a bakery were to be found at various times but these have also now been converted to private houses. Today there is only a sub-post office run in the entrance hall of a Victorian terrace house.

At the crossroads with the B5150 Chester road, Churton also had two inns. The Victorian White Horse is still thriving and very attractive inside, but the Old Red Lion, with black and white timbers, was partly destroyed by fire in the 1930s and is now a house. The stones which formed the mounting block for horses tethered at the latter can now be seen at Highway Farm.

Nothing remains of the old stone cross which stood in the centre of the crossroads. From 'the Cross', Hob Lane runs west, becoming a track to the river Dee at Almere, where there was once a ferry with a flat-bottomed punt. Hob Lane and Pump Lane to the east divide Churton into two parishes: Churton-by-Aldford and Churton-by-Farndon. Churton, despite its name, has never had a church but it does have a small Methodist chapel opened in 1832. Once thriving with two Sunday services and a Sunday school, this has only a very small congregation today.

The largest house in the village, Churton Lodge was possibly a hunting lodge, dating from the 12th century and belonging to the Church. In Victorian times a Mrs Maylor had the facade rebuilt so that the building was turned round. She also built a folly in the grounds and some village houses.

Clotton

Clotton is on a busy main road and was once a coaching stop on the route from London to Wales and to Parkgate. The latter, at the time, was the major port for the crossing to Ireland.

Close to the boundary with Duddon there is an outstanding example of a 'cop' (a hedge standing on top of a sandstone wall), forming an enclosure within which many 17th century clay pipes and pottery items were found, indicating occupation. Further examples of cops can be found throughout the village though many have fallen into disrepair and have become grown over with vegetation. South of the village are examples and evidence of medieval field patterns.

Directories published more than a hundred years ago show that a wheelwright, tailor, shoemaker, butcher and blacksmith were apparently all trading successfully. There was also a flourishing hand-made brick factory.

By the 19th century there were many freeholders and only two large landowners – Lord Tollemache and the Countess of Haddington. There was a National school in the village which was functioning between 1822 and 1873 and served the children of Clotton Hoofield, Duddon, Burton and Iddenshall. The closure of the school followed the building of a new school in Duddon, though the old one still stands and is now a residential dwelling.

Clotton being on a busy main road, it was well served by three public houses – the Red Lion, the Tollemache Arms and the Bull's Head. Of these only the latter has survived with the others being converted to houses.

Today Clotton retains much of the character that prevailed over a hundred years ago with its farmhouses and dwellings, many of which have been painstakingly preserved by their owners. There are several examples of Cheshire's famous black and white houses in the village, such as Wynnstay House, Clotton Cottage and Townhouse Farm. There is also Georgian architecture, an example of which is Clotton Hall.

Agriculture is still important to Clotton though less so than it once was. An interesting point about the history of Clotton is the reversal of ownership of its lands. During its early history there were just a few large landowners, then in the 19th century there was a swing towards reduction in unit size and increase in freeholder numbers, but now as pressure on agricultural industries mounts, a reversal to this trend has come about as small farms are swallowed up by larger holdings and the farmsteads become purely residential. Clotton is not isolated in this occurrence though, as other neighbouring villages suffer the same fate and become so-called dormitory villages for other industries. Development has been stabilised and the character of the village preserved by the fact that Clotton is now in a conservation area.

Coddington ༀ

Coddington in Roman times was said to have been quite an important staging post to Viroconium (Wroxeter). This was a distinct parish long before the Norman Conquest of 1066. The first church of Coddington was built when Christianity was established here in circa AD 655. Many of the church registers were destroyed in 1820 when a manservant of the rector set the rectory on fire. He was caught and taken prisoner as he was entering Chester with a stolen surplice in his possession, and was hanged for arson.

The mill is mentioned in the Domesday Book, the site probably in a small adjoining meadow. On the site of the present Mill House and orchard stood the village green where in Edward III's reign, Hawise, widow of Sir Ralph Botelier, claimed a market every Monday and a fair yearly on the eve and day of the Exaltation of the Holy Cross, 14th September.

In a field near the church, called the Mud Field, there is an artificial mound which is an ancient tumulus, perhaps the 7th century burial place following a fight between the Mercians and the Britons (Welsh) in the days of Penda, King of Mercia.

Now Coddington is a hardworking farming community and is very much a tranquil backwater. Even the ducks who frequent the village pond are so 'laid back' they sleep in the road, oblivious to everyone!

Comberbach ✤

Comberbach is situated in the parish of Great Budworth, which also includes Cogshall and Marbury. The village is still noted for the Spinner and Bergamot Inn, which is thought to have been named after two race-horses belonging to Smith-Barry of Marbury Hall. Soul caking was regularly performed here until the Second World War and the tradition has been revived and is practised by present day villagers, who have formed a mummers and morris dancers group.

Cogshall or 'Cockshalle' (Coggs hyll in 1086) had a 14th century corn mill which was in use until 1880 but no longer exists.

The 13th century Marbury Hall was privately owned until 1930 when it became a country club, having been largely rebuilt in 1843 in the French style. During the Second World War there was an army camp and a prisoner of war camp on the estate. Subsequently, the Hall was purchased by Imperial Chemical Industries, who housed their employees in the huts. It was completely demolished in the 1960s and now the site of the house and grounds has been developed into a country park by the Cheshire County Council.

There are several interesting legends connected with Marbury Hall. One concerns a white horse, *Marbury Dunne*. Lord Barrymore purchased the horse as a wedding present for his wife and wagered that it would travel from London to Marbury between the hours of sunrise and sunset. *Marbury Dunne* galloped home within this time, but collapsed and died. The horse was buried in East Park and its gravestone bore the inscription,

> 'Here lies *Marbury Dunne*
> The finest horse that ever run
> Clothed in a linen sheet
> With silver hoofs upon her feet.'

On occasions Marbury Mere has been frozen over. In February 1938 Lord Barrymore had two sheep roasted on the ice and these were cut up and distributed with bread and rum to 4,000 people. There were two bands and the festivities continued into the next day. In the 1940s, many people were able to skate on the mere and one man drove across on a motor-bike and sidecar.

Many people in Comberbach have lived in the village all their lives and have watched the village grow from a small group of thatched cottages near the crossroads to a community of several hundred houses, incorporating two housing estates. There are several working farms in the area, but most inhabitants work elsewhere.

Inevitably, there have been village 'characters' and one who is remembered was Albert Johnson, the local undertaker and wheelwright, whose sign read 'Body-builder and Undertaker'. He carried his steel measure everywhere, even to the local inn, in order to be ready to measure a potential 'customer'!

Compstall ✁

Compstall was only a handful of stone cottages and small farms on the Cheshire/Derbyshire border until around 1820, when George Andrew, an enterprising millowner and cotton manufacturer from Lancashire, saw the possibility of harnessing the plentiful supply of water available in the area to spin cotton and weave cloth.

Over the following 20 years or so, he built a large mill with feeder canals and reservoirs, and constructed a massive water-wheel to provide power for the looms. This wheel was known as 'Lily' and was the biggest in the country, being 17 ft wide and with a diameter of 50 ft. Unfortunately, this has disappeared and now cars park where once it stood. But an impressive weir which Andrew built on the river Etherow, three quarters of a mile upstream from the mill, and which powered the wheel, still today tumbles down its stone staircase and fills the valley with its roar.

As the business expanded, Andrew built terraces of cottages for his growing work-force. All the streets were named after members of his family – Andrew Street (of course), John Street, Montagu Street (after his son-in-law who became half-owner of the mill and estate), George Street and Edith Terrace. This last street was rather different. It was built for foremen and clerical staff, each dwelling having three bedrooms and its own privy instead of the usual two bedrooms and shared privy. This terrace is still called 'Quality Row' by the older Compstall residents!

The average millworker earned about ten shillings a week for a 60 hour week, and most families lived 'on tick' (credit). Wages were paid fortnightly and bills settled at the local shops (known as 'badge shops') fortnightly in arrear. The 'shop book', which recorded the customer's credit, became an indispensable item in the worker's household.

In the mid-1860s, George Andrew built his workers a reading room (now Compstall Liberal Club), where they could relax and be quiet. Not inappropriately, the village mortuary was below them in the cellar! Every day a boy from the Andrew household brought the daily newspaper by horseback from Stockport, and it was placed in the reading room at 6 pm, presumably when Andrew had finished with it. About the same time, he also provided the village with the Athenaeum (now a branch of Stockport Borough Libraries). This was a substantial building which became the centre of the community and the venue for concerts, meetings and dinners.

It might be thought that after a long six-day working week, followed by church services on Sundays, for Andrew had helped build both a Wesleyan chapel and the Anglican church of St Paul in the village, the Compstall people would have neither the time nor the energy to enjoy themselves in any other activities. On the contrary, they formed a prizewinning brass band, a flourishing dramatic society, a football club and a cricket club which is still playing today on the same ground as in 1860.

After the General Strike of 1926 and the depression of the 1930s, many mill-workers left the village, or travelled to neighbouring towns to work, consequently Compstall was no longer the close-knit community it had been. The Andrew's business was absorbed by bigger firms, some parts of the mill closed, and although modern machinery was installed and synthetic yarns introduced, the mill finally ceased production in 1966.

Over the years Andrew's cottages had deteriorated, and in 1952 there was a serious proposal to demolish the whole village. Almost unbelievably the houses still had dry midden-type toilets, and sewers would have to be laid before modern sanitation could be brought in. Fortunately the Stockport authorities reconsidered the case, and the cottages are now modernised and in great demand. The village has also been enlarged by a small residential development.

The woodlands and waterways and reservoirs of the Andrew estate, where the family had reared and shot pheasants, and fished for trout, formed the perfect foundation for a country park. The local authorities and the Conservation Trust bought 60 acres at first, but further purchases have resulted in the present 240 acre Etherow Country Park.

Cotebrook 🐾

Cotebrook, or more correctly Cote Brook, derives its name from the custom of 'coteing' or penning the sheep ready for washing in the brook which flows beside the Alvanley Arms.

At one time Delamere Forest covered a great part of Cheshire and as it was designated a Royal hunting forest, medieval inhabitants of Cote Brook would have been subject to the harsh justice of the Forest Courts if they had been caught committing such heinous crimes as keeping a greyhound, taking timber or ploughing the land. By the 19th century the Foresters had become a benevolent society whose officers still held the ancient titles.

Cotebrook has two pubs now, although at one time there were several houses where ale was brewed. One, The Buggin-in-the-Bush, is said to have been so named in order to frighten away law-abiding villagers (a buggin being an evil spirit) so that the nefarious doings of the customers went undisturbed. This same 'buggin' was also blamed by cheesemakers if the cheese failed for any reason.

The Alvanley Arms was rebuilt in 1663 as a coaching inn and later refronted. A hundred years ago the landlord was famous for his gaming cocks, but more recently it was shire horses that were bred there.

The Fox and Barrel used to be called the King's Head, but one day when hounds were running past Tom's Hole, the fox bolted into the cellar of the pub where it hid behind a barrel. It is not known at what date this happened, but it must have been toward the end of the 18th century. Later one landlord, Mr Alfred Bickley, was a successful racehorse trainer.

Cotebrook has a long association with horses and in particular with the Tarporley Hunt Club. Their annual race meeting used to be held on the Wednesday of the first week in November at the training ground at Gorselands, on the A49 just beyond Sandiford Lodge. The racecourse was first used in 1812, the change from the previous venue being due to the enclosure of Delamere Forest. The course is still in existence and used as a private training ground by a local trainer.

The sandstone church of St John and the Holy Cross was built by subscription in the late 19th century to the design of the architect George Edmund Street. The east window is by Kemp, as can be seen by his wheatsheaf 'hallmark' which he has worked into the corner of the window. The Primitive Methodist chapel was built in 1847, following a tradition of non-conformism in the area. It is said that followers of John Wesley held meetings on Luddington Hill.

Many village names are the same as in the parish register of 1557. The Cheshire surnames of Foden, Bratt, Dunning, Holmes, Cubbon, Done and Ackerley can be seen on the current electoral role – however, the agricultural activities are in the hands of only a few. Gone are the cheese rooms attached to the farms, cheese production being transferred to the large milk factories. Older residents remember the 'ringing' of the cheese tubs or vats with which the dairymaids accorded their satisfaction at the completion of the day's batch of cheese.

Nowadays a garage, a craft shop and a garden centre together with the post office stores have replaced the saddler, the shoemaker and the bonnet maker who once ran their businesses in Cotebrook. Sadly there is no school where once there was a maintained school as well as at least one dame school. But some things never change, and it is still High Billinge which is the last sight of land one sees when sailing away from Liverpool.

Croft

Croft village, originally known as Croft with Southworth, is situated about two miles east of Winwick off the A49.

In the year 1212 Croft was held by Gilbert de Croft, who possessed the manor now known as Southworth Hall. The original building, destroyed by fire in the 1930s, was replaced by the present Hall which stands at the side of the approach road to the village from Winwick.

Croft was originally within Lancashire county and was mainly a farming community, having a blacksmith, wheelwright, hamper maker, and a brewery. Weaving was also carried out as a cottage industry. The population has increased from 800 to 2,000 since the 1960s, due to some limited housing development.

In Lady Lane there were originally three churches, one at each end and one in the middle – Roman Catholic, Unitarian and Church of England. They were all built within twelve years of each other in the early 19th century. The Roman Catholic church is now a designated building. The Unitarian chapel has been demolished, but the churchyard has been preserved.

There were originally four public houses, the Horseshoe near to the smithy (now demolished), the General Elliot, the Plough and the Joiner's Arms. The Joiner's Arms has been demolished and there is now a petrol station on the site. The Plough near to the northern entrance of the village still retains the old tethering rails at the front. These rails were used by farmers returning home by horse and wagon from Wigan market after selling their produce. The horses of necessity knew the way home and the 'ports of call' along the route!

During the Second World War two Naval camps were temporarily established in the village, and Croft was host to some evacuees. Houses now occupy one of the old Naval camps.

Today, although on the border of major motorways and commercial development, Croft village still retains its quiet charm, with one grocery shop, a post office, a butcher's shop and also a craft shop.

Crowton ॐ

The village of Crowton consisted of four medieval manors – Crowton, Answort, Onston and Ruloe.

Ruloe is believed to have been the meeting place of the Hundred of Roelau (one of the eight Anglo-Saxon administrative areas of the county) and was mentioned in the Domesday Book, but from the middle of the 13th century, this meeting took place at Eddisbury and Ruloe was abandoned. Even today there are many public footpaths and narrow roads radiating from Ruloe, all of which are likely to be at least 900 years old.

Two adjacent fields near the moated Crowton Hall have the name 'Prison Bar Bank'. During the 16th and 17th centuries Cheshire men were famous for their performance of a very boisterous game known as 'Prisoners' Bars' (the OED defines it as a boys' running game).

Evidence of medieval strip farming has been discovered recently in all of Crowton's former manors, except Ruloe. The evidence in Answort manor is regarded by historians as particularly significant and provides a classic example of a small medieval community which lived and worked in a well-planned landscape with peasants' crofts on each side of the lane and their reversed 'S'-curving strips (these arise from ox ploughing) beyond. Some of these strips were enclosed by hedges probably in the 15th century and some during the 17th century.

The old stone houses, dating from 1686, in the centre of the village, were originally known as the pauper house and later the almshouses. There has been a working mill in the village since the Middle Ages, but there are signs of an even older settlement, thought to be pagan, in a field in Answort, and footpaths still lead to this area.

The area known as Pickerings lies some one and a half miles from the main village. The houses lie in a snug hollow between the bottom of the hill in Crewood and the River Weaver Navigation Canal. The set of white terraced cottages known as Pickerings O'Th'Boat were built to house the Irish labourers who had been brought in to help build the Dutton viaduct. This railway bridge, 1,400 ft in length, was opened on 4th July 1837, the construction being built 'without loss to life or limb'. These labourers, denied access to the local hostelry, promptly erected their own – 'Pickerings Boat Inn'. Trading ceased owing to the riotous behaviour of the customers, and the property is now a dwelling known as Lilac House.

Locals crossed the river here by means of a bridge which was wound across from the island side by the bridge keeper. A canalised river, goods such as salt, corn, cinders, manure and timber came to and from Pickerings via the Weaver. Coal was unloaded and weighed at the wharf and it was carried away for domestic use. Gilbert Gerrard had a salt warehouse on its bank near Pickerings in the 17th century, the salt no doubt travelling along the salt packhorse route.

Fascinating to note, a law still exists stating that to swim in the river Weaver on a Sunday is an offence punishable by deportation to the Colonies!

Cuddington & Sandiway 🌿

Cuddington and Sandiway existed as separate villages from before Roman times and did not officially come together until 1935. Since then they have grown to form a large and thriving community. In the past the villages were very much involved with Vale Royal Abbey, the largest Cistercian settlement in England, begun in 1277. The round tower on the A556 is closely linked with Vale Royal and is in fact a gatehouse and not a dungeon or hiding place for King Charles II, although this popular belief is far more romantic.

The Wilbrahams moved to the area from Nantwich and built the beautiful Delamere Lodge, later known as Delamere House, on the fringe of the village. One of the later Lady Wilbrahams in the 19th century was known to ride around the village distributing red flannel, puddings and soups. The house was demolished in 1939 and the area used by the US Army during the Second World War. The 100 acre site has been developed and now forms a new community within Cuddington and Sandiway in the form of Delamere Park, a unique residential area with its own leisure facilities. Another well known family in the area were the Thompsons, who were connected with the salt trade and were responsible for the building of such houses as The Hunting Box, Cuddington Grange and Abbotsford.

A famous son of Cuddington and Sandiway must surely be the Victorian architect John Douglas. He was born in Norley Road and set up a practice in Chester in 1855. He built the imposing Gothic house Oakmere Hall, Sandiway manor, now a delightful residential home, and of course the church dedicated to St John the Evangelist. This is built in a mellow Perpendicular style.

One villager known more for his antics than his building prowess was Charlie the Barber or Mr Charles Stainton, who rode to hounds and even played football riding on a bicycle. His shop was in School Lane which he opened in 1933, and he boasted that he could do 30 shaves before 9 am.

A four-legged character of much renown must surely be *Blue Cap*, the foxhound who was entered for a speed trial in Newmarket in 1743 and won. So much was he revered that one of the local inns was renamed after him. A poem was also written in his honour. Quite a distinction for a foxhound.

A major event which had a great influence in the peaceful village was the coming of the railway. This was opened in July 1870 and the main line, Chester to Manchester, still serves the village well. The branch line to Winsford now forms the peaceful walk known as the Whitegate Way.

Down the A49 is the Creamery which is now a major producer of yoghurt and provides employment for many villagers, although most seek employment much further afield.

Culcheth 🐚

Culcheth's name first appears in Norman times. Medieval happenings included the building of Culcheth Hall, the family home of the lord of the manor.

Later, in the Civil War, a Protestant neighbour won a victory for the Roundheads near the present Raven Inn. This was Lieutenant-Colonel John Holcroft, whose daughter Maria married the most notorious local character, Colonel Blood, who nearly stole the Crown Jewels in 1671. The marriage register with their signatures was luckily saved when Newchurch parish church was destroyed by fire in 1903.

The building of the Liverpool to Manchester railway coincided with a scandalous number of illegitimate births in the village. This must have helped to produce the total population of 2,091, which was entered in the 1841 census.

Now Culcheth has around 8,000 people. In 1974 it finally became part of Warrington after being part of Leigh, then of Golborne. It is still a village surrounded by working farms. Since 1946 Atomic Energy has created many jobs in Culcheth and at nearby Risley. Warrington, Manchester and the Wigan area are other centres of employment and there is a plastics factory in the village.

Newchurch parish church, which gave its name to part of Culcheth, began as a Tudor chapel of ease for Winwick church, although the Catholic Culcheth squires ignored it and had their own chapel. The fire at the old church in 1903 caused great excitement. A passing train driver helped to raise the alarm with his locomotive's whistle. Sadly the horse-drawn fire engine was too late, but a new building was ready by 1904.

The parish hall began as a Sunday school in 1821. Beside it is a shopping complex which is on the site of the 17th century Sundial House, which was in its time a school, a workhouse and a lock-up with one cell!

Business seems to be flourishing in Culcheth at present, with a new coffee shop, some fine new restaurants and a complex of small specialist shops. Culcheth pubs have a habit of changing their names – the Bricklayer's Arms is now the Cherry Tree and the Harrow is now Rakes.

Newchurch Hospital began as the Salford Cottage Homes for Salford orphans. It is set out like a tiny village in its own grounds and for 50 years it has been a home for the mentally handicapped. Its residents are very much part of Culcheth, walking, shopping and visiting friends. Volunteers of all ages help with hospital activities and there is a popular fete at the hospital each summer.

Daresbury 🦋

Daresbury lies to the south of Warrington, a peaceful village built along part of the old Roman road, but now bypassed by the main road to Chester.

Daresbury was, and still is to a large extent, a farming community, although most of the farms are in the nearby hamlet of Newton-by-Daresbury, now separated from the village by the M56 motorway. Perhaps the most interesting building here is Black Jane Farm, no longer worked as a farm, but formerly a farm and local alehouse. It derived its unusual name from the dark gypsy-like lady who dispensed the ale to the locals.

Newton Cross once stood hundreds of years ago on the common land. It was believed that if the stones from the cross were removed a curse would fall upon the farms and all the farm animals would perish. As long ago as the early 18th century, even though the cross had been reduced to a few large stone blocks, this fear still existed and rather than disturb the stones the farmer would plough around them. This 'curse' was eventually lifted when the construction of the motorway necessitated the temporary removal of the stones.

Newton-by-Daresbury was the birthplace of Charles Lutwidge Dodgson, better known as Lewis Carroll, the author of *Alice in Wonderland*. He was born in 1832 at the parsonage in Morphany Lane, son of the vicar of Daresbury. The building, one and a half miles from the village, built on the glebe land, was burned down in 1883 and today the site is commemorated by a stone plinth along the roadside.

Although there was a church in the village as long ago as 1159 the present church was restored in 1872, with a tower which dates from 1550. In 1934 a stained glass memorial window was dedicated to celebrate the centenary of Lewis Carroll's birth. As well as portraying Carroll himself with Alice, the lower panels of the window are made up of illustrations from the *Alice* books.

The village school, surmounted by the 'Alice' weather vane crafted by the last village blacksmith, dates from 1600, founded by Richard Rider of nearby Preston Brook. The old school still serves the children of Daresbury and the surrounding villages, catering for about 80 children.

Adjoining the village inn, built on the site of an old coaching inn, is the Sessions Room. Here from 1841 the Daresbury Petty Sessions were held once a month until 1911 when they transferred to Stockton Heath.

Daresbury Hall, a fine Georgian residence, was built about 1760 by George Heron, who purchased the manor of Daresbury in 1756. Since 1959 it has been owned by the National Spastics Society. The Hall is one of the few sources of local employment.

Although very much an old-world village very little altered by progress, Daresbury's most outstanding landmark, which can be seen for miles around, yet not from the village itself, is the white concrete tower of the Daresbury Laboratory. Overlooking the Bridgewater canal, the laboratory was opened in 1967 and belongs to the Science and Engineering Research Council.

The Lord Daresbury Hotel on the outskirts of the parish is another modern landmark. Built alongside the motorway, the hotel stands on the site of the former Blue Coat school.

Each year at the beginning of September the village hosts the Hatton Show, the only village show in Cheshire still under canvas. The show was in existence in 1894 and was originally held in the nearby village of Hatton but since the Second World War has been held in Daresbury.

The character of the village has changed little over the years and has been unspoilt by modern development. The names of the houses – Coachman's Cottage, Cobbler's Cottage, Sexton's Cottage, The School House, reflect an age gone by. Strangely enough the present village has no shops. The post office, once also the village shop and bakery, was closed a number of years ago, and only the village inn and smithy remain, the latter no longer worked by the village blacksmith but by an agricultural and horticultural engineer. In 1851, 157 people lived in the village and surrounding area, and today the number has only risen to 370.

Darnhall

Darnhall lies in the rural heart of Cheshire, yet close to the M6 and convenient for Manchester Airport, Warrington, Shropshire and North Wales. If you expect a church and shops, you will find none of these in the Darnhall of today, for the sprawling developments of overspill Winsford have encroached on what was once a rural area of outstanding beauty.

Of the local hostelries, the Raven Inn has connections with William Corbett, an 18th century occupant of Darnhall Hall, whilst at Wettenhall are to be found the Boot and Slipper, formerly the Royal Oak, and the Little Man of Wettenhall.

Darnhall itself boasts a mill, dating back to 1829, which with its twin water-wheels was fully operational until 1970, and a school, the charter of which goes back to 1662 when Elizabeth Venables, wife of the commander of the land forces that captured Jamaica for the British, left £220 in her will to her son to employ a schoolmaster or mistress to educate the people of Darnhall.

The origins of 'The Knobs' are as elusive as the dappled woodland shadows. It is said variously that they stood at the beginning of the drive to the Grange, that they were a tollgate, or that they were made from stones from the 17th century grammar school and mark the place where it stood.

Darnhall was the dairy farming heart of pastoral Cheshire, but because of the decline of farming in recent years, of the 14 prime dairy farms that flourished then, some are no more and others have turned the land over to other uses. But the terrain remains basically farmland and its people of farming stock. No one can forget the outbreak of foot and mouth disease in the 1960s which started here, and the burning pyres which could be seen from as far away as Beeston.

Darnhall is of the 'Vale Royal' where Edward I, the first English Earl of Chester, in thanksgiving for his life having been spared from shipwreck and drowning, fulfilled a vow to build an abbey for 100 white-robed, black-cloaked monks of the Cistercian order. Started in 1266 as Darnhall Abbey, the monastery moved to Vale Royal after a few years and thereafter the manor of Darnhall was the scene of much strife between peasants and Church. Indeed the severed head of one luckless monk, John de Boddeworth, was used as a football by his executioners.

Nearer the present day, the final occupants of the Hall from the end of the 19th Century were the Verdin family, proprietors of the largest salt mine in the area, landowners, philanthropists and general benefactors who at one time had 4,000 acres of Darnhall countryside in title. Sir Richard Verdin, the last occupant, died in the 1970s. People still remember the villagers being invited to his 21st birthday celebrations and recognise their debt, and indeed that of Winsford, to the beneficence of his family.

Although the Second World War left Darnhall relatively untouched, it did not escape unscathed. A searchlight battery in a 14 acre field behind Moors Farm deceived German bombers into thinking they were approaching Liverpool and several bombs and incendiaries destined for the docks of Liverpool and Birkenhead fell harmlessly on the green fields below.

The searchlights and the soldiers who manned them are long since gone, to be replaced by an extra-terrestrial satellite telescope controlled from Jodrell Bank, receiving messages from a world that was old long before W. H. Verdin planted the magnificent avenue of horse chestnuts lining the route to the Hall.

Davenham

Tradition says that Davenham was a place of worship in remote ages before the Christian era. The Celts are said to have practised their religious rites here and there is also a tradition that later, St Wilfred established a church here during his journeys through Cheshire.

The hillside along the river Dane at Shipbrook and the land between Davenham church and the by-pass road are said to be the sites of long barrows, the burial place of Saxons and Danes who fought a battle in the vicinity. East and west of the village are Roman roads, branches of the old Watling Street, one leading from Manchester to Chester, now called Chester Road, and the other a branch of the same road leading to Kinderton and Congleton, now called King Street. On the Davenham road connecting these two highways, at one time there could be seen three large stones, one in Hartford Road, one in Church Street and one on Shipbrook Hill. These are believed to have been used as markers by the Romans in planning their roads.

The first recorded mention of Davenham is in the Domesday Book, where it is called Deveneham. Most of the land in Davenham eventually became the property of John Hoskin Harper, who was the chief land-owner during the middle of the 19th century. A memorial erected to his memory can still be seen at the junction of London Road and Fountain Lane.

The Norman church was replaced in 1680, when a spire was erected, and in 1795 Dr Cotton, Dean of Chester and Rector of Davenham, added the chancel. In 1841 reconstruction of the present church of St Wilfred was begun; the church was lengthened, the nave and the aisles widened, the north and south transepts, organ chamber and vestries added. The spire has twice been struck by lightning, in 1850 and again during the 1980s.

The Wesleyan chapel was erected in 1856. Prior to that time the cottage adjoining the Oddfellows Arms had been used as a chapel and was called the Wesleyan meeting house. Mr Thomas Dutton, a stonemason in the village, made the first baptismal font and carved on it the faces of the twelve Apostles.

Sport has always been popular in Davenham. Football has been played in the village for generations. In 1886, Davenham played Crewe Alexander for the Cheshire Senior Cup and Davenham won by two goals to one. For years a terracotta replica of the cup was mounted above the parish notice board in the village, as a reminder of that happy day.

Cricket has also been popular in the village. The first record in the possession of the club, is the fixture list for the 1877 season. The cricket and football clubs are thriving to this day, and they play on the ground owned by the parish.

Dean Row ✺

A signpost off the busy A34 road at Handforth points to Dean Row, one and a half miles away. The village is bounded at one side by the river Bollin, perhaps named from the Wilmslow family of Le Boleyn.

Dean Row chapel, built about 1693, which was originally Presbyterian and later became Unitarian, is said to be the oldest Nonconformist place of worship in the county of Cheshire. The grounds are entered through a lychgate, the chapel now being scheduled as an ancient monument. Nearby a Methodist chapel, opened in 1849, now houses a firm of instrument makers. It is said that when the choir and musicians went carol singing in 1887 the night was not without adventure, since one fell into the river, another slipped into a pump trough and yet another knocked a spigot out of a water butt, releasing floods of water over the singers' feet! Let us hope they raised a lot of money for their new hymn books.

Until its internal modernisation and extension, a row of hooks to tether horses could be seen across the frontage of the Unicorn inn, where a Napier Court used to be held once a year, for tenants to pay their rents. Close by is the Dean Row smithy, built in 1840, with a warehouse added to store agricultural implements brought in for repair. The smithy still operates, though in a smaller way. Across the road was the village shop, now part of a private residence, but once noted for its home-made humbugs. Not far from the smithy is the 'Wheelwright's Cottage'.

Other industries included handloom silk weaving, done mostly by women who walked the five or six miles to and from Macclesfield to fetch raw materials and to return the finished articles. Hat making was

Dean Row Chapel

another cottage industry, and there was a tannery which also produced size and glue from the hooves, although they had to end this production because residents complained of the smell. Brickmaking made use of local clay.

A school built in 1861 was sometimes hard put to make ends meet because local farmers employed their children as labourers at busy times and school levies were not paid. The school became redundant when others were established not far away, but the adjoining school house was occupied by the minister of the Unitarian chapel until fairly recently, when that and the school building were sold to be converted to a private home named 'Chapel Grange'.

Old customs included 'boon day', when the locals gave a day's work to help a new tenant farmer. Ploughing matches also took place, and 'Riding Stang', which was beating on tins outside the house of any man who ill-treated his wife.

Delamere 🌿

Although there is a very beautiful parish church of St Peter, an excellent school, a pub and a post office, these are so scattered that Delamere tends to be thought of as a district rather than a village.

The community centre in Station Road is the hub of social life, and the bowling club has gained quite a reputation; but having the forest on the doorstep is Delamere's main claim to fame.

Once Delamere was full of game and in the days when Sir John Done entertained King James, 'deer both red and fallow and fish and fowl in the meres abounded'. As well as deer in the forest, wolves, boars and foxes roamed.

The Old Pale Farm stands at the top of Eddisbury Hill and about it curve the ramparts of the old Celtic fortress. In AD 915 Ethelfleda built a stronghold there against the Danes. Centuries later a hunting lodge arose on the hill, known as 'The Chamber in the Forest', from which the cruel medieval forest laws were enforced.

Oakmere was at one time the largest lake in Delamere and legend has it that Mary Ann Hollingworth 'the old woman of Oakmere' lived on the shore of the mere in a cottage made from a whale's ribs. She arrived one day in a donkey cart and was given permission to settle there. The year was 1815, superstition was rampant and wild stories of every kind were circulated about her. The truth appears to be that she was an English woman who had married a German and gone to reside in Hanover. Her husband having subsequently died, she returned home and was waiting to be joined by her son.

Watching the road for him one evening, she saw a man approaching whom she assumed to be her son. He stopped at a nearby cottage to speak to someone there and the mother hurried inside to prepare a meal for him, but although she waited until darkness fell, he did not appear. Next morning, gazing anxiously across the lake, she saw men carrying a sack which they dumped in the water. Alarmed that something dreadful had befallen her son, she persuaded the authorities to investigate, and sure enough, the sack was found to contain the body of a man, but not her son's body; he arrived next day!

There are many such tales of mystery surrounding Delamere, and even today the Forest occasionally yields up a sad secret.

Dodleston 🦋

Dodleston village is just five miles from Chester, at the foot of the Welsh hills. It is mentioned in the Domesday Book of 1086, a value of 40 shillings being put on Dodleston manor, castle and moat. The castle served as a watchtower on the Welsh border but only the mound remains in the churchyard today.

The church of St Mary was endowed by Edgar, King of Mercia in AD 980 and the village celebrated a millenium of worship with a flower festival. On Sunday mornings the church bells ring out as they have done since pre-Reformation times.

There has always been a strong connection with the Grosvenor family and the village has many cottages built for the estate workers. They have the date and a 'W' in the brickwork, but no front doors. This, it is said, is because when the agent of the estate knocked on the door he was always told to 'Come round the back' – so no more front doors were put into estate cottages.

The first stop after school is the village shop where sweets, groceries, newspapers and all the news can be had. The shop was once a Methodist chapel where Sunday school anniversaries were celebrated with great singing, and where harvest produce was sold for a penny. At one of the cottages home-made ice-cream was churned – and they say there has been nothing like it since.

During the Second World War the chapel was used as the headquarters of the Home Guard – one member put a bullet through the roof while cleaning his gun! They used to drill in the school yard and their proudest moment was when an enemy plane came down nearby and they stood guard over it.

As in all communities characters abound. The church choir was one of the best around but there were some members who wouldn't sing when the wind was in the north. Another villager refused to milk the cows on his billiards day; one poor soul had so many children that she used to tuck them up under a pig net – 10 in a bed perhaps? Then there was the doctor's surgery, held in a rented room, where the consultations were hardly private as the spinsters who owned it used to listen in!

There were varying occupations among the locals; agricultural and estate workers who walked to Eaton Hall and ran their own smallholdings to supplement their incomes. Each cottage had its own pump and pig sty, and some villagers kept cows tethered at the side of the road – that meant tending their own cows both before and after their day's work. There were two shoemakers and a carpentry firm who made altar rails for the church as well as coffins. Today dairy farms surround the village – there is even one right in the centre.

Duddon ✣

Duddon is still a very cosy little village. It is situated on the A51, eight miles from Chester, with views to the south of Beeston and Peckforton castles and Peckforton hills, and to the north of Kelsall and Willington hills. The village was once mainly a farming community with many of the residents working on the farms and living in tied cottages. Now many of the dwellings are owned by people employed outside the village.

Over the past few years a number of new properties have been built, mainly on two small housing estates, these being on either side of Back Lane, and also many smallholdings and farms have been modernised. The village was once on the edge of Delamere Forest, the small wood at Duddon Heath forming the boundary of the forest.

Duddon Old Hall, a black and white building, has belonged to the same family for generations. It is not mentioned in the Domesday Book. Looking from the Old Hall the Victorian school can be seen on the main road. The name has recently been changed to St Peter's school from Clotton Hoofield School.

St Peter's church, also over 150 years old, stands next to the school. The land for these buildings was given as a gift by the Baillie Hamilton family who lived at Arderne Hall, Tarporley. Opposite the church is Church House, which used to be a long low country cottage, but which has now been been extended and modernised.

The beautiful, white cottage adjacent to the school, known as 'Old Mother Red Cap', was the first public house in the village. On being renovated, holes were found in the wall in one of the rooms for the customers to rest their pint mugs. The present public house is in the centre of the village and known as the Headless Woman – it derives its name from the legend that a maid working at Hockenhull Hall, Tarvin, was approached by Cromwell's soldiers to hand over her mistress's jewellery. When she refused, the soldiers beheaded her. She then walked with her head tucked under her arm through a tunnel from Hockenhull Hall to Duddon Wood – the public house is said to be haunted. For many years an effigy of a headless woman stood in the garden of the public house but it was stolen. The figure was originally brought by Captain Clayton, the landlord in the 1930s, from the stern of a ship on which he served.

Along the road from the Headless Woman is Mill Lane, a very narrow lane down which Duddon Mill is to be found – a farm owned for many years by the Stanyer family. The mill wheel is still in position and the common brook still runs by the farm. The farm is now used as a fruit farm.

There is a village shop, where a taxi service used to be available and which is now also a post office and general store. 'The Bakery' also used to be a shop owned by the Price family.

Off the A51 down The Hook/Burton Lane is the hamlet of Burton. Here stands the 17th century Burton Hall. Legend has it that John Bruen, the preacher, used to call there and preach the gospel, and then went on across the fields to Stapleford Hall, to preach there, where he had his own pulpit and little chapel. Stapleford is divided into two, known as Bruen Stapleford and Foulk Stapleford.

Coming out of Stapleford one enters a lane known as 'Dan Bennett's Lane'. At the end of the lane an oak tree stood until the mid 1980s and it was this tree on which a local resident, Dan Bennett, hanged himself. Many elderly people always said that this little area was haunted.

Many farms in the village were for years owned by the France-Hayhurst family but in 1940 the farms and cottages were sold to the farmers themselves. During the time the farms were tenanted the tenants paid their rents every three months to the estate office which was and still is Stapleford Cottage. It was a great day, as everyone sat down to a meat and potato pie lunch.

Dunham Hill 🌿

Situated high upon a sandstone outcrop, some six miles north of Chester and just off the A56, in a quiet residential 'backwater' unspoilt by extensive housebuilding, stands the old walled village of Dunham o' th' Hill.

In 1917 the estate was offered for sale by public auction, but as insufficient bids were forthcoming the sale was withdrawn and later sold privately to the late Colonel Vernon of Shotwick Hall. After his early death the estate was again offered for sale and was bought partly by existing tenants who became property owners virtually overnight.

The Old Hall was situated at the summit of the rocky hill where now stands a row of houses named Old Hall Cottages, built by the Earl of Shrewsbury in the 19th century. The entrance to the Old Hall still exists in front of the cottages, with wide sandstone steps flanked by rough sandstone gateposts.

Undoubtedly this part of the village was the hub of a closely-knit and partly self-supporting community, consisting mainly of farmers, farm labourers and some artisans, such as a blacksmith, saddler, stonemason, cabinet maker, a tailor and even a rush-light maker! The main street, which was then part of the Chester to Warrington road, bore evidence of having been cobbled in later years, and cuts through the sandstone rock nearly all the way.

Several 16th and 17th century houses still exist and are solidly constructed of sandstone with wattle and daub interior walls. One such house, Elder Tree Cottage dated 1589, was reported to have been an old coaching inn with a sandstone cellar where barrels of ale were kept cool on a raised platform. Most of the older houses contain cellars hewn out of the sandstone rock. Two other coaching inns were The Legs of Man, close by Highfield Farm and now demolished; and the old thatched Wheatsheaf Inn which stood by the roadside in front of the new inn of that name.

Plum trees with lovely juicy red plums, locally named 'Orleans', still grow in some gardens. Tradition has it that a ship carrying a cargo of plums from Orleans met its doom at Ince and the plums 'salvaged' by the local populace found their way here!

Until 1916, when mains water was made available, water was obtained from several spring wells, and in the middle of the village stood the old village pump which the majority of residents used for general needs. Ponds were used to provide animals with drinking water on their way through the village, one being at the entrance to the new County primary school, hence the name of the nearby house, Poole Cottage, and another at the entrance to Talbot Road. Both have now been filled in.

Not until 1861 did the Church of England have their own church, St Luke's, built by local subscription for £800. Before then the inhabitants had to travel down Church Lane to Thornton-le-Moors, where weddings and funerals also took place. Inside St Luke's church hangs a large gilded cross which formerly hung in Chester Cathedral for many years until being given to Dunham Hill in 1921.

Today a modern mini-market with sub-post office has superseded

86

three shops in existence at the turn of the century. One wonders what residents of that bygone era would think of the sliced and wrapped bread that has taken the place of bread baked in the old communal bakehouse!

Dunham Massey

Turn off the busy A556, down Charcoal Road (named for the charcoal pit once there), to Dunham Massey.

The pattern of the lord of the manor owning the Hall and park, the village, the cottages for workers on the estate, and the farms, has changed little from earliest times. In 1976 the National Trust inherited Dunham Massey on the death of Roger Grey, tenth Earl of Stamford. It became, in effect, lord of the manor, but the atmosphere, and other things, altered.

A bypass was built, the village was spruced up for the many visitors to the Hall, and some cottages were sold. New faces, new names, new occupations. But it was, and still is, a farming area, of a high standard. The fields and hedges are always a joy to see, and a field of rape against a grey sky with the striking painting of the chemical tanks at Carrington in the background makes a good photograph.

The 'Big Tree' is old and much cosseted. Of nearby cottages, one is dated 1730. Big Tree House, with its beautiful bow windows, was once, like its neighbour, a farmhouse.

St Mark's parish church was built in 1864 and villagers are proud of its new extension. Nearby are the only village shop and post office, the Axe and Cleaver, and the village hall. Over the canal bridge, some of the farmhouses were built to the same style in the 1870s.

Coming back from the bridge, you will pass the Rope and Anchor, Manor Farm (once the dower house) with its wonderful wrought iron gates, and the Vine, with its skittle alley.

The village hall is a gem, once Little Heath school, built in 1759 by the will of Thomas Walton, and converted in 1965 to a fine meeting place. Its green is a far cry from the once rough field. Trees and shrubs border the cut grass, and the car park is tarmaced and neatly edged with setts.

The Rose Queen festival was started in May 1967 to raise money to help run the village hall. Now it is a 'Rose Queen Festival and Country Fair' held in June, still on the village hall green. The Bridgewater Canal, once used by horse-drawn boats to carry goods, and passengers from Manchester to Dunham Massey for a day out, now gives pleasure to anglers, canoeists, and cruising clubs, the club boats being decorated for the festival.

Legends? Well, the stone lions on the pillars at the Hall gates are said to wag their tails when they hear the clock strike one!

Dutton ✺

Dutton, recorded in the Domesday Book as Duntune, has always been and still is a farming village. Although there is no village centre, not even a church, Dutton has much to commend it.

The river Weaver flows through the meadows, and in 1735 the first lock was constructed at Dutton. The present lock was rebuilt in the middle of the 19th century and Dutton Locks was at one time a very busy place coping with boats carrying salt, and later ICI chemicals, to Liverpool. Nowadays the river traffic is mainly pleasure craft and a few sea-going vessels, transporting soda ash for glassmaking.

The Trent and Mersey Canal, opened in 1766, meanders through the fields. One of the main cargoes on this stretch of water was china clay. This was brought from Cornwall to Liverpool and then carried by narrow boats to the Potteries. Manufactured china goods for export were brought back on the return journey. New Brook Farm, at the side of the canal, had at one time a shop for the bargees. The canal tunnel which connects Dutton with Preston Brook is one of the longest in the country.

With the coming of the railways a viaduct was built to span the Weaver valley. Work commenced in 1834 and the 22 elegant sandstone arches, which are filled with cotton wool to assist resilience, took over ten years to build. They are a well known landmark.

In the reign of King John, Hugh de Dutton, who lived at Dutton Hall, was given the 'minstrilsie' of Cheshire. This meant that all musicians in Cheshire had to pay him and his successive heirs an annual licence fee for the privilege of playing their instruments. These proceedings, held at Chester, always ended with the proclamation 'God bless the King and the Heir of Dutton'! In 1934 Dutton Hall, a beautiful magpie building, was bought by Dewars the whisky family, dismantled brick by brick and rebuilt in Sussex.

After the First World War, in 1919, the village, comprising 2,355 acres, was bought for £114,000 by Cheshire County Council from the local landowners – the Talbots of Aston estate – and the land was divided into 50 smallholdings. Tenancy of these small farms was for ex-servicemen only and this resulted in a completely new village community.

A large Victorian workhouse stood at one end of the village and until recently, when it was demolished, tramps walking the roads were an everyday sight. An isolation hospital was also accommodated here – today it is a geriatric hospital.

A school was built in 1880 and was used as the social centre for all village activities. A Sunday school took place here every week for over 50 years. The closure of this building in 1983 was a severe blow to the village.

Bartington, a small adjoining hamlet, has always been connected with Dutton, both villages having one Parish Council. Bartington has a small Methodist chapel, where people have worshipped since 1840.

Although there has been very little development in either village this century, Bartington has two sites for mobile homes and in 1971 Runcorn New Town industrial estate came to the outskirts of Dutton.

Eaton (Tarporley) 🦡

A small friendly village where traditional black and white thatched cottages nestle side by side with modern houses.

It is set in a pleasant situation below the hill where once a Bronze Age hunter left his axe head, where a wealthy Roman built his country villa and in the Middle Ages a hall with double moat was occupied by the lord of the manor.

An abundance of wells and streams served the inhabitants with water until the late 1930s, the Anglo-Saxon name 'Eaton' meaning a settlement or village by water.

Where once the eight farmhouses in the middle of the village provided work for the villagers who patronised the farrier, saddler, wheelwright, baker, tailor and cobbler, there is now only the post office, which has been in the same family's hands since stamps were first issued.

In the centre of the village, where tradition has it that a medieval preaching cross once stood, a new cross to commemorate the Queen's Jubilee was erected in 1977. This spot was once the venue for the May Day celebrations but these have now moved to the new school which serves the needs of three local villages.

Education in Eaton started in dame schools in cottages, and then in 1806 Thomas Hough built the first school. He supported it at his own expense and left £1,000 in his will to continue this support. A new school was built in the 1960s and the old school and school house have been divided into two houses. An open book still decorates the doorway of the school house with the inscription,

'God is Truth, The Word is Truth
The Spirit is Truth, and Love is Truth'

The village hall, The Jessie Hughes Institute, was built in 1926 and named after the wife of the then Tarporley rector.

The sound of the farrier's hammer on anvil can still be heard occasionally from the smithy across the green, but the predominant sounds at the present time are of machinery constructing the two new golf courses on the outskirts of Eaton. Leisure pursuits are coming to Eaton where once long hours of labour on the farms was the order of the day.

Eccleston 🌿

Eccleston is situated some two and a half miles south of the city of Chester. It appears in the Domesday Book as 'Eclestone'.

Gilbert de Venables, first Baron Kinderton, included the village in his estates in the Hundred of Broxton, and the Venables and their associated family of Vernon were the owners of the manor until it was sold in 1758 to Sir Richard Grosvenor of Eaton, from whom it descended to the present Duke of Westminster, the sixth bearer of that title.

There is evidence that the site was occupied by the Romans – in the 19th century a hoard of Roman coins was found close to a mound north-east of Eccleston church, together with 'a great quantity of bones'. Watling Street passed through Eccleston en route for the 'Old Ford' (Aldford) over the river Dee to the great Roman brickworks at Holt.

During the Civil War a Parliamentary garrison was established at Eccleston, its purpose to blockade the road into Wales, and to create a point from which to lay siege to Royalist Eaton. The village church suffered considerable damage during the Parliamentary occupation. The original 14th century church was replaced by a new building in 1809, the south wall of its nave remaining in the old churchyard.

The present church of St Mary, the third to be built, was consecrated in 1900, and was the gift of Hugh Lupus Grosvenor, the first Duke of Westminster. He is said to have instructed the church's architect to 'build me a small cathedral', and a magnificent red sandstone church was the result. Sadly, the Duke died in 1899, the year the church was built, and his sculpted figure is the church's grandest monument. Beneath the church lie 47 members of the House of Grosvenor, their names headed by an Elizabethan, on a brass panel in the church.

The first Duke played a large part in the management of the Eaton Stud at Eccleston and succeeded in winning the Derby in 1880 with his horse *Bend Or*. The name was bestowed as a nickname upon his grandson, who succeeded to the title as the second Duke in 1899. The Eaton Stud has continued to flourish, and in more recent times has had connections with some well-known horses, including the famous *Arkle*, winner of the prestigious Cheltenham Gold Cup in 1964, 1965 and 1966.

Though part of the Eaton estate, Eccleston has not been spoilt by an excess of estate architecture, the stone and brick houses blending well with the chateau-like edifice built for the estate agent and the village's Tudor-type cottages. A stone shelter, the pumphouse, with a tiled roof, is set in the middle of the village, and the village school built in 1878, has been modernised and enlarged so that it is now attended by children from neighbouring villages as well as from Eccleston. The church gates, originally made for Emral Hall by the skilled Davies Brothers of Wrexham, were placed in their present position as a memorial to the second Duke, who died in 1953.

The stretch of the river Dee which borders Eccleston was a favourite haunt of Edwardian boating parties and picnickers, and a ferry across the river was operated for many years by the descendants of the original ferryman James Harnott, usually known as 'Jimmy the Boat'.

A story, which may be apocryphal, asserts that the reason that the village now lacks a public house is because the inn which occupied the site of the present post office was closed on the orders of the Duke. He apparently considered that the villagers he saw drinking on his return from Sunday morning service would have been more profitably occupied had they joined him at his devotions.

Elton ❧

Between Ince and Thornton-le-Moors, lies the village of Elton, being some nine miles from Chester.

Mentioned in the Domesday Book, Elton is now worth far more than the 38 shillings it was valued at in the reign of King Edward the Confessor.

With the coming of the giant Shell complex and the power station, came the people, the new housing estates and the shops. Elton now has a sizeable population. In the 1950s the villagers made an enormous effort and raised money for a community centre where the various functions of the village could be held.

To the north on the skyline can be seen the huge cooling towers and lofty chimneys of the power station, the warning lights on which shine at night like huge rubies suspended in the sky. To the east of the village can also be seen the large chimneys and works of the Shell complex, with the flame constantly burning on the gas outlet, looking for all the world like a huge Olympic torch.

There is still country life amid the industry. You can take a quiet walk and admire the huge hawthorn trees laden with white blossom, the dandelions in the hedgerow competing with the dandelion clocks swaying in the breeze like thistledown, the tufted vetch struggling to see the light through the masses of cow parsley and the elderberry trees, a boon to the home wine maker.

An interesting item of the past is one of the four brass plaques in the church at Ince relating to the death of John Wright of Elton, who died on the 17th January 1706. His house with houseplate 'JWM 1705' can still be seen in the village.

Elworth 🦊

Although the parish of Elworth only came into existence on 9th March 1847, the land has a history which goes much further back in time. Remains of the old Roman road have been discovered in recent house building projects. Indeed, one street which is on the site of the road was named Roman Way.

A thatched pub, the Fox Inn, had a reputation for good ale, and did much trade with passing coaches, and farmers on the way to Sandbach market, but it was the coming of the railway which led to the formation of Elworth as a village. The station was once an important junction for Northwich, the Potteries, Manchester and Crewe. The canal, too, was another important means of communication.

The development of industry began when George Hancock, one of the great Victorian engineers, began building agricultural machinery. There was no competition in the area, and there was skilled labour from the railway town of Crewe, which helped to make his venture the success it became. He was joined by Edwin Foden, who eventually gained control and gave it the name of Foden's Motor Works as he went on to develop steam and later diesel lorries. Brine pumping, Pring's wire works and other small businesses in the vicinity of the railway station were established. Houses were built to accommodate this work force and the village as we know it was created.

Edwin Foden's keen interest in the Elworth Silver Band led him to reform it in 1902, and rename it the Foden Motor Works Band. Under the conductorship of Fred, and his sons Harry and Rex Mortimer it went on to achieve world renown, and a special vehicle known as 'Puffing Billy' was built to transport the bandsmen to their various engagements. With the collapse of Foden's, the sponsorship of the band passed to Britannia Building Society, under whose name it still performs.

As the firm of Foden's prospered a recreation club was built complete with bowling greens, tennis courts and putting green. The church and chapels were already established and also a school. The Co-op store was built with an upper floor used for various social functions. The quality of life in the village was good, the headmaster of the school and the religious denominations providing many activities for the enjoyment and recreation of the villagers.

In the post-war boom the British Legion added yet another venue for leisure. Sport was centred round the cricket club and the football teams, such as Moston Magpies and Elworth Bachelors. Foden's too, had their own teams and all were well supported. The Flashes formed because of land subsidence due to past wild brine pumping provided good sport for anglers. But hard times were ahead.

Elworth Hall caught fire and had to be demolished, much of the farmland being sold for housing developments. A supermarket came, and the Co-op closed down. New schools were built, one on the Elworth Hall estate, and the old school building is now a church hall.

Foden's collapsed, throwing so many out of work. The British Legion closed, as did Foden's recreation club, its fine old bowling green turf rolled up and sold, and the building itself succumbed to fire. A small housing estate now occupies the site.

An American company took over the motor works, streamlining the production, buildings and manpower. Many of the redundant work shops have been converted into small units and are slowly progressing. Other small units are being built on the outskirts of the village too.

There is still some beautiful countryside. The disused 'Knotty Railway Line' has been made into a country walk and has retained its wild flowers, with 'jack sharps' swimming in the ditches along the pathway. The Flashes are the home of many species of water bird, under the protection of a full time warden, and the canal is populated with leisure craft.

Farndon 🦜

Farndon, which is mentioned in the Domesday Book as Ferendon, lies on a Roman road and it is very likely that there was a ford or ferry here from Roman times until the bridge was built. The first bridge was probably made of wood and was replaced by one of stone in 1345.

There is a legend that two Welsh princes were thrown over the bridge and drowned. It is said their ghosts can be seen and screams heard on dark nights.

During the 7th century, Chad, Bishop of Lichfield, visited the area, which was part of the Diocese of Lichfield at that time; consequently the church was dedicated to St Chad. Part of the church was destroyed by fire and rebuilt in the 1600s. The Barnston chapel contains a unique window called the Armorial Window, showing the arms of the Gamul, Mainwaring and Barnston families, who were all involved in the Civil War.

At one time, the church floor was covered with rushes renewed each year. Today, at Rushbearing, the graves are all dressed with flowers.

In AD 924 King Edward the Elder died at Farndon after dealing with a revolt. His body was taken to Winchester for burial.

John Speed, a famous son of Farndon, was born in the village in 1542. He was a tailor by trade, but later became a renowned cartographer and historian. Later in life, he moved to London with his family; it is reported that he had 18 children. He worked in London until his death in 1629 and he is buried in St Giles, Cripplegate, London.

The Barnston Monument, an obelisk which stands on the edge of the village, commemorates a Major Barnston who fought in the Crimean War and was killed in the Indian Mutiny.

Strawberry growing was, for many years, the main occupation of Farndon. It thrived between the two World Wars, but never quite recovered after the Second World War, when much of the land had to be ploughed up to provide grain. During the 1920s and 1930s, men and women used to flock into the village to pick the strawberries; they were known as 'Dodgers' and were accommodated in huts provided by the growers.

The United Reformed church was destroyed by fire in April 1957, but was rebuilt and dedicated in October 1958. The chapel house has a Flemish gable.

There are still black and white houses in High Street and Church Lane, the ones in High Street having thatched roofs. A small building called 'The Lock-up' is believed to have housed the fire engine at one time but is now used as a garage. There are three public houses in the village, the Raven, the Nag's Head and the Greyhound. There was one other, the Mason's Arms, until it closed in about 1936. A local rhyme of the 19th century went thus: 'The Mason's Arms will lose its charms, the Raven it will fly. We'll turn the Greyhound upside down and drink the Nag's Head dry'.

Farndon's brass band has been in existence for about 100 years and has had success in various competitions. It plays in the Groves in Chester during the summer.

There is a sports and social club on the outskirts of the village which was built with the help of voluntary labour. This was opened in February 1978. It caters for all social activities, with tennis courts, a bowling green and indoor sports.

Since the 1960s, the village has trebled in size, the majority of people commuting each day to the towns surrounding Farndon. Some barns in the centre of the village have been converted into a craft centre. A WI market is held every Wednesday morning in one of the rooms and is very successful.

A local rhyme refers to the four local villages as 'Holt Lions, Farndon Bears, Churton Greyhounds and Aldford Hares', but, although the Lions in Holt comes from the Roman word 'legion', no satisfactory explanation has been given for 'Bears' being allocated to Farndon!

Fearnhead 🐾

Fearnhead is situated on the main road betwen Warrington and Leigh.

Walking down the main road of Fearnhead village today is vastly different from what it was 80 or so years ago. Then it was a tiny community where everyone knew everyone else, doors were kept wide open all day and neighbours talked over garden gates during the evening while men folk would tend their gardens or allotments. One or two kept a few chickens which provided eggs and now and then a Sunday lunch.

There were three main roads meeting at what is known as Fearnhead

Cross, where stood the post office and village store. Nowadays this old landmark has gone to make way for progress, this being a new road, complete with shopping centre, library, high school, medical centre and community centre occupying pride of place.

Down Fearnhead Lane stood a row of small cottages and here was the barrel works – 'tub thumpers' they were called. The cooper made wooden barrels with hoops round them. When this place closed it was opened up again by another member of the Dilliway family on much bigger premises at the far end of the village. Of course, every community must have its pub and Fearnhead's is the Farmer's Arms.

Next to the pub is the wire works which hasn't altered one bit since those far-off days. Only a handful of men are employed and the same ones have been there for many years.

The school playing field was made into a golf links. This was a favourite place for golfers from miles around until the Second World War came and then it had to go and in its place was built 'Canada Hall', the camp for Canadian air personnel. The North Cheshire College of Further Education now stands where Canada Hall used to be.

A feature of the brick pits during the winter was the skating – to the accompaniment of an old gramophone. There always seemed to be a good thickness of ice on the pits and music and laughter would ring all around. This particular spot has been made into an anglers' paradise and, surrounded by landscaping and a children's play area, is a very pleasant place to walk.

A corn merchant stood near the garage and here the miller would grind the corn before it was transported by lorry to various destinations. This was later turned into a wheelwright's, when the previous owners retired, and also served the community as undertaker.

No village is complete without a duck pond. Situated at the end of Cinnamon Lane near to Mather's Farm (Mr Mather being the local JP at that time) and joining up with a country lane, Crab Lane, which skirted the community, it was a peaceful little oasis – a few trees, a rustic seat and of course the ducks. The pond is still there but not nearly so idyllic a setting as it used to be. Leading off down a tree-lined avenue from Crab Lane is Enfield Hall, which was haunted by an old lady who used to sit by one of the windows knitting.

Frodsham 🐝

Overton Hill is an outstanding landmark formed over a million years ago of red, brown and yellow sandstone, rising to 365 ft with a panoramic view overlooking the village to the Mersey estuary, sweeping round to the Welsh hills. In 1865 some enterprising person built the Mersey View pavilion and pleasure grounds on the summit, with swing-boats and donkey rides.

The parish church of St Lawrence was built in the 12th century on the site of a previous Saxon church. The interior was once described by visiting historians as a 'magnificent little cathedral' – the belfry is comfortably furnished for the ringers of the eight bells.

William Cotton, vicar of St Lawrence from 1857–79, a person of note, was an authority on honey bees, having introduced them to New Zealand while serving as chaplain there. He had a Maori welcome inscribed on the front doorstep of the vicarage. A well-known character, he travelled accompanied by his parrot, Papagay. In his memory there is a carving of a bee in the church. The bee is also used on the school badge and on the Parish Council chairman's chain of office.

Traces of Roman camps were found in Bradley and Woodhouses. It is a farming area, where many locals working as labourers lived in 'tied' cottages. Poaching was rife – their meeting place was the Rag and Louse Inn in Five Crosses.

Frodsham is a small community of 10,000 residents. There are two main thoroughfares – Main Street, which boasts being one of the widest roads in England, and Church Street.

Each Thursday a market is held in Main Street, the origins of which go back to the 11th century.

In medieval times Frodsham was a thriving port with salt coming from mid-Cheshire by packhorses, then by river to Liverpool and beyond. Cheshire cheese was also exported and a warehouse was built on the river bank to accommodate this. A small shipbuilding and repair yard was established in the early 1700s. Most of the boats were sailing flats and barges which were used on the river Weaver.

Two well-known characters were Joseph Kydd and Joseph Martin. In 1881 Joseph Kydd opened a grocer's shop and later a jam works, Kydd & Kydd, which unfortunately closed in the late 1960s. Joseph Martin emigrated to America but never forgot his native village, and when he died in 1921 he left 5,000 dollars for a charitable fund in his name.

One of the earliest schools was the Frodsham grammar school, followed by the Church of England National school for girls in 1835. Small private schools were soon established, one being the Manor House, whose most famous pupil was Prince Warabo, son of Chief Ja Ja of Opobo, who unfortunately took ill with pneumonia and died in 1882. He is buried in the parish churchyard.

At one end of the Main Street is the 'Brookstone', an 'erratic' boulder. This stone is thought to have been deposited by glacial action from the Lake District about 10,000 years BC.

Frodsham has a surprisingly large number of public houses, 14 in all. The oldest licensed house is the Queen's Head built in the early 17th century. The Bear's Paw was built in 1632, a bear's paw being the crest of Earl Rivers of the Savage family, who were the lords of the manor of Frodsham.

In Main Street are a number of 17th century timber-framed cottages, some still retaining their thatched roofs. The oldest surviving cottages, possibly built in the 14th century, stand on The Rock on the original road through the village. The Georgian houses remain in all their glory, little altered from the time of being built.

Castle Park was one of the well-known buildings rebuilt in the mid 1700s on the site of the castle which was burned down in 1654. In 1851 it was bought by Joseph Stubs, who employed the well-known landscape gardener Edward Kemp to lay out the gardens. These gardens are now for the use of the people of Frodsham.

Frodsham Marshes, which lie to the west between the M56 and the Manchester Ship Canal, are of great importance to ornothologists, and though nearly 200 different species of birds have been recorded, it is still not designated as 'Green Belt', much to the alarm of local people.

Gawsworth

The parish of Gawsworth is set in a beautiful part of Cheshire, between the hills at the eastern edge of the county and the flat land of the Cheshire Plain. It is named as Goursourde in the Domesday survey of 1086, and it is thought there was a settlement here in Neolithic times. Much of the present modern housing lies just off the Macclesfield to Congleton road in an area known as the Warren.

The Hall and church are probably on the site of an old wooden chapel and stone manor house where the de Orreby family lived when they were

Gawsworth Church

granted the manor of Gawsworth for 'one caparisoned horse'. The Fittons, who owned the manor for 400 years, rebuilt the Hall, the church, and the old rectory, and landscaped the surrounding area as a large park covering several square miles; four of the original five fishponds still remain. The area immediately round the Hall is surrounded by a long wall dating from Tudor times and includes a medieval tilting ground. Recent excavations have shown that this area may have been designed as an Elizabethan garden – perhaps in an attempt to attract Queen Elizabeth I to visit Gawsworth.

The tombs and effigies of four generations of the Fitton family are to be seen in the attractive sandstone 15th century church of St James with its eight-spired tower, winged dragon gargoyles, and armorial bearings of 15 ancient Cheshire families carved on the faces of the tower. The church was restored in the 19th century and is at present undergoing further repairs.

Mary Fitton, daughter of Sir Edward Fitton, is said by some authors to be the Dark Lady of Shakespeare's sonnets. She became a maid of honour to Queen Elizabeth I at the age of 17, but was later sent from court in disgrace, giving birth to a stillborn child. Her ghost is said to haunt the Old Rectory.

Another Gawsworth character was Samuel 'Maggotty' Johnson, last of the paid English jesters, also known as Lord Flame, after a character in a play he wrote and performed in at the Haymarket theatre in London. His ghost is also said to haunt the village, riding on a white horse. He is buried in 'Maggotty's Wood', now owned by the National Trust.

Gawsworth has had its share of drama. A fierce struggle over the inheritance of the manor of Gawsworth, involving forgery, seduction and divorce, ended in a duel in which both participants, Lord Mohun and the Duke of Hamilton, were killed.

The present owners, the Roper-Richards family, have done much to restore some of the important buildings in the village – the rectory, the Little Manor, once a cruck barn, the Old Rectory – but most of all Gawsworth Old Hall. This dates from the 15th century and was an unusual quadrangular shape until reduced in 1860 to the size we know today, making it one of the easiest of the Cheshire Halls to live in. It is now open to the public and is increasingly well known for its open-air theatre in the summer.

It is pleasant to stroll round the village and see the interesting buildings – Gawsworth Court, the gate house with its 20 inch thick walls; the rectory which has served as the village school, post office, shop and parish reading room; the New Hall, begun by Lord Mohun, recently an old people's home and now being converted into private dwellings; the Old Post Office – the oldest shop in Gawsworth, which has been in the same family for three generations; the White House, formerly the village school; and the Harrington Arms – a Queen Anne building which has changed little since it was built. With its cobbled forecourt, farm at the rear, and old oak bar, it is a homely and comfortable hostelry. At the other end of the parish is the only other inn – the Rising Sun.

Gawsworth now has a modern primary school, and a small row of shops. The parish hall and scout hut stand by a pleasant playing field with tennis courts and a children's playground. The war memorial, old water pump and market cross are on a small green which in spring is covered with snowdrops, crocus, cyclamen and miniature daffodils under oak and copper beeches.

Glazebury

Glazebury is the most northern village in Cheshire. It is an example of 19th century ribbon development, and was originally known as Bury Lane.

The oldest family in the area are the Holcrofts, who resided at Hurst Manor, which later became Hurst Hall. Prior to 1700, twelve generations of Holcrofts had lived there, and they were staunch Roman Catholics. The Hurst Holcrofts possessed a corn mill at Hurst Mill Bridge, as early as the beginning of the 14th century. Although the mill is no longer there the bridge is still a landmark of the village. The most noteworthy of the Holcrofts was Maria, daughter of Colonel John Holcroft. In 1650 Maria married Colonel Thomas Blood, whose claim to fame was his attempt to steal the Crown Jewels.

In 1830 the Duke of Wellington rode through Bury Lane, in a coach pulled by George Stephenson's *Rocket*, which was the first passenger train in the country – the line running from Manchester to Liverpool. The engineers of the day had racked their brains in an effort to get a solid formation across the yielding bog and marshland. After thousands of tons of ballast had been swallowed by the greedy swamp, and no progress seemed to have been made, Stephenson tried hurdles, made from the birch trees which grew plentifully on the Moss. On these hurdles was placed cotton waste, six inches deep, and layer after layer was used, until the line held good. This wonderful engineering achievement, of putting a railway line across the Chat Moss, had cost a guinea an inch.

Most of the village is, however, built on sandstone, and water was obtained from wells. Many tales have been told about the Cock Clod well, often submerged in filth from the river Glaze, and the unwary drawer was liable to get a frog, or worse, in the reddish-brown water.

Near the well is a packhorse bridge, Wash Bridge, which is one of the finest examples of a packhorse bridge in the vicinity.

Fifty years after the railway had been constructed, families travelled to the Glazebury Moss, with horses and carts, from Banks near Southport, 30 miles away. Their life was very hard, living in wooden huts on the moving peat, but they started to make the raw moss into what it is today – a great fertile expanse of land, which supports a market gardening industry. It is among the top three lettuce producing areas in the United Kingdom. Whilst Glazebury may not be known by many people, they would know of it, if their salad could talk!

The village Church of England school, built in 1882, which replaced other smaller schools in the area, still provides primary education, and a meeting place for village organisations. The two churches, Anglican and Methodist, maintain a true caring tradition for village life.

Goostrey 🐝

The history of Goostrey can be traced back to Saxon times. St Luke's church is a dominant part of the village and one of the few remaining churches with a moat, albeit without water.

However Goostrey for a long time had a church – but no churchyard. Bodies had to be taken eight miles away to the mother church at Sandbach, across the river Dane. The land was marshy and subject to flooding. In 1530 a licence was granted giving permission to the villagers of Goostrey to bury their own dead, providing they still paid the fee to the mother church.

Legend, backed by old church accounts books, says that the huge yew tree outside the church door provided arrows for the Cheshire bowmen, and in 1365 records show that land was granted to two archers for distinguished conduct at the battle of Poitiers.

The showing of gooseberries is a celebrated custom of the area. To take part you must be an accredited member of the society and be prepared to have your berries examined during the growing period, even though you would never dream of cheating! It is a serious business when the catchweights and pennyweights come out on show day, but a wonderful feeling when you are declared champion.

In 1956 in a field on the northern side of Goostrey, Professor Bernard Lovell was responsible for the setting up of Jodrell Bank, at that time the world's largest radio telescope. Known locally as Lovell's Saucer, the landmark can be seen from most parts of Cheshire. In the exhibition centre, pieces of rock brought back from man's first landing on the moon, one of the space suits and samples of space age technology are on view to the public, whilst the planetarium offers an insight to the heavens. In the grounds of Jodrell Bank stands the arboretum belonging to the Botany Department of Manchester University – old and new sciences side by side.

In the early 1960s things began to change in Goostrey. Planning permission was given to build houses and over the succeeding 25 years the village population grew from 600 to just over 2,000. The move north of some of the large chemical and computing companies and banks brought with them the commuter. With the building of the motorway network and its proximity to Ringway airport, Goostrey found itself an ideal place to be.

Grappenhall ✆

Both old and new buildings combine to make up the village, which has a seven and a half mile boundary. In 1977 the ancient custom of beating the bounds was revived after a gap of 56 years. The north side is now fully developed, but on the south it is still farms and woodlands. These stretch into the distance to give it a peaceful and tranquil air.

The old part of the village is entered by two hump-backed bridges over the Bridgewater Canal and the street between them is known as Church Street. This for the most part is still cobbled. Although its thatched cottages have long since gone, the existing buildings blend in and one feels on entering the village, that one has stepped back in time.

The sandstone-built Ram's Head, with an old sun-dial on the wall, and the cream-washed Parr Arms with its hanging baskets and coat of arms over the door, and the stocks just outside, all help to keep this illusion. The stocks were still in use as late as the 19th century, and were the responsibility of the verger. The Parr Arms was formerly known as the 'Barry Arms'.

The church of St Wilfrid dates back to the 12th century and is built of sandstone, which came from a local quarry. It makes a very impressive feature and is surrounded by an interesting graveyard. The earliest gravestone to be read is of the Drinkwater family of Thelwall dated 1624. Another is marked with the skull and cross-bones, commonly thought to be a pirate's grave, but in fact the grave of a plague victim.

The old rectory is now a home for the elderly. The new rectory opposite the church was built in the early 1800s and is of Gothic design. Many garden parties, fetes and social occasions take place within its walls and gardens throughout the year.

The original Grappenhall Hall stands in its well kept grounds with tree-lined avenue, and is now a special school for boys. This was the home of the Greenhall family and private theatricals used to be performed there. The sandstone wall which surrounds the grounds has been a feature of the village street for many years.

The village school was built in 1846 and, despite renovations, retains its charm and identity. Its playing field extends to the Bridgewater Canal, which is cut in a loop around the village thus making it free from heavy traffic. The first school was attached to the church and this was built in 1627 and paid for by subscriptions. The outline of it can still be seen on the west wall underneath the Cheshire Cat.

During the summer months narrow boats of all lengths and assorted cabin cruisers pass through the village or are moored along the towpath. The towpaths are kept in good repair and offer some lovely walks, linking with footpaths and lanes through this part of the county.

There are still some of the original buildings associated with the cutting of the canal in 1759–65, including a small grain warehouse or store for local farmers who made use of this new mode of transport. This is now a private house, as is a grander house built for an official to oversee this section of the canal as it was built.

The church hall, or as local people call it, 'The Large Room', is opposite the Parr Arms and was built 150 years ago. Sadly several thatched cottages were demolished to make this possible.

The shops have gone from this part and are now all on the other side of the canal. There was once a tollgate on Knutsford Road but the gate was removed in 1876 and the toll cottage pulled down in the 1960s.

There used to be a smithy at the bottom of Broad Lane and it was here that the iron work for the church was made. The initials GF (George Fairhurst) can still be seen on the ironwork of the doors, he being the village blacksmith at that time. Also in Broad Lane there used to be a workhouse made up of several cottages. These were mostly demolished in the early 1900s.

Great Boughton
& Boughton Heath

In 1086 Great Boughton and Boughton Heath were well-defined by the remains of Roman Watling Street (A51), the lane to Christleton, marshy Caldy brook, and the steep slopes dropping down to the Dee. The Dee marked the Welsh border and for the following century there were periodic raids by the Welsh – probably no more than cattle rustling, which was common along the border well into the Middle Ages.

The land was owned by the Benedictine abbey of St Werbergh. In the 12th century it administered the leper hospital of St Giles founded by Earl Ranulph III of Chester near the hamlet which became known as Spital Boughton. It would not have been permitted in the city, but here there was land for the hospital, a chapel and graveyard (now 'the Mount').

In Elizabeth I's reign, gallows and a whipping post stood on Gallows Hill – a very steep bank of the Dee – a place of public execution for Chester until 1801 (today a public garden).

In 1555, Protestant martyr George Marsh was burned at the stake and his ashes interred in the hospice graveyard. In 1679 Catholic priest John Plessington was also martyred there. An obelisk erected in 1898 commemorates them both.

There are tales of reported witches being bound in barrels and rolled into the Dee down Barrelwell Hill, from the gallows to the river. If they drowned they were believed innocent; if they survived this was attributed to the protection of their satanic powers, proving their guilt, so their tormentors could look forward to an execution to follow. Of a later date, Stocks Lane past the heath tells its own story.

Bull baiting frequently took place in Boughton Heath until 1833; the sport was banned in Chester 30 years earlier.

Chester city was held for the King in the Civil War and, when siege was threatened in 1643 by Parliamentarians encamped at Rowton, defensive measures necessitated the demolition and burning of buildings which might afford cover. Boughton was razed to the ground, including the chapel and hospice. The siege developed and in 1644 the beleaguered garrison attempted a sortie to the east – a disaster which cost the Royalists 140 men, some of whom are buried in the graveyard at the Mount. This little plot continued in use until 1854 and is all that remains of pre-Civil War Boughton.

In the 1770s the Shropshire Union canal from Chester to Middlewich was constructed through the northern part of the district, and the subsequent trade increased the size of the village. By the late 18th century the road linking Great Boughton to Chester was developing attractive houses on the north side, with views across the river to Wales. Many ledges in the high riverbank were levelled and built upon with romantic disregard for sound foundations. Boughton Hall was the largest of the houses round Filkins Lane in their own grounds.

The tithe map of 1849 shows the Heath as an area of land (almost 18 acres) crossed by several tracks. The Heath was 'enclosed' in 1859, the tracks becoming lanes whose names still persist – Heath Lane, Becket's Lane, Bachelor's Lane – the open space being fenced and parcelled out. Five acres along Heath Lane/Poorhouse Lane (now White's Meadow) was taken by the Tarvin union workhouse. The trustees, doubtless mindful of Christ's reminder that the poor are with us always, undertook to maintain the fences of this plot 'for ever'.

A large brickworks is shown at the end of Bachelor's Lane, its size suggesting it was a major employer of labour, but it had totally disappeared by 1911. The workhouse was demolished in the 1960s and replaced with sheltered housing.

St Paul's church, built out from the highest point of the Dee bank, is a feature of the area with its spire and steep roof (1898), a few yards from the shops and public house (1900) opposite the Mount.

Today, Boughton and Boughton Heath continue as a popular residential area, but the Heath and lanes remain in name only.

Great Budworth 🎋

Argued by some to be one of Cheshire's loveliest villages, Great Budworth, or the village on the hill, lies three miles north of Northwich and eight miles south of Warrington, overlooking Budworth Mere. Its name derives from Saxon times, meaning Budda's enclosure.

Its character results from the almost unchanged square-framed cottages, closely packed on either side of the main High Street. With names such as Goldmine House, Noah's Ark and Cob Cottage, the houses are all individually styled, built of local brick or black and white wattle and daub, with wooden front doors leading directly onto cobbled pavements, while the varying pitch and heights of roofs support a wide range of

Great Budworth

chimney design. Because of this very original and charming setting the village is a popular location for films and television dramas.

In the past, the White Hart, Ring o'Bells and Saracen's Head have all been alehouses but are now converted to homes, and today the George and Dragon is the local inn, with its ornate wrought iron sign hanging over the porch.

Before the arrival of mains water in 1934 the village obtained its water from a pump at the bottom of High Street, which was later enclosed by a pumphouse, built in 1869 by Rowland Eyles Egerton Warburton, composer of the verse inscribed above the pump. He was known as the 'Rhyming Poet of Arley' and wrote verses which can still be found today on nearby houses, signposts and in the George and Dragon porch.

At the top of High Street, by the church wall, remain the village stocks, which were frequently used up until 1854 to discourage vagrants from other parishes.

Passing through the lychgate, erected in 1921 in memory of those killed in the First World War, one enters St Mary's church, a fine example of Perpendicular Gothic design, dating from the 14th century. It was built from local sandstone by the Norton priory and in the 15th century the clerestory and tower (now housing eight bells dated 1733) were added.

Adjacent to the church is the parochial school building founded by Sir John Deane in 1600, which has been a reading room, library, men's club room, and became the Sunday school when the new school was built in 1857. During the 19th century there were five schools in the village, today there are two.

Industries which flourished in the 19th century included brickmaking, saddlery, shoemaking, and clock-case making in Clock Cottages.

A wake to commemorate the dedication of the church of St Mary and All Saints is still observed on the old date of 11th November. The custom of eating flummery, or furmenty, a mixture of boiled wheat, milk, sugar and spice, was observed in some households on Wakes Sunday. School children had two days holiday and a dance and parish social were held. Today villagers are entertained by nearby Comberbach Mummers performing the local soul caking play. This is based on an ancient ritual with Death and Resurrection as its theme. Characters include the 'Letter-in', Quack Doctor, Dairy Dout and Beelzebub. A real skull with bones strung together is used for 'The Horse', which enables the mouth to open and the teeth to snap.

Today Great Budworth is a changing village, old names that have been here for generations have disappeared, but a village atmosphere is still maintained. Great care is taken to ensure that all alterations and extensions to cottages are in keeping with this charming old-world village to preserve it for the enjoyment of future generations.

Great Sutton 🌿

The village of Great Sutton lies some six miles from Chester. It existed as a quiet agricultural community, virtually unchanged for centuries. There is in fact evidence of very early inhabitation in the district. In the early 1950s an axe head dating from between 1000 and 500 BC was discovered in a garden in Church Lane. This artefact can now be seen in Chester's Grosvenor Museum. There is also a local legend that a long-lost Roman road to Meols ran through Great Sutton and nearby Capenhurst. No evidence remains of this, however.

In 1845 the population of the village was 203 people living in 69 dwellings. By the close of the century the population had not greatly increased, the village now having 336 inhabitants. Today the population swells weekly as modern private estates cover the once fertile farming land. This building joins the extensive council estates built in the late 1950s and early 1960s.

The village of the 19th century contained several names of thoroughfares familiar to the residents of today. Green Lane for instance, though now unrecognisable with modern private housing and having had its course altered, originally acquired its name because it led to an area called 'the green'. In addition, Whetstone (Whitestone) Hey probably gained its name from a rock or pillar of stone. The modern Whetstone Hey gives its name to a home for the elderly and a built-up housing area. The ancient Salter's Lane however, has sadly disappeared. This is thought to have been a remnant of the 'Salt Way', that ran along the village borders and along which salt was transported from the Cheshire 'Wiches', to Shotwick.

One of the most attractive features of old Great Sutton still surviving is the 'Manor'. On the main road to Chester, and now a home for the mentally handicapped, it was once the residence of Peter Owen, a local landowner and benefactor. The Owens also constructed Manor Cottages, the attractive dwellings on the opposite side of the New Chester Road. They were built at the end of the 19th century and beginning of the 20th for estate workers.

Great Sutton and neighbouring Little Sutton were incorporated originally into the parish of Eastham, not having a church of their own. Church services were once held in the shippon of Church Farm, which formerly stood on the corner of what is now Sutton Way and Old

Chester Road. The present church was completed in 1879 and in 1880 the parish was officially divided from Eastham.

The building beside the church was formerly a school. It was built by Peter Owen in memory of his late wife Eleanor. It was always called the Eleanor school and now it serves as a church hall and is still affectionately 'the Eleanor'. The former school and the church are both attractive sandstone buildings.

The main street of today's Great Sutton contains two hostelries, the modern Bull's Head built on the site of a former inn, and the White Swan, which still looks much as it did in its days as a coaching inn. The Swan or 'Mucky Duck', as it is known locally, was once called the Black Swan, which perhaps explains its nickname.

While the village has been somewhat overshadowed by its giant neighbour Ellesmere Port for a number of years now, it has still managed to retain its own unique qualities. It offers a pleasant and attractive place to live with a long and interesting heritage behind it.

Hale ❧

There appears to have been a Domesday settlement in Hale, some evidence of which came to light near Queens Road and Hermitage Road.

Hale Moss was where the 'fragrant sweet rush' grew in abundance, but by 1870 the quality of the sweet rush and grass had deteriorated and the Moss was abandoned to vagrant gypsies, led by 'Emperor Boss'. The rest of Hale Moss was fenced into areas, drained and cleaned up and, in the 1920s used for housing.

The first Urban District Council offices were at Thorn Grove, Albert Road but, in 1913, were moved to a building in Ashley Road, which was originally a girls home, built in 1883. These offices were next to the drill hall, whose polished wooden floor used to resound to the steady tramp of the Cheshire Regiment's boots – well remembered for being amongst the first men drafted in the dark days of August and September 1939 at the beginning of the Second World War.

Alas, all this has gone, together with the individuality of the shops, the personal service given, and the grocery orders delivered by cheerful, whistling youths on carrier bicycles. However, when developers tried to acquire the pretty, flower-bordered bowling green, local citizens banded together and personally contributed to the cost of legal representation, as apparently this land had been a gift to the people of Hale. Nowadays the present residents can enjoy this little oasis, right in the centre of the village.

The old Hale cinema, which boasted a licensed bar and restaurant, is well remembered by the older residents. Unfortunately it was a privately-owned cinema, which died like many other smaller cinemas. A block of flats has been built on the site.

Hale station, both before and during the Second World War, was a very pretty one, with flower baskets and gardens in the summertime and polished benches and good coal fires in the winter to cheer the passengers. The goods yard was full of thriving businesses and, in earlier years, horses were stabled behind the now Cheshire Midland Hotel, with a smithy in Brown Street.

One Hale character was Mr James Goodier, who used to sit, resplendent in bowler hat, fancy waistcoat and clogs, near Hale railway crossing. He had worked on the railway all his life and knew every driver and guard who passed through. He was a great believer in herbs, and people used to go to see him with various aches and pains, and were given bunches of comfrey leaves to boil and drink to ease their ailments. Unfortunately one day a spark from a passing engine set fire to his comfrey patch, growing on the railway embankment. He was sadly missed when he died at a very old age.

At the far end of the village there is an old inn called the Bleeding Wolf. Legend has it that the last wolf in Cheshire was sighted at that spot. Visitors to Hale these days must think the people a rude lot when, asking directions, they are told to 'turn left at the Bleeding Wolf'!

Halton 🦊

The residents of Halton village thought they would be completely swamped during the 1960s by the joining together of the twin towns of Runcorn and Widnes to form the new Borough of Halton. At the same time the New Town of Runcorn was started and the new houses and buildings, including the 'Shopping City', proliferated around the village itself. However, the village has managed to retain much of its identity.

Main Street, which runs round the base of the castle, is almost unchanged.

The Methodist church stands at the far end of Main Street, at the bottom of Castle Road. The castle (built in the 11th century) was reduced to a few ruined walls during the Civil War, but the remains are well preserved, and stand out at the top of the hill. The Castle Hotel next to the ruins incorporates the old courthouse on the upper floor, with access by steps outside the main building.

The present church (St Mary's), just below the castle, replaced the original in 1820; but the stone vicarage was built around 1650, and the recently restored library in 1773.

Following Main Street back to the top of Halton Brow, the Seneschal House, a medieval building of great beauty, has been in continuous occupation and it is kept in immaculate condition by the present owner. Opposite stands an ancient inn, the Norton Arms.

Mention must be made of nearby Norton Priory, which was built by Augustinian friars in 1155, but at the Dissolution of the Monasteries was purchased from the Crown by Sir Richard Brooke. The family had close ties with Halton, where they were regarded lords of the manor. Early this century the family left and the house fell into decay. It was demolished in the 1930s, except for the crypt and a wall with a statue of St Christopher. These have been recently incorporated into a tasteful and informative museum, with the grounds displaying the finds of an archaeological dig with many interesting remains.

Village activities, in addition to the two churches and the two inns, include a British Legion and a lively Women's Institute, as well as various other clubs and societies.

Although so near the recent urban areas, it is considered by present residents that Halton village can still be regarded as portraying the characteristics of busy village life.

Handbridge

From the city walls of Chester one can stand on the Bridgegate and look across the river Dee to Handbridge. It was at this spot that the Romans on their way to Wales found a ford and later built a bridge. The pleasant park with its tall trees conceals a Roman quarry and a shrine to Minerva. This same vantage point gives one a view of the Old Dee Bridge and the weir, an ancient causeway built by Earl Hugh of Chester (d1101), for power to drive the watermills. So successful were these mills that by the early 17th century there were eleven water-wheels, six for corn, three for fulling cloth, and two for raising water. All this activity made Handbridge into a hive of industry; no wonder the Miller of the Dee was such a happy man.

The 'bridge' in Handbridge is another clue as to the reason for its existence. There is no sign of the Roman structure but during the Middle Ages several wooden bridges were swept away by floods. King Richard II therefore gave grants for repairs to the bridge and authorised tolls for rebuilding it. These tolls were not abolished until 1885. This was the main road into Wales, at that time still unruly. The Welsh for Handbridge, Treboeth, means burned town and it is easy to imagine the inhabitants fleeing across the bridge to seek refuge in the city walls when the raiding parties descended from the hills.

The present stone structure, seven irregular arches, dates from the 13th century and looks as though it was built in a piecemeal fashion. From here one could watch on a summer evening the activities of the salmon fishermen as they rowed their boats out into midstream. The method of fishing was to play out the seine nets until the boat had come full circle. Standing on the bank they then hauled in hand over hand until a great mound of netting piled up beside them. Tension mounted as the last bobbing corks approached the bank. The anti-climax when the net was found to be empty – that is, nearly always – was felt by all, but occasionally one could tell by the extra care taken that there was a catch. Flashing silver in the mud the fish would struggle desperately to get back into the river. Just once in a while they would be too strong for the men and slipped from their grasp.

The street where the fisherfolk lived was known as Stye Lane. Now called Greenway Street, it is an interesting cobbled way with picturesque quaysides leading down to the river. Not much fishing goes on now and the families have left the street but the stakes where they dried the nets can still be seen.

A guide book of the 19th century gives this description of Handbridge: 'narrow steep streets, built on a red rock almost exclusively inhabited by the lower orders'. It was indeed a rough place full of taverns and groups of hovels known as 'courts'. Besides the fishermen the local inhabitants got their livelihood in trades associated with the Dee mills – there were skinners, tanners, and workers at the tobacco and snuff mills run by the firm of Nicholls. At the end of the bridge there was a needle factory and beside the Red Lion in Overleigh Road, a rope walk, the length of which can still be identified.

Being so close to the city and also to the countryside, Handbridge is no longer a haunt of the lower orders. The former inhabitants would smile to see their humble cottages done up by young professionals who enjoy being able to walk to work. Retired people and young families also like

113

living here as they value the village atmosphere. The old originals, however, of whom there are still a surprising number, cherish their reputation for mild eccentricity and never cease to wonder at the prices fetched for houses in their street.

Hargrave & Huxley 🐚

Six miles south-east of Chester in the rural area between the roads to Whitchurch and Nantwich, lie the villages of Huxley and Hargrave. Strictly speaking the civil parish which includes Hargrave is known by the medieval sounding name of Foulk Stapleford. The two separate civil parishes are now linked in the same ecclesiastical parish based on Hargrave church.

The river Gowy runs through the district and there is evidence for there having been at least four watermills on this stretch of the river.

A local legend about the origins of Hargrave church and school says Thomas Moulson, a schoolboy from Hargrave, could not return home one night from Tarvin school because the river Gowy was flooded and he spent the night sleeping in a haystack. Next morning he vowed that if ever he became rich he would build a school at Hargrave. As in another famous legend, he found wealth in London and became Lord Mayor. In 1627 he kept his promise and built a combined school and chapel at Hargrave.

There has been a strong tradition of nonconformist worship in Huxley. To commemorate the opening of the New Connection chapel in Huxley of 1842, a tea party was held when a large booth or tent was erected in the field opposite the chapel. It was skilfully contrived and richly decorated with evergreens of almost every description, with a light covering to protect from the heat of the sun or falling showers of rain. The day was beautiful and the company numerous. Six hundred and forty tickets were sold at one shilling each and about 800 persons were refreshed with the beverage which cheers but does not inebriate.

One of the oldest houses in the village, Higher Huxley Hall, has a carved oak Elizabethan staircase, two presumed priest holes and a south facing 'leper' window. Some old inhabitants say that a ghostly lady rides a white horse at midnight through the horsewash. A late 13th century bronze stirrup was found when new drains were dug.

The other extant manor house is Lower Huxley Hall, which is moated. The house commands a clear view of Beeston Castle and was garrisoned by Colonel Thomas Croxton for the Parliamentarians in the 1640s while the castle was held by the Royalists.

Some form of fair, traditionally held on the nearest weekend to the feast of St Peter, was held in Hargrave from at least Victorian times. Within the memory of the present inhabitants it included a rodeo for both horses and bullocks and cart-horse racing. At one fair a gypsy won the five shilling prize sitting back to front and holding onto the bullock's tail! Since 1985 this fair has been revived as 'Happy Days' with floats, stalls, games and sports.

Having been predominantly farming communities for most of their history, the villages are now attracting more residents who travel to work either in Chester or in the industrial areas to the north of the county. Despite the closeness to Chester the area still offers facilities for country pursuits and the many footpaths are used by ramblers.

Hartford 🌿

Hartford dates from pre-Roman times and probably got its name from its situation near a ford across the river, on the rough track through Delamere Forest to the salt springs in Northwich a mile and a half away.

With the coming of the Romans, the track grew into a branch of Watling Street and must have seen regular traffic of salt traders and Roman soldiers. Hartford is mentioned in the Domesday survey and by then it had grown into a small hamlet. Throughout the Middle Ages it continued to be just a clearing along a trade route, walled in by the forest. The villagers must have been awe-struck by the glimpse of a world of riches, colour and splendour when the soldiers and baggage train of Edward I marched and lumbered past their cottages en route to Vale Royal Abbey from their triumphant Welsh campaign.

Hartford records two bits of excitement during the Civil War. Colonel Morrow, a Parliamentarian much respected by both sides, is said to have received the wound from which he subsequently died during an incident in Hartford in July 1644; and there was also a skirmish on the village green before the battle of nearby Winnington Bridge when the Royalist forces of Sir George Booth were fleeing from the Parliamentarians under John Lambert. One of the village's present housing developments has roads named after the famous men of the Civil War.

In time the forest receded and considerable areas of common land developed on which the villagers grazed their cattle. During the Industrial

Revolution wealthy manufacturers from the growing towns nearby came to make their homes in Hartford. These included the chairman of the Grand Trunk Railway and it was because of him that mainline trains were stopped at Hartford, even though it was only a secondary station. It is interesting that these houses of the industrial giants of yesterday are now occupied by their present-day equivalents – notably North West Gas, NW Water, the Borough Council and a well-known hotel chain.

With the coming of Brunner Mond (later ICI) to Winnington, the character of Hartford began to change. It was sufficiently close to the works and yet sufficiently rural to attract new inhabitants and the population increased rapidly. In 1921 it was 894, in 1931 it was 1,420, in 1965 it was 2,753 and in 1981 it was 3,958 – a pattern of growth which is continuing.

Today it is still regarded as a desirable place to live and its inhabitants come from all walks of life. Apart from the huge increase in the number of houses, one of the most conspicuous developments in Hartford has been its growth as an educational centre. Not only is there a large independent school, but also a campus housing the Mid-Cheshire College of Further Education, Roman Catholic and County primary and secondary schools and two schools for children with special needs. These stimulate the life of the community and their grounds have preserved acres of virtual parkland.

Hatherton ❧

Hatherton is a country district or parish rather than a village. The centre is four miles south-east of Nantwich and the A529 passes through Hatherton to Audlem.

Haretone, as it was called in the Domesday Book, had at that time a manor house, two farms and a lodge, and was owned by William Malbank.

The original Hatherton Hall was demolished and a farmhouse built on the site. The house is now a private residence and the farm buildings have been converted into a large home with a separate entrance from the farmhouse. The Cliffe family moved from Hatherton Hall to Hatherton Manor Farm, where they are today.

There are two Methodist chapels in Hatherton, one with a house attached on Crewe Road, is still used for worship. It is also the polling station for local and general elections. The other chapel on Audlem Road was built in 1900 and ceased to be a place of worship in 1968.

The very large white house known as The Broomlands, stands in an elevated position from the A529. It is now divided into several dwellings, and was formerly the home of Mrs Walkden, a local landowner. The Broomlands' stable block was a hospital for sick horses during the First World War. Reg Johnson worked for the army looking after the horses. The stable block has been converted into cottages, one being the post office and stores.

Tommy Davies lived at the aptly named Bank House, built up to the road, on the top of the bank at Oaks Corner. He earned his living as general carter. A wheelwright named Manning lived at Rose Cottage, Audlem Road. Jimmy Pover, a noted 'character', lived further along Audlem Road near the Hankelow boundary. His home was the white tollgate house and he worked as a cattle drover.

Stapeley House was the Rural District Offices until the reorganization of Crewe & Nantwich Borough Council. Colonel Christy-Miller of the 'Christy Hat' family lived there. Christy's became well known for their excellent quality hats of all types, including protective hats for horse riding and the police force.

Stapeley Water Gardens, started by Mr Ray Davies in a small way, has grown to international proportions. Visitors arrive by coach and car to see the varied attractions.

Hatherton is still a very rural district with only four new homes being built since the 1960s. The farms are now owner-occupied but at one time formed part of the huge Delves–Broughton estate.

Hatton juxta Daresbury ✒

It was in the early years of Henry III's reign that Hatton received its first known mention in history, when Geoffrey, son of Adam de Dutton, gave their township to William, son of Hothy of Hatton.

There was a significant outburst of building in the early years of the 18th century when the ancient 'messuages' were consolidated into modern-type farms. In 1708 Little Greenside was built and, soon after, the nearby Greenside Farm. Holly Bank dates from 1709 and a plaque on the wall of School House ascribes it to 'P.I.E. 1710'. Pepper Street Farm (since 1912 renamed New House Farm) and Hatton Hall Farm both date from about this time.

It was in the year 1709 that a John Picton of Manchester, in his will, gave the residue of his personal property and a croft in Clay Lanes to the poor of the township. Later £63 was deposited in the Savings Bank, the interest from which provided coal and calico for the poor of the village. The Picton Charity is still in being but has been rendered largely ineffective in recent decades.

Samuel Bagshaw's 1850 *History, Gazetteer and Directory of Cheshire* gives Hatton's population in 1801 as 241. In 1831 it had risen to 392. By contrast the 1931 census records a population of 297 and this had only increased to 329 by 1981. Bagshaw also gives the number of dwelling houses in 1841 as 82. Currently there are 122 in Hatton.

As the generations passed there evolved a community almost entirely tied to the land as farmers, farm labourers and their families. They comprised an extremely tight-knit community, somewhat in-bred, tending to be cut off from and impervious to outside trends and influences. Movement outside the village was rare and so was marriage. The First World War did little to alter these characteristics since farming was a 'reserved occupation', though one minor outside influence was the annual arrival of potato-picking gangs of Irishmen who worked with the village women to dig and bag potatoes. They were accommodated in 'paddy shants', a feature of most farms of the time.

By the early 1930s there had been little significant change over the centuries. True, an infants school had been built. There was also an Anglican chapel with a village hall attached, but there was no electricity, no street lighting, and no gas (nor is there a gas supply today). There was no public transport except for a bus which ran shoppers to Warrington and back on Saturday mornings. Supplies of bread, greengrocery and paraffin were brought in by travelling salesmen, though there was by now a small village shop, a post office and the Hatton Arms inn (which appears on the Ordnance Survey map of 1873 as The Red Lion). Since the end of the 19th century fresh water had been brought to each house through lead pipes but before this time water was drawn from wells, a number of which were to be found in back yards, and there was a town well for public use, still to be seen in the garden of Wellbrow Cottage.

Very few villagers now work on the land. The village school has long since been turned into a dwelling place, as has the chapel and village hall.

It is apparent that the sleepy, charming, restful, old Hatton is becoming a 'dormitory village'. Even now the Warrington New Town development is reaching out across the surrounding fields to Hatton – and in a very few years could destroy it.

Haughton 🪶

Haughton is a township and small village 15 miles from Chester and six miles from Nantwich. It lies in the heart of the dairy farming area, where cheese was made on many farms up to the end of the 1950s, and farming is still the main occupation.

The property of Haughton Hall is believed to have formed part of the lands granted at the Conquest to Robert Fitz Hugh, one of the most powerful of the Norman barons. By Edward II's reign it had passed into the hands of Robert de Halghton. In this family it remained until the middle of the 18th century, and the name gradually developed into Haughton. The original old wood dwelling was taken down and replaced with the present fine brick Hall.

Although Haughton does not have a church, it does have a mission room built by the Brocklebanks, used for monthly services. It has for many years had its own post office and public house, the Nag's Head.

The population of 130 remained fairly unaltered, due to restriction in building, until recently when some farm buildings have been reconstructed into dwellings.

Helsby 🪶

Helsby's history goes back 2,000 years, when Iron Age tribesmen – probably of the Cornovii tribe – constructed a hill fort on top of Helsby Tor (464 ft high), a northern frontier post of their tribal territory. Helsby itself was built at the foot of the hill above the level of the undrained marshland.

In medieval times, the great Forest of Delamere reached as far as Helsby and beyond. Even when the forest receded and much of the common land became cultivated, there were still many trees. Nowadays the surrounding land is under cultivation and the only remains of the common land are on the hill itself. The marshes which stretch northwards to the river Mersey, where the early inhabitants kept their cattle, are now more extensively drained than hitherto and turned into agricultural land. The M56 motorway was built on this land in 1971.

The rocky escarpments on the hill have a strong resemblance to a man's face. This part of the hill is a favourite haunt of rock climbers and is a recognised training place. Guide books quote, 'As long as Helsby wears a hood, the weather's never very good'.

In the latter part of the 18th century the mail was carried on horseback through Helsby. In 1795 the postboy was stopped and his mail bags stolen by a man named Lowndes. Three years later Lowndes was seen and identified in Exeter and brought to Chester for trial. He was convicted and sentenced to death, his body to be gibbeted on Helsby Hill.

Unlike many Cheshire villages Helsby is sadly lacking in any architecture of note. One house worthy of mention is Hillside, a house of unknown age, but from the existence of powder-closets leading from the bedrooms, it would appear to be Georgian. When Mr Fairich, who lived here, was the Mayor of Chester, Charles Kingsley came to spend a few days with him. He liked Helsby and wrote in a letter, 'They have no east winds here'.

Quarrying was a thriving industry on the south side of the hill in the 1870s. The stone obtained was used in the construction of Liverpool Docks, Birkenhead Docks, Liverpool Custom House, many churches in the area and a number of buildings in Chester. It was also used for repairs to Chester Cathedral. Nowadays there are two industrial units. The main industry is cablemaking, which came to the village in 1887, known then as the Telegraph Manufacturing Co, and now as BICC Electronic Cables.

Today Helsby is a growing village (population 4,350) with a church, Methodist church, high school, two primary schools, library, community centre, old folks' sheltered housing, health centre and of course, station, but it still remans an agricultural area with many farms with milk cattle as well as growing cereals and the famous 'Cheshire' potatoes. There are also many clubs and societies ranging form Brownies, Scouts and Girl Guides to the Tuesday Club for Senior Citizens.

On Good Friday the three churches hold a service on the top of the hill when a wooden cross is erected at noon and remains on the hill all day. One of the village primary schools has revived the old custom of maypole dancing and there has also been a successful revival of the Hill Races.

Henbury & Broken Cross 🌿

Henbury, three miles from Macclesfield, is a fascinating village, mentioned in the Domesday Book. It was known as Henbury in 1383 though the name has varied frequently through the centuries. Over the years most of the people have been tenant farmers of the Hall, or farm labourers.

However, without its neighbouring village of Broken Cross, Henbury would by now almost certainly have lost its identity.

Broken Cross village, with its assortment of small shops and its clock of considerable age, has been at the centre of a very busy crossroads for over a thousand years. It is thought that at one time there may have been a cross in the village centre, or perhaps its name arose from the nature of the crossroads, which did not form a regular intersection, though now they are joined by a modern roundabout.

Here on the turnpike road from Macclesfield to Knutsford, crossed by the older salters' route, stood the toll house. Money, fraudulently

Henbury village in winter

minted in the village by a coining gang, is thought to have been passed on here. Many of the villagers were basket makers, gathering the withies locally. On Saturday mornings the children used to deliver the baskets to the customers, mainly on the farms. Another occupation was weaving and the weavers' cottages still stand in the village.

It is recorded that children from Broken Cross Sunday school, which is now demolished, walked in procession with other Sunday schools in Macclesfield to celebrate the coronation of Queen Victoria in 1838. The Methodist church built about 1880, recently modernised and extended, has a flourishing congregation.

The district of Henbury is still a farming area with comparatively large farms, but a commuter estate has grown up around the church.

The church of St Thomas, built in 1844 as a daughter church of Prestbury, was only licensed for marriages in 1870 when the local squire's daughter was married. It is beautified by the engraved glass doors in memory of Sir Vincent de Ferranti of Henbury Hall, founder of the electronics firm. The slender broach spire can be seen from quite a distance across the fields. A recent signature in the visitors' book is that of Sarah, Duchess of York, when she attended a baptism service in 1989.

The modern church hall is used by a number of organisations including an amateur dramatic group. Plaques in the entrance hall show that Henbury has won a number of Best Kept Village awards.

Burial mounds have been found at Bearhurst Farm and excavation took place in 1966 when a burial urn was unearthed containing the remains of a male aged about 18 years.

An elderly resident remembers his mother relating how she and other women sat on stones in a circle making bricks at Brickbank Farm. Here, in 1971, when a field was ploughed some large stones were discovered. Later excavation revealed the remains of a stone circle measuring six metres in diameter. The circle had an alignment with the mid-winter rising sun. Could these brickworkers have been unwittingly using a prehistoric site as their work place?

Pale Farm, with a typical Cheshire black and white house and a mere, on the boundary of Henbury is a very beautiful spot. ('Pale' here meaning boundary as in 'beyond the pale').

The present Henbury Hall, built between 1984–86 on the site of the 18th century hall in the Palladian style, and planned by Sir Vincent, but it was not built until after his death. By the gate of the lodge, now a private house, stands a famous tree, believed to be the largest sycamore in Cheshire. The Plague Stone, originally in a rather unpleasant spot known as Sugar Pit Dump, has now been moved nearer to a gate leading to the Hall. Legend has it that the stone used to turn over at midnight! The grey squirrel was first successfully introduced to Britain in Henbury Park as a game animal, but little thought seems to have been given to the damage it might cause in years ahead.

Whirley Hall, on the old turnpike road, is a late 17th century brick house on the site of a much older hall. There have been many alterations and it is now the home of Sir William Mather of Mather & Platt Engineering. There is an old local saying that 'a pig and its litter would cross the road twice a year', and here the villagers used to sit by the roadside awaiting this event.

The Henbury high school, which is situated at Broken Cross, helps to combine the two villages and maintain the continuity of this pleasant rural area as it moves steadily into the modern world.

Higher Bebington

People who were, and still are, born in the immediate village are known as 'firbobs'. This comes from the fircones of Storeton Woods across the way.

Higher Bebington had been established as a village for many years but it was not until 1859 when the Higher Bebington Local Board was formed that its growth really began. It now has a sizeable community.

There are still a number of old, interesting buildings. The 'Royal Oak Chambers', now occupied by a firm of architects, dates from 1739. Until recent years it was a tiny public house. Outside there was a hedge that was trimmed into the shape of a large armchair!

The original school building stands on School Lane. Built in 1845 it closed its doors in 1913, when the new larger school was opened in Mill Road. The old school was reopened as the Methodist chapel and over the years has been renovated and is popular with the villagers.

Higher Bebington's parish church is a graceful building standing on Kings Road, called Christ church. It was built in 1857–59 of the local 'Keuper' stone. Its steeple and bell tower were added in 1885. Alongside in the 1920s was a golf course, where local people used to caddie for the rich golfers (the local golf course is now situated in Brackenwood Park).

Victoria Hall is the village hall, opened in 1897 to mark the Diamond Jubilee of Queen Victoria. It was extended in the 1970s. Originally 'magic lantern' slide lectures were held there. Today, however, sees a wide selection of events, from playgroups to attic sales.

Occupations have been many and varied over the years. The last farmer was probably farmer Howard, in the 1950s, who would plough his Town Lane fields with his two shire horses. The smithies were very important for shoeing the horses and making tools. Cobblers kept everyone well-shod. Carpenters did the major wood work and the thatcher and tilers looked after the roofs. Carters delivered goods of different types. The mill, built about 1808 close to Storeton Quarries, provided the flour for baking.

There were a number of wash-houses, most famous being Granny Everard's in Kings Court. It was demolished long ago and the Co-op replaced it. Outside, the tree that once grew at Granny Everard's door still stands.

Quarrying brought many jobs to the area, blasting, or digging on the famous Storeton Tramway that travelled to the river Mersey past Lever Brothers soap factory in Port Sunlight. Keuper stone, both red and grey, was quarried and used for buildings all over Bebington and beyond.

In 1838, footprints of a prehistoric reptile, known as a Cheirotherium, were discovered and the fossilised prints are now displayed in Christchurch and the Williamson Art Gallery in Birkenhead.

Higher Hurdsfield 🪶

In 1286 the village was known as Hyrdesfeld, meaning 'open land at a hurdle'. The first mention of Higher Hurdsfield (as opposed to just Hurdsfield) was in 1301.

In the past there has been coal mining here, evidence of which could be seen on the Kerridge Hills between Higher Hurdsfield and Rainow. Cotton and silk were also part of the industry of the village.

John Wesley preached at a farm in Higher Hurdsfield – his first visit to Macclesfield. People from a large area crowded into that farmhouse, after a day's walk to get there and another long walk back.

Leisure pursuits of those days included cockfighting and dog fights, and people from Macclesfield came to take part and to watch.

The Macclesfield Canal which was started in Bollington in 1826 was finally completed in 1831 and this altered the boundary between Higher Hurdsfield and Macclesfield itself. The boundary had been Higher Fence Road and now the toll bar was removed a few yards to just beyond the canal bridge.

The Sunday school was originally started in a farm and other buildings in 1808. It was not until 1811 that the school on the turnpike road to Whaley Bridge was built. Education on the basics of reading and arithmetic took place, as well as religious instruction. The Sunday school is now a community church. During the week it is used by the Parish Council, the Bridge Club, WI and the Youth Club, besides occasional meetings of different bodies.

In the village today there is a large private estate on the east side of the main road, with the original part of the old village being around the main road and the outlying farms.

Higher Walton 🌿

Higher Walton is a picturesque village lying to the south of Warrington. Gabled houses and a few modern houses lie along a straight stretch of road through the village.

A wayside lychgate and a black and white gable leads to a lovely 19th century church in 15th century style, built by Sir Gilbert Greenall, a Lancashire MP and founder of the Greenall dynasty. The church of St John Evangelist is built like a cross with a sturdy central tower and spire. All the woodwork is richly carved, the reredos with the figures of the Crucifixion, the Centurion and Mary Magdalene and the Four Evangelists. The face of St George in a window transept is that of the eldest son of the Greenall family, who was killed in a motor accident in 1928.

Sir Gilbert Greenall, later to become a baron and founder of the famous brewing firm, also built Walton Hall, which was the family home, and Walton Old Hall, which was eventually used as a dower house by Frances, Lady Daresbury. The Hall was sold to the Warrington Corporation in 1941 to pay death duty demands. Later, dry rot was discovered in part of the Hall and so a wing was demolished. It was the end of an era when the Hall closed, for it employed many people, who were housed in the estate houses in the village built specially for them.

The land surrounding the Hall, which was in the region of a 170 acres plus 20 acres of ornamental gardens, is now available for public use, and is skirted by the Bridgewater Canal. There used to be a stonemason's yard by the hump-backed bridge, where the sandstone was cut and shaped for use on the estate houses, giving them a distinctive appearance.

The Walton Arms was originally a public house and farm combined, from where milk was delivered twice daily to the surrounding area.

Eventually the farmland was sold to make way for a dual carriageway and the village was cut into two. The vicarage and school house are now situated across the main road from the village. The Walton Arms had a very notable 'Mine Host', George Duckworth the England and Lancashire wicket-keeper, who coined his own delightful utterance of 'Owzat' when he made a brilliant 'catch'. The Cheshire Hunt met regularly at the Walton Arms until the Second World War to enjoy their stirrup cup before setting off to chase the fox.

The original post office was situated near the Bridgewater Canal and the post-mistress of that time delivered mail to the Irish navvies who were cutting the Manchester Ship Canal. The stop at the post office was a recognised collecting point for fodder for the barge horses, after it was weighed at the weigh-bridge which was alongside.

Holly Hedge Farm has the ghost of an old lady, often seen sitting in one of the armchairs. Research has shown that she is probably the ghost of a lady who lived at the farm in the late 18th century, who, unfortunately had a tragic end due to a fall down a flight of stairs. Although no ghosts have been seen at Grange Mill House, voices have been heard as if in deep conversation. This is a building of note, having been originally built in 1192. The land was given by the Knights Hospitallers to the priory to be used as a mill.

Frances, Lady Daresbury made sure that the daughters of the workers at the Hall were taught the fundamentals of home-making. Besides a thorough grounding in the three 'R's she ensured that the girls could bake a good cake (a Christmas event) and sew a fine seam. This was done by the girls making a hand-sewn garment, starting it in the New Year and having it finished by Easter so that it could be judged by her ladyship and Mrs Oddy the headmistress. The winner was then presented with a sewing machine. The girls also made their own overalls in blue zephyr material, taught by Mrs Oddy and two members of her staff. The boys were taught until the age of seven, then they went to either Daresbury or Stockton Heath school. The old school house is still standing but is now a private residence.

High Legh 🌿

High Legh stands 240 ft above sea level, on the escarpment overlooking the Mersey, midway between Knutsford and Warrington.

During the reign of Henry II, the manor was rented in two parts, to two families, who assumed the local name, they became known as *Legh* of East Hall, and *Leigh* of West Hall. Each family had its own chapel, both of which are still in existence, one of them being now the parish church of St John, and the other St Mary's, the private chapel of the Cornwall Legh family. In 1912 the Leighs of West Hall sold out to the Leghs of East Hall. Both Halls were taken over by the Army in the Second World War, and were demolished in 1962. When the army moved into the Hall, the Cornwall Legh family moved to High Legh House, where they still reside, Mr Charles Cornwall Legh being the present squire. The name Cornwall was added in 1730, when George Legh married Anna Maria, daughter and heiress of Francis Cornwall, Baron of Burford.

The old village consists mainly of farms and cottages, built in the 18th century, a few Victorian houses, a modern council estate, and a group of houses built for army personnel, later taken over by the prison service, and now mostly in private ownership. However some 16th and 17th century houses still exist.

St Mary's chapel is probably the oldest building in the village, dating from 1581, and it may have replaced a chapel mentioned in the Domesday Book. Built of sandstone, it contains some fine carved oak. The parish church of St John, an attractive black and white building, was originally the West Hall private chapel. It is the third building on this site, and was built in 1893.

The Independent Methodist chapel in Northwood Lane, was once a gamekeeper's cottage. The movement was started in High Legh in 1783, by Betty Okell. The Congregation met in her farmhouse kitchen, and was known for many years as 'O'Kells Meeting'. A direct descendant, Mr David Okell, still worships in the chapel. The famous African missionary, Robert Moffat, worshipped here when he was under-gardener at High Legh Hall in the early 19th century. He received his call to the mission field when walking home from a Revival meeting in Warrington. His daughter, Mary, became the wife of David Livingstone.

The village stocks are still in existence, though they have been restored in recent years. There is no record of any miscreants who were punished therein. High Legh Sports have been a flourishing annual event from 1875. Cricket was once a popular feature of the village, and the ground was maintained by the squires for generations, but it has now been taken over for building a new estate – 'The Belfry'. Now there is an indoor bowls club in the village hall, and an outdoor crown green has recently been laid.

High Legh continued as a mainly farming community until 1962. Since then there has been considerable building development on the sites of the two Halls, and due to the close proximity of two motorways, Ringway Airport, Manchester, Liverpool, etc, High Legh is a popular residential area for people in many walks of life. These newcomers entered into village life, and when the old primary school was converted to the village hall, the new residents joined with the villagers in the many practical tasks that were required.

Holmes Chapel 🦢

Holmes Chapel, or Church Holme, was originally just called Holme. It has come a long way since it was just a church and a few cottages in the middle of a wood.

A fire on 10th July 1753, burned down 18 of the 20 houses; only the church, the two cottages behind and the Red Lion escaped. Even the lime trees in the churchyard were scorched.

St Luke's church is the product of many centuries. It was originally half-timbered, later having brick walls added. In 1705 the church was extended and three plaster ceilings were constructed. Then in 1935, due to the need of repair, the ceilings were removed revealing the beautiful timber in all its glory. The following doggerel once graced the vestry walls:

> 'Whoever rings with Spur or Hat
> Shall pay the Clerk a groat for that.
> Whoever swears or bell turns over
> Shall forfeit fourpence if not more.
> If any shall do ought amiss
> Three pence the forfeit is.
> Observe these laws and break them not
> Lest you lose your pence for that.'

The Methodist chapel on Knutsford Road was built in 1900. John Wesley on a journey with two friends from Oxford to Manchester, on 16th March 1738, preached to the customers of the Red Lion.

The Catholic church on Macclesfield Road used to be a school. There was another school at Cranage and the post office in London Road was a 'School for Young Ladies'.

128

Thomas Hall from Cranage bought the Hermitage in 1702 and was a great benefactor to the village. He built the bridge over the Dane down Coach Lane, now Hermitage Lane, also a cottage on Macclesfield Road. Romper Lowe lived in the cottage, and was notorious for smuggling salt across the river Dane to avoid taxes, hence the name Saltersford. It is said that the salt was forded across in coffins.

Saltersford Hall was built in the late 18th century, and was owned by the Toler family. It has had various uses through the years, being a reformatory, approved school for boys, agricultural college and a Home Office school.

Grannie Mandeville started the first May Day celebrations in 1879 and Miss Elizabeth Mandeville was the first May Day Queen to be crowned. The present-day Mandevilles still run the bakery on Macclesfield Road. Old Mr W. Mandeville baked a 'Fertility Bread' which was eaten far and wide, and Dr Lionel Picton recommended it to all infertile ladies; the success rate was apparently very good!

At Michaelmas time the children of the village took a can to Massey's Mill, where they were given wheat. This was taken home to their mothers who mixed the wheat with honey, spices, brown sugar and water. This was cooked slowly overnight and eaten in the morning like porridge.

The shopping precinct stands on the grounds and site of Sandiford House. Today Holmes Chapel, being close to the M6 motorway, is a commuter area. Sadly, farmland has disappeared, making way for estates, shops and a comprehensive school.

Hooton 🌿

The manor of Hooton (ie the estate) passed through various families until 1310 when William de Stanley inherited through marriage, and with it went the Master Forestership of Wirral with its badge of office, the Wirral Horn.

The old Hall at Hooton was built in 1488 and was replaced in 1778 by a mansion in the Italian style built of Storeton stone. In 1847 Hooton was purchased by Richard Christopher Naylor. He vastly extended the Hall but in 1875 the contents were sold by auction, and it is said that the sale lasted nine days. After years of neglect the Hall was demolished in about 1922.

Before Speke Airport was opened, the parkland of Hooton Hall gained fame as an aerodrome. It was the HQ of Liverpool Aero Club and also a base for Scottish Air Services, while its hangars still housed fighter planes of the First World War and later homemade versions of that strange plane, the Flying Flea, whose controls really were operated by large rubber bands! Somewhat more modern planes were seen when the RAF took over during the Second World War.

Hooton was also the base of the Wirral Draghounds whose Master, Major Lockett was a well known local character. It is said that he often took his horse into the club, where he bought it a bottle of beer which the horse drank clamped between its teeth! The Major did much charitable work and is said to have used the champion jockey Fred Archer's boot as a collecting box!

One of the great social events used to be the Hooton Races which took place at Hooton Park. Cottagers living on the lanes to the park would serve teas in their front gardens to passers-by.

Hooton Park was the venue for the Cheshire Show for several years. Alas, it is now covered by the Vauxhall motor factory. As for other local industries, Hooton was mainly known for its extensive brickworks and a glue manufacturing company, both now defunct. There is a small industrial estate but Vauxhall's is now predominant, being a major unit of the British car industry. Unhappily, Hooton cannot boast a post office or even a single shop.

Hidden in the woods which line Hooton Green is the gas works which lit Hooton Hall. A short distance along the Chester Road stand the Chester gate lodges to Hooton Park which, together with the semi-circle of columns which join them, are all that remain of the 1778 building.

Next to them is St Paul's church with its bands of red and white sandstone, granite pillars and unusual dome, which was consecrated in 1862. The entire cost of the building (£5,000) was borne by Richard Christopher Naylor. Nearer Hooton crossroads is the Roman Catholic church of St Mary of the Angels. Until Hooton Hall passed out of Stanley hands, the local Catholic community worshipped in the private chapel of the Hall. In 1876 Sir John Massey Stanley Errington, the last of the old family of Stanley of Hooton, decided to use money he had been awarded in a lawsuit in France to build a church here.

Hooton does have a village hall. This was due entirely to the local people who, after the end of the Second World War, raised sufficient funds to buy the field on which it stands and to have the hall erected. The late Brigadier Sir Philip Toosey is well remembered locally for his generous help in bringing the scheme to fruition.

Hooton is reputed to have more than one ghost, including that of a headless airman who was decapitated on the airfield in 1936 by an aircraft propeller. A lady in white also haunts the nearby drive to Hooton Hall.

Hough

Hough is a small village in the south of the county adjacent to Shavington and Wybunbury, and is within the latter's ecclesiastical parish.

Until the 1960s Hough was just a hamlet, comprising a string of small cottages and farms along what is now the A500, with a village inn (the White Hart), a shop-cum-post office and a smithy. The shop and inn still flourish, but the smithy doors closed when the tractor replaced the horse. Gone are the days when Blacksmith Farrell was busy at his furnace, a row of horses tied up outside waiting to be shod, and a cluster of children at the entrance watching him at work.

The lanes forking out from the end of the village by the Swill brook were interspersed with farms and some cottages, with agricultural and domestic work on these farms the main source of employment. The industrial expansion at Crewe, approximately five miles away, eventually created alternative and more lucrative employment which many turned to.

Back Lane has only recently reverted to its original name, having been known for nearly a century as Murder Lane. In March 1890 two young brothers in their teens named Davies, who lived in the village, lay in wait one night for their father who regularly returned home along this route in his pony and trap after visiting the hostelries in Crewe, coming home under the influence of drink, violent and terrorising his wife and family. The boys attacked and murdered him. They were brought to trial; the elder was hanged, but the younger being under the age of 18 was reprieved and sent to prison.

The Methodist chapel is situated in Cobb's Lane, built in 1860. Services have been held there ever since. It is not licensed for marriages, and being the only church within the parish, no weddings can take place in the village. There is no school in the village either and the children travel to neighbouring villages for their education.

A little further along Cobb's Lane is Hough Heath, now referred to as the Common – a small tract of land which had an abundance of wild flowers including the rare cotton plant. It also attracted many species of wild birds which nested among the small shrubs and trees – the nightingale could be heard late in the night during the summer months. Gypsies often camped here using it as a resting place on their way from one fair to the next. They could be seen sitting around their camp fire at night, rabbit cooking in the cauldron, the men shaping pegs from willow twigs, which they first stripped of bark, the two finished pieces then being bound together with bands of multicoloured tin cut from empty cans. Before they left their women-folk would hawk the pegs around the local houses. Today the Common is a pleasant picnic and recreation area, fringed with trees with a perimeter path around it.

Hough Hall is an attractive moderate-sized residence of its type, standing in well kept grounds and gardens, surrounded by many varieties of beautiful mature trees, on the south side of the A500 as one enters the village. Part of the house dates back to the 16th century and the dining room still has the original Queen Anne panelling. A new wing was added at the beginning of the 20th century. The Hall was originally the dower house, the first Hall being set further back but this was destroyed by fire. Some 30 years ago a second residence was built within the grounds, and with the old walled gardens, tennis court and farm now forms 'Hough Gates', so named because the magnificent wrought iron gates from the original Hall made during the reign of James I, stand at the entrance to it.

During the period 1970 to early 1980 extensive property development took place in the village, trebling the population. A new M6 motorway link was opened in 1987 only one mile from the village enabling people to travel much greater distances to their work and this has brought many new people to reside in the village, pursuing a wide variety of occupations.

Huntington 🦢

Huntington, which lies some two miles to the south of Chester Cross, is an old settlement with early associations with the Church.

In AD 959 Edgar, King of the Mercians, granted land at Huntington to the religious community of St Werburgh. More than 100 years later – in 1086 – the Domesday Book records that Huntington (Hunditone) was held by St Werburgh's church in the City of Chester.

The manor passed out of the hands of the abbey of St Werburgh in 1538 to Doctor Thomas Lee or Legh, and later to the Cotton family, who acquired extensive estates in and around Chester. The name Cotton is still remembered in the nearby parishes of Cotton Abbots and Cotton Edmunds.

For some 400 years Huntington remained an agricultural community with a small population. In 1811 it had 16 houses and a population of 124; by 1871 there were still only 21 houses and 119 people. In 1931 Huntington's population was only 144, but between then and the Second World War some 250 houses were built and the population grew to around 800. In 1989 a second wave of housing development was completed and there are now some 900 houses and 2,200 people.

The growth of population inevitably led to problems. Primary education was initially provided either at Aldford school or at a city primary school, and secondary education was virtually non-existent. Pressure from the community resulted in Huntington County primary school opening in 1957, and the opening of Christleton high school shortly afterwards completed the structure of the education service.

Other developments have included an Army camp, misnamed Saighton camp, which was built in the 1930s and which, at peak, accommodated upwards of 2,000 soldiers. Today its future seems uncertain.

In the late 1960s plans for using the river Dee to provide water from Tryweryn and Bala for use in Liverpool were completed, and a major intake and water treatment works was built in Huntington. From here water is piped across country to Liverpool and Merseyside.

Local government in Huntington was for centuries in the control of the Justices and Quarter Sessions. The parish until 1936 lay in the Tarvin Rural District, and from then until local government reorganisation in 1974 was part of Chester Rural District. Since 1974 it has, of course, been a part of the extended City of Chester. Its first Parish Meeting was elected in 1894, and it was succeeded by a parish council which provided the impetus for establishing a village hall shortly after the Second World War, and acquired a playing field in 1976 – now known as the Jubilee Playing Field.

Until very recently Huntington for ecclesiastical purposes was in the parish of Bruera. When the mission church of St George was demolished, Huntington became part of the parish of St Paul's, Boughton. In 1987 a new parish, of St Luke's, Huntington, was established, and the building of the first parish church began.

Ince

Ince is a small Cheshire parish whose boundaries comprise seven miles of water and a mile and a half of land. An old-world village, its known history began when St Werburgh's remains were brought to Chester in the 10th century. The small community which was founded to serve her shrine, was endowed with several granges, Ince being one. The Benedictines who took over Chester, took over Ince, and the remains of their priory are here to be seen. The long 14th-century chancel of St James' church dates from monastic use. After the Dissolution of the Monasteries, Chester Cathedral continued to pay £4 6s 8d a year to the vicar of Ince until this century.

The building of the railway made the centuries-old ferry redundant. The Ship Canal built through the parish made access to the Mersey for shrimp fishing (a staple but unreliable and uncomfortable industry) difficult and industrial growth gave more stable jobs to the men of Ince. In the last few decades the Stanlow refinery has extended across the marshes right into the parish. The site of Ince Hall with its once beautiful gardens is now occupied by oil tanks. On the Frodsham side there are the Ince power stations and Shellstar, and over 400 acres owned by Shell, destined for more industry.

The village remains a quiet oasis of peace surrounded by industry. It still has an outlook on river and mountain, wood and plain; and the church, whilst boasting no striking architectural features – no wealth of ancient woodwork or treasures – has a simple charm and an atmosphere of prayer that endears it to those who love simple places and simple things.

On the village square there is a lamp to commemorate the coronation of King Edward VII.

Irby & Thurstaston

Irby is a small village situated in the Wirral peninsula, surrounded by pleasant countryside crossed by public footpaths, with heathlands, Thurstaston Hill and the Dee estuary close by. The village has a busy shopping centre with all amenities.

The 'by' ending of the name denotes that a settlement here dated from the days of the Viking invaders. A Norse longboat features on the badge of the local primary school.

Most of Irby is in the parish of Thurstaston, a tiny village recorded in the Domesday Book as Turstanetone. There has been a church there since the 12th century. The present sandstone building of St Bartholomew was rebuilt in 1885. In recent years the parish has grown considerably with new housing developments taking place, necessitating the building of the daughter church of St Chad in Irby village.

Thurstaston Hall stands close to the church, and Irby Hall, a sandstone manor house with a half-timbered facade and the remains of a moat, is close to the main village street. The history of both houses dates back to the Norman Conquest when Hugh Lupus, nephew of the Conqueror, became the first Norman Earl of Chester. There was another important house at Thurstaston, Dawpool Hall designed by Norman Shaw. Sadly the house has been demolished.

A number of old sandstone farm buildings remain but very few are working farms. Sheep graze in the fields and horses kept for riding occupy the outhouses. The majority of the working population commute to the local towns.

Outside the library is a replica of the village stocks. Irby Club in Thingwall Road stands on the site of a farmhouse once known as The Rookery, and Irby has a flourishing cricket club which was founded in 1948 and a park with bowling green, tennis courts, football pitches and a children's playground.

A windmill was first recorded at Irby in 1291 and the Irby Mill Inn now stands at Mill Hill crossroads on the site of cottages which stood next to a windmill demolished in 1898. On the edge of the village is the Anchor Inn, once a 17th century sandstone cottage.

The church is entered through a lychgate erected to the memory of Thomas Henry Ismay, founder of the White Star Shipping Line, who died in 1899. He was very rich and influential and when the railway line threatened his peace and quiet he had it re-routed to run along the shore away from his home. Likewise, he caused a cutting to be made through the sandstone rocks at Thurstaston so that the main road could be re-routed. The country lover is thankful for both happenings.

Wirral Country Park, which was once part of the West Kirby to Hooton railway line, contains fishing ponds, nature trails and a visitor centre along with magnificent views over the Dee estuary to Wales. There is also a caravan park and camping site at Thurstaston.

The National Trust owns the area of heathland known as Thurstaston

Common, Thurstaston Hill being possibly the most visited beauty spot in Wirral. In the middle of Thurstaston Common is Thor's Stone, a large red sandstone block where, it is said, pagan sacrifices were made by the Vikings.

Kelsall 🌿

Nestling beneath the sandstone ridge which runs across Cheshire from Helsby to Beeston, Kelsall has been home for many settlers. There are remains of a Bronze Age castle on Kelsborrow Hill, probably one of a number of hill forts on the track linking Wales to the Pennines. Indeed Kelsall's past and present development is closely linked with roads. The Roman Watling Street passed through Kelsall en route to the salt towns where salt was collected to pay the wages (salarium) of the garrison at Deva (Chester).

Parts of Watling Street can be traced around the village and in 1969 Kelsall Women's Institute members successfully cleared the Hollow Way which is thought to be part of Watling Street but had become blocked with garden waste and other rubbish. Sadly, despite efforts by other village groups over the years, dumping has continued.

During the 1960s and 1970s Kelsall became a village divided by its road as an unending stream of traffic passed up and down the A54, headed by heavy lorries toiling slowly up the hill. Now a new bypass offers fantastic views of Cheshire from Beeston to the Mersey.

There are not many very old houses in Kelsall, probably because of a fire which destroyed most of the village in 1738. However, there is an old farmhouse in Frodsham Street, thought to be 17th century and a thatched cottage, thought to be 16th century, in Green Lane. The old 18th century gaol opposite the Royal Oak which was obviously built before the days of prison reform, has been preserved by incorporating it into the boundaries of a new house built just behind it.

St Philip's church was built in 1860 to plans drawn up by Sir Gilbert Scott. There was also a church school and a schoolmaster's house but when the County primary school was bulit in 1935 the church school became the church hall and is now home to a firm of design consultants.

The present Methodist chapel overlooking Chapel Green was built in 1884 together with a day and Sunday school. The Methodist chapel schoolroom, now being extensively modernised, is used for WI meetings and Sunday school.

The names Quarry Lane and Quarry Stores give a clue to the activities in the village during the late 18th and early 19th century when several quarries were excavated and provided work for the local community.

A number of mixed farms and several thriving fruit farms and nurseries take advantage of the fertile soil and sheltered aspect to retain agricultural links and skills. Recently a firm making exclusive solid wood furniture has taken over buildings at the corner of Hollands Lane and is thriving.

The present village is fortunate to have two post offices, two butchers, a pharmacy, a general store, greengrocery/fish shop and four pubs – the Royal Oak, the Morris Dancer (formerly the Globe), the Forester's Arms and Th'ouse at Top (formerly the Farmers' Arms).

Kelsall's chalybeate (mineral) springs are frequently mentioned in books about Cheshire and have a reputation for promoting good health and longevity – many residents reaching 90 years or more. However, the lady who fell down a well, and is reputed to haunt Old Coach Road may not have agreed!

Willington Hall, Kelsall

137

In contrast to Kelsall's rapid growth – 3,000 inhabitants in 1989 and likely to expand even more with new housing developments – Willington, Kelsall's nearest neighbour, has remained predominantly rural. Its country cottages with pretty gardens looking over the Cheshire Plain towards Beeston and Peckforton, seem content to slumber in the sunshine or stand up to winter's storms and not be hustled into the modern world. The scenic valley known locally as 'Little Switzerland' leads down to the attractively situated and sympathetically modernised Boot Inn. Off Chapel Lane there is a row of almshouses built by the Tomkinson family of Willington Hall. The chapel which gives the lane its name has now been converted to a residence.

Willington Hall itself was built in 1829 and is a handsome brick mansion in an Elizabethan style, standing in impressive grounds. It is now an hotel – its setting, decor and atmosphere making it a popular choice for wedding receptions. It also provides a perfect rural background for hounds and horses of the Cheshire Hunt when they meet there during the season.

Kettleshulme

Kettleshulme, set amid the circle of hills and lying in the deep valley of the Todd, has a worthy place in the Peak District National Park.

The name, Kettleshulme, was first recorded in 1285 but it probably has Viking origins. The area must have been well known in Saxon times, as evidenced by the Bow Stones which are thought to have Saxon religious connections. The Salt Way from Nantwich and Middlewich through to Sheffield and Chesterfield brought travellers over Reed Bridge and along Flatts Lane. The Swan Inn probably gave refreshment and rest after the toll had been paid at Flatts Lane. Gap Lodge was also a toll house. Kettleshulme continues to be the hub of footpaths in every direction and attracts a stream of ramblers throughout the year, as well as young climbers bound for Windgather Rocks.

Until 1921 Kettleshulme was in the parish of Prestbury but, following boundary changes, became part of the parish of Taxal with Kettleshulme. Originally it was St John's church at Saltersford that cared for worshippers, and many Kettleshulme folk still make an effort to walk the four miles by road or over field paths to join in the summer services at the church (called Jenkyn Chapel), especially on the occasion of the harvest festival.

Taxal church, however, provides much of the evidence that we have of early history and property. They hold the record of the Thomas Ouffe Charity which has helped the poor since 1628, particularly benefiting apprentices and students to this day. Thomas Ouffe, originally an orphan and cared for by a local couple, prospered as a builder and later built Clayton Fold, up on Stocks Brow and, on his death, left the estate to the poor of several parishes. He was also responsible for donations of bread to everyone at Christmas.

In 1856 the present school was instituted on an Anglican foundation. Once a month Church of England services are celebrated there by the rector of Taxal.

From the 18th century Methodism had a large following in the valley and, for many years, Methodist preachers gathered at Pym Chair, in the open air, and attracted large congregations. They often used Chapel House on Saltersford road as a headquarters and collected sufficient funds to build a more permanent chapel, first at the 'Cotton Shop' in the village and then, in 1815, the first real chapel at Brookbottom.

Both silk and cotton were woven in the local cottages and around 1797 William Brocklehurst of Gap House erected a two-storey building alongside the Todd Brook at Lumb Hole, to be used as weaving rooms. The building was twice burned down and finally rebuilt in its three-storey form by John Sheldon in 1823. The wooden water-wheel was replaced by an iron one, and a large beam engine and hand-fired gas retort was installed. The building was first used as a spinning and weaving mill but developed into a candlewick mill, which was worked as a going concern until 1937.

Spinning and weaving have long disappeared but horticulture has now been developed. The village nurseries now specialise in pansies and violas, in trees and bushes and in primulas and bedding plants.

Kettleshulme folk have produced considerable voluntary labour over the years to improve their village. A supplementary water scheme was piped down from below Windgather Rocks. The library was built in 1876 and extended to become the War Memorial Hall in 1921, and continues to provide an admirable village centre.

The prize for the oddest fellow in village history would still be awarded to Amos Broadhurst of Priest Farm, whose beard grew to 10 ft long and was proudly displayed on special occasions!

Kingsley 🖋️

This 'much sought after' village lies in the north of the county and extends from the river Weaver to Delamere Forest. Ancient in origin, dating back to Saxon times, it is a rich source of material for local historians. Old mansions and manor houses – Kingsley Hall, Crewood Hall, Peel Hall and Catten Hall – still enhance the village, having been demolished and rebuilt over the centuries, whilst Kingsley Mill is still a going concern, carrying on a tradition started in pre-Norman days.

Throughout the ages the villagers of Kingsley have had a reputation for independence, as exemplified by their staunch Parliamentarianism during the Civil War and in matters of religion, by early institution of a Quaker meeting house, a Baptist chapel and Methodist chapels. The Quaker meeting house was built along with a burial ground as early as 1686. It is now a private residence. The Baptists had a chapel in Chapel Lane but this has now vanished without trace. There have been various Methodist chapels over the years; the first was built in 1787.

The parish church of St John the Evangelist was consecrated in 1851. The tower, with its clock, dominates the approach to the village from Frodsham, whilst across the road lies the cemetery with the Kingsley and Newton war memorial. The old vicarage has been sold and replaced by a modern residence.

At one time there were three schools in the village but now there are just two – the Church of England school (originally a board school), near The Cross and a state primary school, built in 1932 in Middle Lane on the outskirts.

The number of shops has declined since the Second World War as improving transport has enabled villagers to make their purchases further afield, but the atmosphere of the village remains. The nucleus now consists of a village store, which is also a newsagent, a post office combined with a mini-market, a garage, a bank – open two mornings a week, a butcher's shop, a ladies hairdresser's and two hostelries. These last two – the Horseshoe and the Red Bull – are long established, the latter dating from 1771.

Whilst still lying in the midst of a typical agricultural area the nature of the village has shown change in recent times. Since the 1960s three new developments of private housing – Hunters Hill, Highbank and West-brook, have been established. Some of the original purchasers still enjoy living there, but there is also a very mobile population, due mainly to the proximity of large industrial conglomerates such as ICI and Shell within easy commuting distance.

For many years, the recreational facilities of the village were catered for by the Kingsley and Newton village institute, housed in a wooden structure which, with time, became somewhat dilapidated. In 1988 this was replaced by a magnificent brick building with modern facilities. Snooker, pool and darts are available and outdoors there is an excellent bowling green and tennis courts.

To provide further recreational opportunities, the incoming population along with the 'original villagers' set up the Kingsley Community Association and worked hard to provide a community centre which was opened in 1976.

Lach Dennis 🦢

Lach Dennis is a suitable name for the village because it means 'wet and marshy land'. Lach Dennis is a farming community, and altogether there are eleven farms in and around the village.

When Captain France-Hayhurst's family owned the land, rent collecting day was 4th September. The tenants would journey to Bostock Hall to pay their rent and they were given a good meal. Captain France-Heyhurst was very well liked by his tenants and his family were very popular in the village. There are just a few privately owned farms in Lach Dennis nowadays and the rest are owned by ICI.

Lach Dennis church of All Saints was built in 1895 and a foundation stone was laid by Captain France-Heyhurst. Other foundation stones were laid by special people who were each given a silver trowel as a souvenir. One of these trowels has been given to one of the parishioners and it can be seen in the church on special occasions.

The village inn, once the Farmer's Arms, is now called the Duke of Portland. This is because King Edward VII used to make frequent visits to Cheshire to ride with the Cheshire Hunt. He would always travel under the pseudonym of the Duke of Portland, hence the reason for the change of name.

There used to be two smithies in the village, one on Hulse Lane and the other on Smithy Lane. Legend has it that Dick Turpin rode through Lach Dennis and stopped at the Smithy Lane forge for his horse to be shod. Smithy Lane is now a public footpath into Hulse Lane. Hulse Lane smithy is still operated by the local blacksmith.

Opposite Common Lane was a small cottage/shop where the lady of the house provided refreshments, cigarettes and sweets to the Cyclists Touring Club and also to the Army tank drivers who used to test drive the tanks made by Foden's of Sandbach during the Second World War. There were setts across from the cottage for the tanks to be parked on while the soldiers purchased their refreshments. Although bombs were dropped on the village, not a great deal of damage was done.

There are two very old cottages in Common Lane called Common Lane Cottages. The first one was the village post office. The postmaster was also the wheelwright and undertaker. Later on in the 19th century, the post office was moved to the new little shop on Holmes Chapel Road. With the advent of the motor car, the gentleman who was the postmaster built a garage, selling petrol and repairing bicycles. This has now been extended by the present owner and is a very busy establishment.

Lach Dennis is a very pretty little village, especially in the spring when both sides of the main street are lined with masses of daffodils and tulips. It has developed quite a lot in recent years and is busy with traffic but it sitll retains a very friendly spirit.

Leasowe ✐

The first recorded building is Leasowe Hall, later renamed Leasowe Castle, which occupies a prominent position on the edge of the sandhills facing the Irish Sea. The oldest part is the central tower, built in 1593 by the fifth Earl of Derby. The castle is now a flourishing hotel.

The other outstanding landmark is Leasowe lighthouse, erected in 1763, and reputed to be the oldest lighthouse in England. It is being turned into a visitor centre and ranger's office for the Wirral Coastal Park.

A very large open air hospital for children was built here in 1914, the inspiration of Margaret Beavan, a notable Liverpool personality. This hospital originally catered for children suffering from rickets, a disease that rapidly diminished with the introduction of free milk in schools. It then became a tuberculosis hospital, and afterwards an excellent centre for the treatment of rheumatism and a much valued burns unit. It now flourishes as a Christian centre, catering for residential elderly folk, a day centre and a playgroup for children of working mothers.

St Chad's church was consecrated in 1967 and was for some years the newest church in the Chester Diocese. The windows of St Chad's are truly magnificent, modern stained glass, very reminiscent of Coventry Cathedral. The Roman Catholic church of Our Lady of Lourdes stands proudly on Leasowe Road, a modern church with an Italian influence.

The local golf course is for 'Men Only', and has been ever since it was opened by a Mr John Bull in 1891. He was a famous golfer of his day, and won the British Open.

Alongside the golf course are the market gardens, which are famous for the production of vegetables delivered to markets in Liverpool the day they are picked. Families who started the gardens long ago, and still actively connected, are the Websters, Crosses, Joynsons and McGills.

Leasowe Common is protected by rights of access going back to the Middle Ages and has long been a 'green lung' for people from the streets of Birkenhead who flock to pitch their tents for the day in sunny weather.

The seashore has been wonderfully improved since the siting of stone barriers covered with strong wire mesh netting, which has resulted in the sand returning to Leasowe Bay. Technicians have come from as far afield as Japan to view this innovation, and many other coastal places have copied this idea.

From the embankment in 1962, history was made, as the world's first hovercraft passenger service commenced here, and plied between Leasowe and Rhyl for a period of eight weeks.

St George's school (now the junior department of St Mary's college), was the first building in the world to be heated entirely by solar energy, in 1961. The designer, Mr Emslie Morgan, a local man, conceived the idea of a giant solar 10,000 ft wall of glass leaves, facing due south, which provides heat in winter, and is cool in summer.

Ledsham ༄

Ledsham is situated on the north-west border of Cheshire and Wirral, six miles from Chester. The village is a predominantly agricultural settlement, recorded in the Domesday Book as Levetsham. It was a small village on the Roman road between Chester and Meols, and covers an area of approximately 800 acres.

During the 19th century the village was dominated by two farms owned by Mr W. Knowles and Messrs T. & C. Davies. Mr Knowles and his family were instrumental in establishing and building the Calvinistic Methodist chapel which was opened in 1855, and is now a branch of the Presbyterian Church of Wales. A Band of Hope was formed in 1864 by

Lord and Lady Radcliffe at Ledsham Hall, as a further means of suppressing the 'evil habits' and the drinking that was found at that time in the village.

In 1908, in response to the Smallholdings and Allotments Act, Cheshire County Council bought the estate from Sir Richard Bulkley and divided it into the first council smallholdings and market gardens to be established in the country.

Ledsham sandstone was quarried and used to build the wall around the village,'now a conservation area. A barn situated at Court Farm is a Grade II listed building. As the name implies, this was once the court house for the area, when Shotwick was a port and prisoners arrived by boat and were brought to the village for sentence.

After the Second World War the armament factory at Capenhurst was bought by the Atomic Energy Authority and land was taken from the Ledsham smallholdings to expand the works, now owned by British Nuclear Fuels Limited. Eleven cooling towers were built, causing the factory to be a landmark from many miles away. In 1981 these became outdated and over a period of about six years they were demolished brick by brick to avoid damage to machinery. The taking of the land and the increased traffic caused some ill-feeling and resentment in the village at the time.

The Hunt used to meet regularly in the village and the Royal Rock Beagles, the oldest beagle hunt in the country, are still kennelled behind the old Ledsham Station Hotel, now the Cheshire Yeoman. This inn was always signposted as being 'The last hotel in England'. Point to point meetings were held and these were well supported by the local people.

Until 1859 Ledsham was part of the parish of Neston, and buried at Neston was John Hancock of Ledsham who died in December 1775, aged 112 years. His wife, also buried at Neston, died in 1799 aged 73 years and must therefore have been 63 years younger than her husband!

Ledsham is now a mixture of the old and the new with the BNFL factory part of the landscape and providing employment for some of the villagers, who are also able to use their sports and social club facilities. The factory could provide a secure future for the youngsters when the smallholdings are no longer able to support a family because of the whittling away of the land for the new link road.

Lindow & Row of Trees 🐚

Whoever had heard of the parish of Lindow before the discovery in 1984 in nearby Lindow Moss of the body of a Celtic Iron Age man, well preserved in a peat bog? Lindow Man, or 'Lindow Pete' as the popular newspapers nicknamed him, now resides in Manchester museum, and the riddle of his death will probably remain a mystery forever. He certainly met with a violent end – killed by blows to the head, then garrotted, and finally sacrificed to the bog.

Although entirely surrounded now by other villages and hamlets (Alderley Edge, Chorley, Row of Trees) and joined to the town of Wilmslow by roads and buildings which have developed over the last 50 to 60 years, the present parish of Lindow still maintains all the features we think of as necessary to make up an English village – the church of St John Evangelist, village school, cricket field, small Methodist chapel, church rooms and village hall.

The village school at Lindow was started in 1863, celebrating its centenary in 1963, to continue for only another seven years. In 1970 a fine new school was built down the road, and the authority for running the school was taken from the Church and handed over entirely to Cheshire Education Committee. Most pupils came from small farming or smallholding families, and many of these local former students look upon their time at the school with considerable affection.

The hamlet of Row of Trees is attached to Lindow although in the parish of Chorley. Thirty lime trees were planted here in the 17th century, and there are many conflicting stories told of their origin. The original trees have since decayed, but during the 20th century have been replanted. One story says they were planted as a guide to travellers, to keep them out of the treacherous Lindow Bog. Whatever the origin, they are a focal point for the village, and surely must have given Row of Trees its pretty name.

For such a small area Row of Trees has many buildings of note. Row of Trees Farm, a lovely black and white building, was built in 1603. In 1665 a lady visited Row of Trees Farm to escape from the Great Plague in London. Alas, she was already a victim of this disease, so she was isolated in an adjoining barn, and fed from the end of a hayfork. She succumbed to the dreaded illness and was buried in a nearby field. A stone inscribed E.S. 1665 was placed over the spot, and can still be seen today.

Davenport House Farm is a beautiful example of an 18th century building with handsome gates, a fine studded door and a carved oak staircase. There are Georgian houses and farms, Victorian houses and Edwardian cottages in both Lindow and Row of Trees.

For such a small area, Lindow and Row of Trees have not been without their interesting neighbourhood characters. During the 18th century, a shepherd became a well-known figure in Lindow. He was noted for his strange and colourful attire, of 'low shoes with large buckles, knee breeches, red vest, brown coat, a large round hat and he carried a crook'. He died in the early 19th century at about the age of 100 years.

Another resident of Lindow, living around 1880, was of a particularly economical turn of mind. He only bought two loads of coal in the space of twelve years. In winter he visited his neighbours every night, shared their fire, and then returned home to his own bed!

Between the two world wars there were still many characters of interest around. In the 1930s an old lady called Mrs Worthington used to sell pikelets, crumpets and oatcakes. She wore a navy blue straw hat with large hatpins rammed in it, and pushed a pram which was lined with spotless tea-towels to protect her wares. Another character was Mr Barton, who used to ring a handbell to inform everyone of his visits. He pushed round a box on wheels, selling bread, buns and cakes.

Little Bollington 🌿

In 1973 the village of Bollington, situated to the north of the county, was prefixed 'Little', thus avoiding confusion with the urban district of Bollington, as both are now within Macclesfield Borough.

Little Bollington is bisected by the Altrincham–Warrington road, the A56. Its northern boundary is the river Bollin and it covers an area of approximately 638 acres.

There are nine farms. Brook Farmhouse, Spode Green Lane, is dated 1749, and Spode Green Farmhouse is of an equal age. Eight of the farms are mixed, growing cereal and root crops and breeding cows, pigs and poultry. The ninth, Arthill Farm, is a market garden growing flowers and vegetables, which adorn the church on frequent occasions.

Holy Trinity church was built to a design by Salvin in 1854. It is built of sandstone, as is the font and pulpit, has a porch in the black and white style, and can seat 150 people.

The first school was built in 1857, again built of sandstone probably quarried at nearby Millington. For many years the little girls attending the school wore 'Red Riding Hood' cloaks and hoods given to them by Mrs Lister of Agden Hall. The Earl of Stamford paid for the education of a certain number of children, the rest paid a small weekly sum.

Of the four pubs in the village, Ye Olde No 3 was built in the 17th century and was the third coaching inn on the York to Liverpool stage coach route. For some time it was known as the Red Lion but the old name was reverted to in the early 1950s by landlord C. Atherton. Another ex-landlord was Ernie Kemp, who was well known for breaking in horses on the small piece of land opposite the pub. If he sold just eight gallons of ale in a week he was satisfied and liked nothing better than to sit and chat with a customer. A picnic area has recently been constructed from the car park to the Bridgewater Canal, along which are moored many pleasure craft.

Little Budworth

Little Budworth lies midway between Winsford and Tarporley and is best reached by way of the coach road from the A49 Warrington–Shrewsbury trunk road. To the north of the village lies Little Budworth pool while to the west lies the common. The village was mentioned in the Domesday Book, where it was called Bodeurde.

The area was extensively wooded in earlier times and was part of the great forests of Mara and Mondrum which covered the centre of Cheshire in the Middle Ages. Little Budworth common represents the last remaining trace of those forests in the parish and has been designated a Site of Special Scientific Interest.

The common has remained untouched for centuries; it has never been built upon or farmed but older villagers remember collecting pine needles for use as bedding for animals and fir cones for fuel. The only disturbance in this secluded area came during the Second World War when American soldiers, camping at Oulton Park, used the common as an assault course and learned how to assemble Bailey bridges for the D-day invasion (an original Bailey bridge remains in use as an entrance to the racing circuit). During this time many beautiful trees were cut down to help the war effort.

Two bombs fell on the burnt-out shell of the Egerton's stately home and finalised its destruction. The Hall had been burned down on 14th

February 1926 and six people lost their lives when the ceiling collapsed while they were helping to remove priceless treasures from the house.

For centuries the Egertons had lived at Oulton Park, providing employment on their estate for local people and playing a beneficent role in village life. Many gifts of pictures, vestments and books were donated to the church and in 1898 they gave the village its own church room for reading and recreation. The first harvest supper was so successful there had to be three sittings. Schoolchildren were marched to the Hall once a year for the Christmas party, when each child received a present from the large tree. Traps were always provided to help transport choir members to Beeston station for their annual outings.

There have been other benefactors in Little Budworth's history. The almshouses at the west end of the village stand testament to the generosity of Dame Isabella Dodds and Ralph Kirkham who bequeathed money to help the poor and needy. Three charities currently provide funds for the maintenance of the almshouses.

The village no longer has its own school and children have to be transported to the nearby village of Eaton but in the 18th century there was a dame school founded by the Egerton family. The Egertons wished to express their gratitude to a small boy, 'Irish' Jack Gawley, who kept them supplied with food during an outbreak of the plague, no other villager being brave enough to approach the Hall.

What of today in Little Budworth? Oulton Park became a racing circuit in 1953 and now includes a racing school. Cheshire Polo Club meet in the parish and have their best polo ground here, frequented by Royalty. Oulton Park Cricket Club plays on an idyllic ground near the Egerton Arms.

Village folk are still involved in agriculture and there are a few tied farms and cottages, part of the Oulton estate, but many newcomers commute to the city each day, returning thankfully down leafy lanes frothing with cow parsley in summer, glistening with blackberries in the autumn and occasionally blocked by drifting snow in the winter.

Little Sutton

The village of Little Sutton stands on the main road that links Chester and Birkenhead.

The area before the Conquest belonged to the secular canons of St

Werburgh and passed to their successors the Benedictine monks, who held the land until the Dissolution of the Monasteries. Unfortunately nothing survives of this time except a fine yew hedge that can be seen in Ledsham Road. It is believed that the monks planted this hedge.

The historian Ormerod records that in 1811 an underground burial chamber was discovered south of the former Hall. This, he believed, was a cemetery belonging to the secular canons. However, this important find was not further researched and valuable historic evidence was lost. The present Sutton Hall, an attractive Georgian building some 60 ft from the Ledsham Road, was built in the latter part of the 18th century and was the home of the White family for many years.

The village contains three inns today, the Black Lion, the Olde Red Lion and the Traveller's Rest. The Black Lion was once a popular coaching inn on the main Chester to Birkenhead road. A small post can still be seen today giving the distances to certain places. Unfortunately the 300 year old inn was demolished in the 1960s and replaced by a characterless modern edifice. The new building does have a ghost however, perhaps a remnant of its former days.

Little Sutton has another ghostly resident. This gentleman gives his name to a thoroughfare that runs from the main road past the rear of the railway station. At the corner of the lane a Mr Antwiss, a Liverpool merchant, had a house with a large garden. A gardener named Walker was engaged to work there. This poor chap hanged himself one day, and his ghostly shade is said to haunt Walker's Lane, wandering up and down in the evenings.

The Olde Red Lion stands at the corner of Red Lion Lane, a thoroughfare once called Poachers Lane. The present pub stands on the site of a former building but it was constructed some years ago and fits well into its surroundings. This inn was once the focal point of village life. The Hunt gathered on its forecourt, and the first National school was held in the club-room adjoining the inn.

The village was always a lively place. Certainly on each Good Friday, when the boys of Little Sutton would fight a mock battle with the 'town boys' from Ellesmere Port. This dispute decided for the coming year the ownership of the area called 'Sutton Valley'. The valley however, was cut in half by the construction of Rossmore Road in 1926. The last recorded battle took place in 1933.

Another popular local custom enjoyed by the youth of Little Sutton occurred during the period in early May when Chester's main race meeting is held. At this time many racegoers passing through Little

Sutton stopped for refreshment at the Red Lion. The local lads would shout this rhyme

'Time, time, Chester Race time –
Cracking nuts and drinking wine.'

As the carriages departed some of the occupants would throw coins on to the carriage steps. If any boy attempted to take this bounty his hat would be hooked off by the racegoers with a stick. The lad would then chase after the coach and eventually his hat would be returned together with a generous contribution inside. It is said that some boys could make up to five shillings on Chester Race days. It is not known how many hats were lost!

Little Sutton, like its near neighbour Great Sutton, has changed from a rural farming community to a residential suburb of Ellesmere Port. In 1889 it had a population of 886. That has now greatly increased with much building by council and private developers. Most of the residents are employed in Ellesmere Port or commute to other areas. Today, however, the old and the new blend together to make Little Sutton an attractive area. There are numerous local facilities including a library, bowling green, ample shopping area and it is also well served by public transport. The station, in aptly named Station Road, is a good example of a Victorian building.

Lower Peover 🦢

Lower Peover, a friendly community, is divided by the district boundary of Vale Royal and Macclesfield, defined in part of the village by the stream, the Peover Eye. References to the village made in the Domesday Book of 1086 suggest that the area was of little value and mostly 'waste'. A somewhat different picture exists today!

The church of St Oswald founded in 1269 and of Cheshire 'magpie' construction with a Norman sandstone tower, dominates the area. Its medieval bible chest hewn from a Cheshire oak tree is possibly of a greater age than the church itself. Lower Peover Hall Farm (a manor house) is mentioned in records dated 1350.

A minor Roman road is reputed to have crossed the village from north-east to south-west and part of the ancient saltway from Northwich to Macclesfield and beyond traverses the area from west to east. The area is

The Bells and St Oswald's Church, Lower Peover

still mainly agricultural and the field patterns little changed. Evidence exists of medieval ridge and furrow ploughing.

The Warren de Tabley Arms, now known as The Bells, has been an inn since 1569. Prior to the building of the church, services were held by a monk from the mother church of Great Budworth in a dwelling which existed on the site of the present hotel. The landlord in 1871 was a George Bell whose family were brewers of beer on the premises and owners of several public houses in the area. His ghost is reputed to haunt the present beer cellar.

Older residents remember local horse races, athletics and a steam fairground taking place at the annual Peover Sports Day. A further annual event was Peover Club Day, when the village members of the Ancient Order of Foresters, a Friendly Society, walked around the township led by a brass band which started from Plumley station, calling at various farms for refreshments and accompanied by village children dressed in 'Sunday best'.

The annual village gooseberry show, held in August under the genial sponsorship of Bert and Lesley Flint at the Crown Hotel, is fiercely secretive and competitive amongst its members. Around the turn of the century when the hotel was part and parcel of Crown Farm, Sergeant Tom Simpson, licensee and farmer serving with the de Tabley Troop of the Duke of Westminster's Cheshire Yeomanry, was acclaimed Champion Swordsman of the Regiment, receiving a silver cup to mark the event. No mean feat considering the size and weight of the cavalry sabre of that era!

Some village craftsmen who are remembered and still have family or relatives living here are Sam Harrop the shoemaker who 'repaired shoes like new', Walter Buckley the tailor, and Gough the wheelwright who had a sawpit, and made wooden wheels later to be fitted with iron hoops by Johnnie Jackson on Smithy Green. Lower Peover corn mill was run by the Lea family and serviced by Taffy Williams, millwright and miller, and Tom Cragg, miller and transport, until its closure in the late 1930s.

Due to the past efforts of an alert and enthusiastic Parish Council and a caring Women's Institute the title of Best Kept Village in Cheshire has been achieved on several occasions. Much effort has gone into tree-planting, bulb-planting and the clearing and restoration of ponds, natural areas and conservation of old buildings. Local craftsmen are keeping alive traditional skills such as thatching, paving and the like, including the restoration of the medieval cobbled road to the church.

Lower Withington 🐌

Lower Withington village forms the southern section of the manor of Old Withington, which was acquired around 1266 by a descendant of the Baskervyles who came over from Normandy with William the Conqueror in 1066. The estate was sold in 1960 to Mr E. Crosby, who rebuilt Withington Hall and still lives there.

Adjoining the Park is Catchpenny Lane – so called because it was used by travellers to avoid paying the toll at Dingle Bank, and therefore a second toll bar was erected to catch the penny charge!

Cheshire Hunt Farm was at one time an inn and the Cheshire hounds were kennelled there. It is now owned by the University of Manchester and has been refurbished to accommodate post-graduate students studying for higher degrees at the Nuffield Radio Astronomy Laboratories,

Jodrell Bank (founded by Sir Bernard Lovell in 1945) where the giant radio telescope was built in the 1950s.

The village green, known locally as the 'Sandhole', is a popular picnic area. Formerly it was used for horse racing during the annual Wakes week in November. Frumenty, consisting of boiled wheat and milk was eaten by everyone during the Wakes.

In 1808 the Methodist chapel was built and still plays a prominent part in village life, often combining with St Peter's church (built 1892) to celebrate special events in the Christian calendar. Rogation Sunday is one such event when both the vicar and minister walk the local fields with their congregations, blessing the fields and the animals and crops in them. In 1870 the Withington Brass Band was formed and every Christmas since then the band and singers have visited houses and farms singing carols and collecting for overseas missions.

For over 100 years the Lower Withington Gooseberry Show has been held at the end of July. The Red Lion Hotel (itself once a medieval moot house) was originally the venue for this event, but in recent years it has been held in the parish hall.

The discovery of silica sand in Withington has resulted in vast quantities being extracted for use in the glass-making, steel, and associated industries, leaving several large water-filled quarries which have been landscaped and now form attractive wildlife sanctuaries. The main quarry buildings are situated at Dingle Bank, where local people are employed in the laboratory, testing, grading and drying the sand before it leaves the site in huge tankers.

Although Withington remains rural, the number of farms has decreased due to the quarrying, and the farm cottages have been sold and transformed into 'desirable residences' – most of them retaining their original exterior character. The village school, built 1870, was closed in 1968 and its pupils absorbed into the new primary school at Marton. The Church Commissioners sold the school, and it is now a large private residence.

With the continuing mechanisation on farms, and the more recent reduction in dairy herds, the need for manual labour has been cut, so local people now find employment at Jodrell Bank, the sand quarry, horticultural nurseries, or move into neighbouring villages or nearby towns. Apart from the conversion of properties, the only new housing has been the building of six senior citizens' bungalows in the 1970s.

Lymm 🌿

'Lime' is the version used in the Domesday survey, and the settlement was evidently well established by then. The present parish church of St Mary the Virgin is the fourth known to have been built on the same site, a grassy mound above the village itself. In 1086 it was one of only nine churches recorded in Cheshire. There are many reminders of old Lymm families in the church, including memorials to the Lymmes, Domvilles, Warburtons and Leighs.

Lymm's best known landmark is its ancient cross, set on steps carved in part from a natural outcrop of the local sandstone, geographically and culturally at the heart of the community. Its history is lost in time, but it may have originated as a forum for itinerant preachers at a time when such ministry was not part of church ritual. Legend has it that John Wesley preached from the steps.

Through the years, the cross has been at the centre of all festivities old and new. The present day May Queen and Rushbearing processions pass by it, the old Horse's Head plays and November Pig Fair were held there, and on Christmas Eve crowds of people gather on the surrounding cobblestones to join local bands and the district WI choir in singing carols.

Parallel development of agriculture, transport and industry has caused continuous change to landscape and lifestyles. Until about 1700 most people made their living on the land but, as the population grew, other work was needed. Quarrying for building stone deepened the existing valley into the steep ravine we see today. Dams were built and the resulting water power was harnessed to drive mill wheels. An old corn mill stood near the site of the present bakery; downstream in what is now a landscaped walk known as Slitten Gorge, a slitting mill cut brittle sheets of cast iron into strips for making nails and barrel hoops. The slitting mill, which was in use for more than 100 years, must have been an important feature of Lymm's economy for most of the 18th century.

Around 1770 the Bridgewater Canal was extended from Worsley to Runcorn, cutting through Lymm and altering the village centre beyond recognition. This brought benefits in the form of quicker and cheaper transport which in turn boosted local industries, particularly fustian cutting. Fustian was a form of rough cotton cloth known as 'poor man's velvet' and was used for making working clothes. Bales were brought into Lymm by barge and distributed to the cutters who worked on the cloth in their own homes, cutting the pile with long-bladed knives. In time, cottages were specially built by the factory owners, with a third-storey workroom extending the length of the terrace.

The 19th century brought rapid change. In 1824 the dam below the church was strengthened for the new turnpike road (now A56) which bypassed the difficult route through the village centre. This new dam flooded the marsh near the church to create a large natural-looking lake, Lymm Dam. Later, the first Lord Leverhulme, planning to transform the dam into a great beauty spot, built the bridge at the head of the lake, planted many trees including the avenues of poplars and improved the lakeside footpath known as 'The Bongs' (dialect for banks). Recently a team of rangers have taken over the care of the dam and are developing it like a small country park.

More changes came with the railway and the Ship Canal. Wealthy Manchester families moved to Lymm, building large houses and bringing businesses and jobs. Several local industries flourished, notably basket making, salt production and gold beating. 'Lymm Pure Salt', advertised in white lettering on red railway wagons, became nationally known. Gold leaf from Lymm embellishes the Dome of the Rock in Jerusalem, the high altar of St Paul's Cathedral and of course our own village church. Gold beating is still carried on here.

The railway and the Ship Canal are now almost disused, and change continues. For most residents, moderate comfort has replaced Victorian poverty. Computing, engineering, catering, transport, rabbit farming and horticulture have superseded older occupations – but Lymm remains a very typical Cheshire village.

Macclesfield Forest 🌿

'Macclesfield Forest' once meant a vast medieval hunting area for royalty but is now usually taken to mean the township, an area of scattered farms and in the centre a cluster of four buildings which formerly included the church, school, parsonage and pub. No visitor to this isolated hamlet would guess that in years past the place was humming with activity when the king visited his hunting lodge with his entourage.

There was said to have been stabling for 600 horses, yet the exact site of 'The Chamber in the Forest' has never been established.

A school of some sort has existed since 1728, but a century later the parsonage became the schoolmaster's house and lessons were more regular. The number of pupils varied between 30 and over 60 and some had to walk several miles to school 'carrying jars of stew and rice pudding over their shoulders.' When the Water Authority took over a number of farms the attendance dropped until the school finally closed in 1960 when only seven children remained.

The church, or Forest Chapel is situated at about 1,300 ft. It was built in 1673 and rebuilt in 1834, and has seen many human stories both happy and sad. It is well known for its annual Rushbearing Service, held on the Sunday after August (the Glorious) 12th when the current Lord Derby was likely to be staying at Crag Hall. Centuries ago rushes were strewn on church floors for warmth. Once a year these were ceremoniously renewed. Nowadays the chapel is decorated with plaited rushes and flowers and rushes are symbolically scattered on the floor. Many visitors attend the service, part of which is held outside in the churchyard. In 1848 windows had to be repaired in both church and school after 'a memorable Rushbearing'. In contrast a note in the register records that 'John Etchells did very meanly order only one bottle of Communion wine' and there was none left for Easter. Others record deaths in the snow: one, as recently as 1939, occurred at Christmas time and was not discovered until early March.

One of the incumbents at Forest Chapel was the Rev Gage Earle Freeman, who had much to do with the revival of falconry in his day. He came to the district in 1856, and remained until 1889. At that time the local grouse were in greater danger from the parson than from the gun. He hawked grouse with peregrines on the moors and killed hares and rabbits with his goshawks. It has been alleged that he actually housed his birds indoors in the vicarage. Four years after moving to the cure of Askham, near Penrith, he died but his body was brought back to Forest Chapel for burial.

Malpas ✥

Malpas is a small township in a mainly agricultural area situated about 15 miles from Chester and six miles from Whitchurch, Shropshire, along the Roman road linking Chester with Wroxeter. The route formed a once much-disputed border between Cheshire and Wales.

Behind the church (St Oswald's) is a green mound which was the site of a small Norman castle. The 14th century church has two chapels, one dedicated to the Brereton family and the other to the Cholmondeley family, both families having featured widely in the history of Malpas. In the church are to be seen some examples of medieval stone carving, attractive stained glass windows, and a 13th century chest.

Malpas has a number of interesting buildings namely the Market House with its Tuscan columns, the tithe barn, a 17th century building, and the Cholmondeley almshouses built in 1721. The Market House is a reminder that Malpas was a medieval borough with permission to hold fairs and a market, although these have not been held since the 19th century.

The Red Lion Inn is an old coaching inn visited by King James I in 1624. In the inn is a chair used by the King on this visit. It is a tradition that anyone sitting on this chair must pay one penny for the privilege or pay for a round of drinks for all present in the bar.

The Alport family of Overton Hall is remembered by the endowment of £500 to endow a Blue Coat charity school. The present primary school perpetuates their name.

Another notable figure, born in the Higher Rectory in 1783, was Reginald Heber who later became the Bishop of Calcutta. During his life he composed many hymns, perhaps the best remembered being *Holy, Holy, Holy* and *From Greenland's Icy Mountains*. He is commemorated by a stained glass window in the church, and the high school bears his name.

Though Malpas today is chiefly engaged in agricultural pursuits such as farming, dairy products and the sale of hay and straw, it is a thriving community able to offer employment in light engineering, coach and plant hire, haulage, building and its allied trades, poultry keeping and promotional advertising.

Marbury ❧

Marbury is situated in the south of the county, close to the Shropshire border, its most notable features being the beautiful, old church of St Michael and All Angels, dating back to the 13th century, and the two meres, one now very small through being overgrown with vegetation and the other, lying just below the church, a large and very pleasant tract of water on which can be seen many wildfowl.

The church has the second oldest pulpit in Cheshire, dating from the 15th century, and many interesting carvings in stone around the outside of the building. Due to the presence of sand in the area the church building is gradually slipping and the 63 ft high tower is now 25 inches out of the vertical. There is a 1,000 year old yew tree in the churchyard, now a mere hollow trunk held together by chains. Legend has it that if the yew tree falls the church will fall also.

The centre of the village is the village green, where an oak tree was planted to commemorate the battle of Waterloo. From the green several roads radiate outwards, along which are some old black and white cottages and The Swan, the local inn for many years. In days gone by these roads had names like Bulgaria Street, Grosvenor Square and Threadneedle Street, the latter so named because the tailor lived there, but now they are mundanely referred to by the places to which they lead.

A few new houses have appeared in Marbury since the Second World War – 14 council houses, originally built for farm workers, and one or two private houses, but the village has remained basically the same for a very long time. Prior to 1810 there was an old Hall in what was known as Tapley's Craft, just below the church and by the big mere, but a new Hall was built in that year on rising ground beyond the mere, with extensive views all round.

Farming, mainly dairying, is still the main occupation of the area, a good proportion of the land being owned by the Duchy of Lancaster, which bought a number of farms in 1945 from the Poole family who, until then, had lived in Marbury Hall. There are, however, people from the village who travel out to work.

A poignant feature of Marbury is the inscription over the lychgate at the churchyard entrance, in memory of those who died in the First World War, which reads:

'Ye who live on 'mid English pastures green
Remember us and think what might have been'.

Marton 🌿

The old village of Marton with its distinctive black and white church is situated on the A34 about four miles from Congleton. Its name derives from a large mere which was drained in the mid 19th century.

Sir John de Davenport granted the estates to his son Vivian and endowed the church in 1343. Effigies of both are in the church porch. The church, dedicated to St James and St Paul, is reputed to be the oldest black and white church still in use in Europe. During restoration in the 19th century medieval wall paintings were discovered on the west wall.

In the centre of the village is the Davenport Arms Inn – local justice used to be dispensed there and the local constable had to report periodically on the state of the stocks and pinfold. Also in the village are several ancient cottages, two of which are still thatched. The Davenport family were Master Sergeants of Macclesfield Forest with power of life and death over malefactors, and their crest, of a felon's head with a rope round his neck, is still on the gable end of some of the properties.

The old smithy is now a private house but at one time was smithy, wheelwright's cottage and home of the local undertaker. One of the cottages was the original village school, later the post office, and the birthplace of William Buckley. Buckley was born in 1780 and was transported to Australia for taking part in a mutiny. He escaped prison camp on landing and spent the next 32 years with a tribe of aborigines, eventually marrying the deceased chief's wife. At 6 ft 6 inches he must have towered over the tribesmen, and had almost forgotten how to speak his native tongue. He died in 1856, aged 76, after falling from a horse, and Buckley's Cave and Buckley's Falls in Australia are named after him, also the saying 'doing a Buckley'.

Another notable feature of the village is Marton Oak – now split into three living trees it was at one time the largest oak in England. It had a girth of 58 ft at the base and its greatest limb measured 11 ft 6 inches.

One of the ancient traditions is the village Wakes fete – formerly a two day event this is now held on the Saturday nearest to the patron saint's day. Before the mere was drained a horse race around it was one of the principal events and a further attraction was the annual cattle fair. One of the highlights in 1939 was the election of a 'Potato King' but in 1976 a Rose Queen was crowned for the first time. Another local custom is the Gooseberry Show, one of the oldest in Cheshire. In 1978 the largest gooseberry on record was entered in this show, and in 1987 the world record runner up was grown by a Marton man.

In 1954 water was brought to the village and this allowed 14 council houses to be built. Since then six old people's bungalows and a new vicarage have been built.

Although mainly a farming community there are now many other occupations including trout farming, horticulture, strawberry growing and the sale of farm produce.

Mellor 🌿

The village has more in common with Derbyshire, of which it was a part until the 1933 boundary changes. It lies on the edge of the Peak District and is only six miles from Kinder Scout as the crow flies.

The older part of the village, Moor End, forms the upper part of Mellor; here are the old stone cottages and houses, many of them several hundred years old. Lower down, red brick houses have been built since the turn of the century, many in recent years for the commuters living here and working in nearby Stockport or Manchester.

The village is dominated on either side by hills. On the one to the north stands the old parish church of St Thomas; the base of the tower dates back to Norman times, whilst the chancel was rebuilt in the 1880s. The church is notable for a pulpit carved from the solid trunk of an oak tree and thought to be the oldest wooden pulpit in Britain (dating back to the 14th century) and for an even older Saxon stone font carved with strange figures.

On the hill to the south, Cobden Edge, stands a large wooden cross, erected some years ago by the local Council of Churches. A procession of hundreds of people from all the churches in the area wends its way each Good Friday in the late afternoon to the cross, pausing on the way for prayers, readings and hymn singing. Near to the cross is a group of cottages known in former days as 'Bongs'. Here John Wesley came to preach several times during his ministry. The oak preaching chair he used is now in the Methodist church.

Until the late 1700s the residents of Mellor were employed in farming and cottage industries of hand-spinning and weaving, but with the advent of powered machinery (mainly water power) several mills were established for spinning and weaving cotton materials. The largest was built by Samuel Oldknow in the valley between Mellor and Marple. His fine mill was a model of industrial architecture and his employees – many of the apprentices being from orphanages – were treated with more consideration than many at that time. He built a large house to accommodate them and they were well fed. He was also instrumental in commissioning the building of the Peak Forest Canal. His mill was burned down in 1892 and very little trace of it now remains, though the mill lodge has been devleoped as a boating and fishing lake, and the house built for his apprentices is now a farmhouse.

Another large mill – Dove Bank, in Moor End – was built by the

160

Waller brothers. This employed about 600 people, many walking in daily from neighbouring villages. In the 1870s there were two fires at the mill and this, coupled with a trade depression, made the owners bankrupt. Other small mills in Mellor also went the same way, and in 1881 a local paper reported that out of 383 dwelling houses in Mellor, 110 were uninhabited, and the population fell from 1,768 to 1,242. From this time until the First World War the village was small, residents working on small local farms or travelling to nearby mills in Strines or Marple. Hardly any trace of the old mills remains, except for the mill lodges. A small wadding mill, built much later (about 1890), is still in production, and employs a handful of people.

Mellor has become increasingly a dormitory village. Many small farms have gone, the land amalgamated with other farms, of which only three are now milk producers. The remaining land, although most of the village is green belt, has been used for building or grazing for horses – there are three riding schools in the village. Mellor has three shops, three public houses, an attractive golf course, a thriving sports club and many societies and organisations, catering for a variety of interests and hobbies.

Mere & Over Tabley 🌿

Mere and Over Tabley straddle the main A50 and A556 roads, and are bordered on one side by the busy M6 motorway.

A mixture of stockbroker belt and farming communities, it is an area with no centre other than the intersection of these two 'A' roads.

The primary school has been closed and is now a restaurant, the smithy has gone, turned into a social club and the local post office and store is once again a private house.

But Mere is noted for its excellent golf course which attracts many celebrities, the club house situated on the site of the Old Hall. The New Hall, home of the Langford-Brookes, is positioned nearby.

Mickle Trafford 🌿

Mickle Trafford is divided from Bridge Trafford by the river Gowy and derived its name from the ford which crossed the river in olden days.

Mickle Trafford is not a village in the traditional way with houses clustered around a village green or church. Until recent housing development took place, it consisted of small isolated groups of houses straddling the A56 for about two miles.

Mickle Trafford is in the parish of Plemstall, which also includes the villages of Bridge Trafford, Picton, Picton Gorse, Hoole Bank, Hoole Village and part of Pipers Ash.

Plemstall church stands on a site where Christian worship has taken place since at least the 7th century. A legend tells of a shipwrecked fisherman who, during the height of a storm, made a vow that if he ever reached dry land he would build a church as an act of thanksgiving and dedicate it to St Peter the fisherman. At that time the area was marshland and tidal. Having found refuge on an outcrop of rock he built his church there.

Another place of interest in the village is the watermill, one of several astride the river Gowy between its source at Beeston and its outlet into the river Mersey.

During the 1950s the mill ceased to be a privately owned working mill and was taken over by the Water Authority, who allowed it to become rather derelict. However, in the late 1970s and early 1980s a trust was formed and it has now been restored. Unfortunately the original mill stream has been diverted but there is a culvert which will allow sufficient water to drive the huge undershot water wheel for demonstration purposes.

The only resident of the parish with any great claim to fame was John Hurleston of Picton Hall, whose family owned Picton and part of Upton. He is believed to have sailed with Drake against the Spanish Armada in 1588 and his portrait was on a postage stamp commemorating the 400th anniversary of the defeat of the Armada.

The Hurleston tomb is beneath the east window of Plemstall church, a large box tomb with rather gruesome recumbent skeletons carved on either side. On the wall above the tomb is a memorial tablet which records the burial of a young wife. Unfortunately time has obliterated the words, which used to read:

> She was beautiful in her person,
> Discreet in her behaviour,
> A dutiful daughter
> An observant wife
> and had she lived a few weeks longer
> might have been a happy mother
> Married 1723 and died 1727, aged 32

162

Today Mickle Trafford is a busy commuter village for Chester, War-rington, Liverpool and Manchester, with housing on the new estates continually changing hands.

Minshull Vernon ✍

On either side of the busy A530, midway between Nantwich and Middlewich, lies the scattered village of Minshull Vernon.

The land is mainly pasture and in former times the area was known for its cheese making. It boasts two greens, Bradfield and Whalleys, and it is from Bradfield Green farm that evidence of a settlement much earlier than the Norman period was found when police frogmen diving in the large water-filled pit there, discovered a Roman bridge and road. This road travels due north and another section of it was uncovered when restoration work was being carried out on the old vicarage.

The parish church of St Peter, erected in 1847 to replace an older one, was designed by Sir Gilbert Scott to seat 200. There is also a Congrega-tional chapel, erected in 1809 and a Wesleyan chapel, built in 1832. The village school was built in 1840 and in 1900 recorded 108 children. The latter chapel and school are now private residences.

Within the memory of some of the older inhabitants many cameos of village life, as it was at the turn of the century, are recalled.

Before the ladies attended the village dances and socials, held in the school room, they were invited to change from their travelling garb into their finery at the nearby farm where the farmer's wife had prepared a fire in the guest bedroom and where the sound of the fiddle and accordion made them hurry to join in the merriment.

On summer Sunday evenings, after church and chapel, folk met together on the greens to talk and sometimes, in order to extend the evenings, would visit neighbouring beauty spots. As one lady recalled, 'let's go and listen to the nightingale in Warmingham Wood'.

Some can remember playing hop scotch, marbles and hoop-bowling down the main street – now the busy A530!

One inhabitant recalled the fun that they had roping after a wedding. As the bride and groom came down the road a rope was suddenly pulled in front of them and the perpetrators requested a coin as ransom before the happy couple were allowed to proceed. Not always did the ropers encounter a happy couple. On one remembered occasion the registrar from Nantwich, who was also a pig farmer, brought the wrong licence to the chapel so the marriage could not take place. However the couple were reassured to know that the registrar's pigs had a licence to prove that they were free from infection!

Nearer to the present day there are many reminiscences from the Second World War: the two children who were killed by a bomb; George Smith, roadman, who was awarded the OBE for bravery; the narrow escape of the late vicar's wife from an unexploded incendiary bomb; and teaching evacuees to knit using stripped hen's feathers for needles.

In 1890 Kelly's Directory gave the population of Minshull Vernon as 318, and probably a similar number live here today. A few new houses have been built but no great changes have taken place. The familiar family names appear in the parish register over and over again and in the spring of 1989 Michael Vernon married Deborah Minshull in St Peter's church, Minshull Vernon.

Mobberley ✤

Mobberley is a village of great antiquity about 15 miles south of Manchester between Wilmslow and Knutsford. It lies in dairy farming country and its twelve and a half square miles are mostly covered by lush farmland. One of its boundary rivers is the Bollin; another, Mobberley brook, winds its way through the parish in a series of tight loops. There are many ponds in the fields caused by subsidence due to the underlying salt beds. It was principally these salt beds which saved the village from becoming a satellite town soon after the Second World War.

Most of the 3,000 inhabitants live in pleasant housing estates and on roads near the shops and post office. This part of the village has recently acquired street lighting on the main road but the rest of the parish is dark at night. There are several small scattered groups of houses and also some remote farmhouses joined to the rest of the village by narrow tree-lined roads.

Mobberley has a long history. It existed centuries before it was mentioned in the Domesday Book under the Anglo-Saxon name of Motburleg. Originally it was all forest, but part of it was cleared by the Romans who built a road through what is now the village. The first church was built about AD 750 soon after the death of St Wilfrid, to whom it was dedicated. The present church of St Wilfrid was started in 1245.

The Old Hall, Mobberley

Because of its long history and the large area it covers, Mobberley has many beautiful and interesting old buildings, some in typical Cheshire black and white, some with thatched roofs and cruck frames, and some in attractive weathered brick. The records of their occupants over past centuries make fascinating reading. Probably the best known, because it can be seen from the main Knutsford–Wilmslow road, is Mobberley Old Hall. It is a splendid building with mullioned windows, built in 1612, and it stands in extensive gardens behind an ancient yew hedge. Saltersley Farm is believed to be the oldest house in Mobberley and has been inhabited for over 600 years. It stands on the eastern border of the village, on the edge of the peat bog where Lindow man was discovered in 1984.

165

In the 19th century there was a six-storey crepe mill which had developed from a much older corn and spinning mill. This must have dominated the landscape. It stood beside a large mill pool created from the dammed-up Mobberley brook. It was pulled down and the pool drained in 1887. Now the large Ilford works is the industrial feature in otherwise rural surroundings.

The Victory Hall, built to commemorate the end of the First World War, is in constant use for all sorts of activities and functions. A flourishing men's club and bowling green are attached to it. There are various sporting facilities but particular pride is felt in the cricket club, founded in 1876. Other amenities range from a primary school to an old people's home, a local railway station and seven public houses. Eleven other pubs, which appear in the old records, no longer exist.

An old tradition, which dates from the time of the manorial court, is the election by the parish council of two burleymen. These are still called in to assess any damage done to crops or private property by straying cattle, and although their assessment is not legally binding, it is usually accepted by both sides.

Moore ꕬ

Moore, and the hamlet of Keckwick, lie in the Mersey valley, 100 ft below the gently sloping hills to the south-east, on the Runcorn road. Passing through also are two railway lines and the Bridgewater Canal, but they are now separated by part of the Runcorn New Town expressway.

The plantation of firs on Keckwick Hill was cleared just after the Second World War, but has recently been replanted. The quarry on the same hill was largely filled in so that the new Chester road could be built. Keckwick has expanded from 13 dwellings in 1871, to 19 today, and will soon be engulfed by new housing from Runcorn New Town, but since it is mentioned in the Domesday Book, it is to be hoped that the name will not disappear entirely.

Most of the land has been drained and farmed for centuries. The Manchester Ship Canal now forms the northern boundary of Moore. The main Runcorn road probably followed the driest route along the valley, and slopes gradually from about 100 to 40 ft above sea level. All the older buildings are on, or near this road. The central part of the village from Manor Farm to Canal Side Cottages is a conservation area, and many trees carry preservation orders. Strangely there are four farms within 50 yds of each other in the centre, and a fifth at the corner with Moss Lane, a short distance away. Of these, only two are now working farms – Manor Farm which dates from 1660, and Rose Farm, bearing a picture of a shire horse above the front door as these are bred by the owner.

Moore Hall, said to be haunted, with its fine late 17th century frontage, also stood very close to the main road, in the angle with Hobb Lane, but was split off from the road by the Bridgewater Canal in the 1760s. This canal, the earliest in Britain, closely followed the 100 ft contour in order to avoid locks. It runs parallel to the road until it reaches the Hall grounds, then swings away through the fields. The little bridges over it are rather too narrow for modern traffic.

Moore looks to Daresbury for its church although services are held in the Milner church institute, which also functions as a village hall and meeting place. Methodism arrived in Moore in 1812, and the Wesleyan chapel opened in 1813.

The present primary school was built in 1965 in Lindfield Close just off the main road near the site of Moore station. The old school in Moss Lane was built in 1877, but is now used by scouts and cubs. There is a shop-cum-post office, a shop-cum-newsagents, a pub, a plumber, a builder, an undertaker and the farms, but most working inhabitants have jobs outside the village. Increasing from 45 dwellings with 344 people in 1871, to 290 dwellings plus two caravan sites, with a population of approximately 1,000 today, Moore is still a pleasant 'backwater'.

Morley Green 🐝

A very rural village with a village green, on which a seat donated by Morley Green WI is much appreciated. Situated three miles from Manchester airport and three miles from the nearest town of Wilmslow, in bygone times it was a place in which peat was excavated and used for fuel. There was also a Quaker meeting place and a brickyard here.

There are around 300 inhabitants and two mobile home sites. Pownall Hall was the home of the Boddington family (the brewers). Morley was owned originally by the De Trafford estate and later properties were sold to private individuals, the largest owner being Mr. A. Lythgoe who bought most of the farms.

A social club is very active with over 400 members, and there is one church (United Reformed). There is no shop and the village post office was closed some years ago. Situated in the Green Belt area, there is no new building permitted.

It is a happy little village, sporting two bungalows on the main road. The owners are great gardeners and their gardens are true showpieces, causing many a car to stop on the green and pause awhile.

Mottram St Andrew 🕸

In 1086 a Saxon named Gamel, is recorded as holding land in Motre. The village was, in 1414, called Mottram St Andrew. St Andrew's Well is in Mottram Wood, from which the Old Hall was supplied with water.

The 13th century Old Hall, the residence of the Mottrums and subsequent families, was a black and white farmhouse originally surrounded by a moat on three sides. The moat still existed in 1880, and although it is now dry it is still visible. The Mottram estate was bought by William Wright, a Stockport landowner in 1738. He built the New Hall in 1753.

The Mottram Hall estate was broken up in 1922, and farms and houses were sold to private buyers. Now the New Hall belongs to De Vere's, and it is a much enlarged hotel and leisure centre.

Cherry Tree Cottage, formerly thatched, had a small mortuary at one end, used by the Baptists from Warford chapel, who buried their dead in an adjacent burial ground behind the then smithy. The earliest burial was 1701. One raised slab records four deaths in one family, all within ten months, accounted for locally by the fact that the family had eaten potatoes grown in the burial ground, and it is said that calves put there to graze met the same fate.

Seams of copper and lead extending from the Alderley Edge mines, produced a rich deposit of vanadium, a rare metal used in the hardening of steel. The ore was given the name Mottramite, and was discovered by Professor Roscoe in 1877.

Mottram Cross, an old butter cross, has a 14th century base and a restored shaft and head, dated 1832, bearing the coat of arms of the Wright family. There are accounts of bull baiting taking place, and a story that the steps served as an auction block when a husband wearied of his wife.

Across the road is the Bull's Head Inn, once a farm with a six day licence to sell liquor. The sign of a bull's head over a crown is the crest of the Wrights of Mottram.

In 1932, electricity and piped water came to the whole village, previously just a few houses had water which was produced by the power of the windmill in the centre of the village. The metal frame of the windmill was given to be used for the war effort in the Second World War. In 1851, the village allotments were awarded to be used by the labouring poor of the township, and today they are still very well tended. There is still no sewerage system in the village, a decision made by the villagers.

St Peter's church, Prestbury, is the parish church for Mottram, so many of the stones bear the names of Mottram families. The Greens occupied one old house for many years, and the epitaph to Ed, stonemason and parish constable, who was shot by a poacher, reads:

> Beneath this Stone lyes Ed Green
> Who for cutting Stone famous was seen
> But he was sent to apprehend
> One Joseph Clark at Kerridge End
> For stealing Deer of Esquire Downs
> Where he was shott and dyd o'th wounds.

Mow Cop

Rising to 1,100 ft above sea level, Mow Cop or Moel Coppa, has been interpreted as 'bald head', 'lofty summit', or 'hill of the cairn'. At one end of the Staffordshire Way, at least six counties can be seen from the Castle, which stands on the Staffordshire/Cheshire border. Formerly known as the Tower and later the Summer House, it was built for the Wilbraham family in 1754. The Old Man of Mow, so called because of its resemblance to a human head, is another landmark, 65 ft in height.

The village was at one time well wooded, and there was an abundance of heather and bilberries. The sandstone was quarried as far back as Roman times, and the cut-out shapes of millstones, or querns, can still be seen. The softer rock was pounded into sand for glass making. Stone walls were well in evidence, and the inhabitants of the stone cottages were, through the ages, quarrymen, smallholders and miners.

Bourne Street was at one time called Baker's Lane, as there was a bakehouse, from where the bread and cakes were delivered by horse and trap. It was possible to buy two penn'orth of Nelson, which was a very tasty sort of currant bread. There were at least 15 shops then, but only two today.

The Odd Fellows public house had the Staffs/Cheshire boundary running through it, so that at closing time, the customers moved over to the side which permitted another half hour drinking time. The same building, once a fustian mill, now manufactures surgical supplies. A former fustian mill in Mount Pleasant, now producing textiles, may eventually become a housing site. There were also two clog making businesses run by Mr Sidebotham and Mr Haycock.

In the wall by the Wesleyan chapel at The Bank and in the alley behind Westfield Road, were communal bread ovens, which were used in turn by the cottagers. Of the numerous wells and springs, many are no longer in use, or they have been covered over. The ceremony of the blessing of the wells is now a thing of the past, the carnivals also. The many springs are responsible for the constant flow of water that runs down Mow Cop, often in the most inconvenient places, causing annoyance to the inhabitants. It is claimed by some that the source of the Trent is here, and not at Biddulph Moor.

The stretch of Top Station Road by the Cheshire View Inn has a 1 in 3 gradient, where Foden's tested their lorries. Cycling and motor-cycle races also took place up Station Road. This same steep slope is now part of the 'Killer Mile' race which starts at the former station and ends at the Castle. It is an annual event and each April finds more contestants participating.

The lengthsmen used to break up stones to fill the many potholes. More recently, lengthsman Eddie Hackney thought that a car parked near the Castle, had been left there in difficulty during the snowy weather. He obligingly sprinkled grit around the car. Later, one of the bus drivers trying to turn his bus near the car, took a closer look at the vehicle. Inside was the body of a woman, murdered by the other woman in a love triangle. So once again Mow Cop hit the leadlines.

Today the heather and bilberries are not so plentiful, and the stone walls and cottages are less in evidence. The present diminished woodland is no longer the main territory of the fox, as he is now often seen in fields and gardens, especially in the Fir Close area. The rabbits are now very numerous, and breed on the site of the former quarry in Halls Road. The village is becoming a commuter area and there is no longer much employment on Mow Cop.

Ness & Little Neston

Ness Gardens has always been the hub of local social activity, going back to the end of the 19th century before Mickwell Brow was built in 1899 for the founder of Bees Nurseries. On that Brow many meetings were held by the villagers. The nursery moved to Sealand in 1913 and Mr Bulley then developed the land as his private garden open to the public day and night, free of charge, and called Ness Gardens.

In the early part of the 20th century, the colliery situated on the Ness coastline was the biggest employer of labour, and caused serious unemployment at its closure in 1926. The land and the village smithy were also a source of employment – the latter known as 'The Providence Works', and owned by a keen Methodist, Mr Joseph Mealor. The three thatched cottages by the works have now been replaced by well built houses, known as Smithy Close. There is only one farm now whereas there used to be three, and only one shop, whereas in the old days there were three plus a bakery owned by Mr Wilde.

The house where Lady Hamilton, mistress of Lord Nelson was born still remains and is the tall house at the end of the village named Swan Cottage. Her father was a blacksmith at the village smithy.

Mr Arthur Behrend lived at Friends Hall and was a member of the Liverpool shipping firm, Barr, Behrend & Co. He wrote the book, *The House of the Spaniard*, a tale of mystery and intrigue inspired by Denna Hall, which is situated overlooking the Dee marshes. This was the home of Richard Summers, son of the founder of the Shotton steelworks. Friends Hall is believed to be on the site of a Quaker meeting place.

A line of roughly hewn rocks on the fringe of the marsh was the only landing stage from the river Dee in the Denhall area. The Old Quay was the home of smugglers and a landing place for Irish immigrants making their way along the marsh and Well Lane on their way to Chester.

A few of the old cottages remain in Ness village, built of Cheshire sandstone, and have a conservation order on them, but otherwise the village is rapidly changing face as property is developed and old Dutch barns become modern residences.

Newton 🦢

The lands of Newton or Newton-cum-Larton, formed part of the ancient possessions of the old Lancashire families of Banastre. In 1240 a silver penny was rendered at midsummer by way of acknowledging their lordship. By the middle of the 17th century, partly by descent and partly by purchase, the largest part of the lands had become the property of a freeholder, Thomas Bennett. He bequeathed 252 acres of his lands to the poor of his native parish of West Kirby.

A farmhouse was erected in Newton in 1768, by a Mr Johnson, Mayor of Liverpool. He set in the wall of the house a china plate bearing his coat of arms, and made in Liverpool china. The plate is still there in the wall and the road where the farmhouse stands is called China Farm Lane.

At the first census in 1801, there were 49 inhabitants, following mostly agricultural pursuits, but only six inhabited houses. After 40 years the village had grown to 53 inhabitants in eight houses.

During the following century Newton grew apace, gaining its first shop during the First World War, a cafe and a shop in 1930 and its first post office in 1932.

Now a parish in its own right, Newton has a modern church, St Michael and All Angels built in 1963, a busy village hall, a guide hall and a large school. With its population following many trades and professions, many of the people living here now travel to Liverpool, Birkenhead or Chester to work. Although there are a lot of residents now, the village of Newton as a separate entity has almost disappeared, being engulfed by West Kirby.

Norley 🦢

The name Norley, or Northley as it was once called, means 'north clearing in the forest', the 'forest' being Delamere. Situated twelve miles from Chester, Norley became a parish in 1836. The 1801 census records 376 inhabitants, and by 1981 the number had risen to 985, with very little change since that date.

Traditionally, Norley has been primarily an agricultural community, interdependent and closely knit. In addition the village has been the home of craftsmen, including the blacksmith, the tailor and the shoemaker. During the 20th century it has housed those who have provided services for the community such as shopkeepers, the coal merchant, the milkman and the taxi owner.

A head forester lived in Gallowsclough Lane and Forest House now stands on the site of the original 12th century house. Hangings were carried out on Gallowsclough Hill and poachers on their way to the gallows would kneel to pray at Gad Bank, a corruption of God's Bank. Cheese Hill was where in the 17th century a game called 'Rolling the Cheese' was played. The smithy stood opposite the present village hall and the anvil can still be seen.

The village has been well served by both churches and schools since the establishment of the first Wesleyan Methodist chapel in 1779, and the first church of St John the Evangelist in 1833, the Wesleyan Methodist Association in 1836 (a group of villagers who had seceded from the main body) and Zion chapel in 1870. Both Methodists and Anglicans organised day and Sunday schools.

Life in Norley had always centred around the church and chapel and in earlier days, the temperance movement. Indeed, so strong was the support for temperance that the village split between those who supported the Ancient Order of Foresters and those who supported the Rechabites. The Rechabites met in the Temperance Hall and the Foresters met in their own hall on School Bank. Their parades were quite grand occasions, and greatly enjoyed by residents.

Life in the village today still centres around the church and the chapel and the old Temperance Hall, bought by the villagers for their own village hall. The village is still steeped in tradition. Many remember with pride Norley's olden days and many still believe local folklore. There is a legend that the ghost of a woman walks from the well steps in Pytchley's Hollow to School Bank just before a death in the village. Others believe that a ghost walks by the Tank Tree in School Lane, and that the ghost of the daughter of a one-time landlord haunts the Carrier's Inn, one of the two remaining public houses, the other one being the Tiger's Head.

Amenities came late to the village, gas was not available until 1987. What has changed, however, is the population of Norley. Though farming is still an important occupation, the residents are now mainly professionals. Hatchmere Lake and the forest are popular tourist attractions and the villagers welcome many who want to share the beauty of this Cheshire village.

North Rode 🦜

North Rode lies halfway between Macclesfield and Congleton, on the north bank of the river Dane, amidst beautiful hills, woods and valleys. Its past is reflected in names like Scissorcroft Wood, Weaver's Hey, Brickbank Wood and Kiln Croft.

The Macclesfield Forest stretched from Marple to Bosley and people lived under the jurisdiction of the church, the hundred court and the forest court. The Davenport family, who were chief foresters, had the right to decapitate offenders caught poaching, stealing wood, or letting beasts stray and the forest harboured wolves as late as 1303. Thus, population was sparse, the land infertile and justice harsh.

Before the building of the church, services were held in the school-room, the village being in Prestbury parish. Problems of travel for burials and baptisms meant that people went to Bosley and Gawsworth. The church, built by the Daintrys in 1846 has a screen, font cover and cross carved by local craftsmen. Other buildings of interest are Colley Mill, dating back to 1444 and later a wheelwright's and Yew Tree cottage, possibly older, home of a forester.

The cutting of the canal in the 1820s and the building of the railway affected life in North Rode. A great celebration, with an ox-roast, marked the opening of the viaduct in 1849. The building of its 20 great arches was accomplished in two years, with considerable difficulties, by 2,000 men, who lived, in very orderly fashion, in shacks by the river. The railway carried milk from local farms to Manchester and also provided transport for passengers.

The village remained self-contained, however, with its own shoemaker, wheelwright, blacksmith, undertaker, joiner and tailor. The farms were working communities. Dobford Farm had three men and dairymaids, living in, besides casual labourers, all fed by the farmer's wife.

True love never did run smooth, as we see from the story of a young lover, forbidden by Mr Dale the joiner, to see his daughter. He hid in the plantation, shot Mr Dale through the cheek and, presumably overcome by his deed, threw himself in the lake and drowned. Another young lady carried on a dual courtship, and on her wedding day the unsuccessful suitor stood up, and declared a 'lawful impediment'. She subsequently married him!

In 1835 a school was built by John Smith Daintry, endowed with money from trusts by John Plant in 1780 and Wade Stubbs in 1821, and run by local managers. North Rode thus had the first 'poor school' in the area. The log books provide a picture of life in the village – the smells from the latrines 'on the pail system', the illnesses – ringworm, typhoid, scarlet fever and the sinister 'itch'. Then there was the 'sad accident' when an infant caught fire at the stove and died from her burns.

The break-up of the estate in 1923 began the village's change in character, with only a few people locally employed. However, there is a strong community spirit and a great assortment of talents, many used for the benefit of the village.

Odd Rode ✺

The district known as Odd Rode is made up of several small villages, namely Scholar Green, Kent Green, Mow Cop and Rode Heath. Running through the area is the Macclesfield canal, now mainly used for recreation, but in earlier times used to carry goods from the Potteries to Macclesfield.

It is mainly an agricultural area, many of the farms having been in the same family for generations, such as Boarded Barn farm, owned today by the seventh generation of Thorleys.

Within its boundaries are the estates of Rode Hall, Ramsdell Hall, Little Moreton Hall and Lawton Hall. The property now known as Rode Hall was bought from the Rode family by Roger Wilbraham towards the end of the 17th century. In 1864 the then Squire Wilbraham was responsible for the building of All Saint's church, Odd Rode. Three schools were also founded by the Wilbrahams.

Close to Mow Cop station is Ransdell Hall, where a salt stream runs through the grounds and is supposed to possess healing powers. It is said the bargees used to collect their drinking water from it. Adjacent to the Hall is the coach house, where a 'walk-in' ice house can be seen in the garden – obviously used in times past for the refrigeration of food. Today it is a Grade I listed building.

About two miles from Scholar Green is Little Moreton Hall, built in the 15th century. It is one of the most perfect examples of a timber-framed, moated Elizabethan manor house and boasts a wainscoted gallery, a chapel, a great hall and a knot garden.

In the grounds of Lawton Hall is an unusual memorial stone. The inscription on the stone says – 'On the death of a bullfinch that sang God Save the Queen when bidden to do so'.

An interesting obelisk known as the Stone Chair stood at the junction of Stone Chair Lane and Station Road, Kent Green. It has been removed for safety to the grounds of Rode Hall. Tradition says that the original took the form of a seated woman with a basket in her hand – which seems to suggest that a market was held here for the sale of farm produce.

Ollerton & Marthall

The villages of Ollerton and Marthall, with populations of about 300 and 150 respectively, are situated two miles south of Knutsford and equidistant from Altrincham, Macclesfield, Northwich and Wilmslow. They are bounded by the hostelries, the Dun Cow to the north and the Egerton Arms to the south.

The Egerton Arms marks the extent of the original Tatton estate and Lord Egerton's coat of arms can be seen on a farm in School Lane, Ollerton. He was considered to be a good landlord and farmers in the area were pleased when they were chosen to manage one of his farms. On days when they went to pay their rent, they could always rely on being provided with a good dinner in the tenants' hall at Tatton.

The A537 runs through the villages and was at one time a toll road with a turnpike gate at the Ollerton crossroads. It has always been a busy road, being a main route from the Mersey basin across the Pennines. The toll bar cottages, dated 1740, still remain, though one was demolished for road widening. The Dun Cow inn housed passing travellers and still has its water trough and mounting block, relics of the days when horses were the chief mode of transport.

Remembered with affection by the older inhabitants of Ollerton are the three friends, Mary Horn, Beatrice Bowker and Jessie Matheson. Starting their working life in domestic service at Beechcroft, a large house on the Chelford Road, they achieved their ambition at the beginning of the Second World War by taking over the Ollerton post office and general store. The old cook baked bread and cooked meats to sell to customers. They were all keen members of the Methodist church (a few houses away and now a private house), and in order to persuade the local children to go to Sunday School, Miss Horn distributed shillings at Easter time to all the children in the village. There is a commemorative plaque to the three friends at the Ollerton crossroads.

The church of All Saints at Marthall is not old, having been built in 1839. Before then the villagers were often buried in Over Peover church-yard, and a bridle way which runs through Bowden Bank Farm was known as Coffin Walk as this was the route the coffins were carried to their last resting place. A noteworthy vicar of the parish for 22 years was Rev Walter Greswell, nicknamed the Hunting Parson. He must fre-quently have ridden the two miles to the smithy at Ollerton where the many horse owners in the area took their horses to be shoed by the blacksmith Mr Potts. Sadly, the blacksmith's forge has given way to a garage.

The days of walking the five miles to Tatton Park daily to work are now over, and commuters travel long distances by car. A sizeable farming community still remains however, with many farms passing from father to son. Recently, part of a farm in School Lane has been made into a nature reserve with facilities for instruction for school parties.

Over Alderley & Birtles 🦜

Over Alderley and Birtles is a small, very rural parish situated between Alderley Edge and Macclesfield. It comprises about 2,800 acres and the lanes wind through beautiful undulating farmland, interspersed with woodlands. Footpaths enhance the area for walkers and there are many varieties of wild flowers and birds.

There is no shop, post office, garage, school or public house, and only about 20 farms, far fewer than in the past.

At one time there was an old, quaint cobbler's shop and the last of the old gentlemen who kept the shop was a real village character. It is said that he was not an early riser, and if customers took shoes to be mended before he was out of bed in the morning, he let down a basket from the bedroom window in which they left their shoes.

Among houses worthy of special mention are Birtles Old Hall, Birtles New Hall, Hare Hill Hall and Whirley Hall. The reading room was built in 1886 by Frank Brocklehurst Esq, who owned Hare Hill estate. In the days when few people had access to books or newspapers, the Brockle-hurst family put them there for parishioners to read. Through the years it has been the social centre for the parish.

St Catherine's church, Birtles, has an unusual octagonal tower, which contains eight bells. It was built by Thomas Hibbert in 1840 and used as a domestic chapel for Birtles Hall. It was consecrated as the parish church in 1890. The precious Flemish stained glass is particularly beautiful.

Up the lane from St Catherine's is the Methodist church, built in 1863. From its peaceful graveyard can be seen the house known as the Black Greyhound, and across from it the blacksmith's building. Last used as a blacksmith's and farrier's around 1930, after the Second World War it was a wheelwright's shop. Having been empty for many years, it is now once again a thriving smithy.

Over Peover 🦢

In early records Peover is spelt 'Peeffer', the original Anglo-Saxon meaning 'a bright river'. The river, though small, provided the mainstay of the villagers' diet, trout, which can still be caught today in the same river, known as Peover Eye. The village of Over Peover, originally and still sometimes referred to as Peover Superior, has a population of about 700.

The village emblem is an ass's head: legend has it that a Crusader was unhorsed in the village and could only procure an ass to replace his lost horse. Since that time the motto has been 'Devant si je puis' (Forward if I can).

Two buildings which attract visitors are the church of St Lawrence and Peover Hall, which stand close together in Peover Park. The older building is the church which dates back to 1450, although very little remains of the original structure and the main building was rebuilt in 1811.

The Mainwaring family, who lived at Peover Hall, can be traced back over 500 years and it is thought that they originally came to the area in the time of Edward I. Peover Hall was originally a half-timbered building and stood in a moated enclosure – the moat remains but very little survives of the old hall. The present Hall was built in 1585 and is a fine example of an Elizabethan manor house, with carved staircase, panelled walls and a long gallery. The last Lady Mainwaring to live at the Hall gave red knitted jackets, known as 'Ganseys', to each worker at Christmas and these enabled her to keep a check on their whereabouts!

Another famous resident of Peover Hall was General George Patton of the United States Army, who lived there during the Second World War and to this day the Stars and Stripes hangs with the Union Jack in the church of St Lawrence.

In 1840 the postmistress, Mary Cooke and her husband Joseph, were murdered by a sailor who jumped ship in Liverpool. The post office was then sited in a house now known as Rose Cottage on Stocks Lane. There is still a village post office and shop which serves the local community.

As many as a dozen stage coaches pulled up daily at the Whipping Stocks Inn en route to London, Liverpool, the East Coast, Scotland and Wales. The journey to London was accomplished in just under three days. The Whipping Stocks still does a flourishing trade. In the 16th century the Court Leet was held in the Whipping Stocks and it is believed that there used to be a medieval fair.

All good villages have a ghost and Over Peover is no exception. Where the Hall stands today there was once a monastery and legend has it that a monk walks the banks of Peover Pool saying his rosary and at midnight walks along Long Hey Lane by Black Pits and opens the gate.

Still very much a farming region, the number of commuters has grown over the years but Over Peover still retains very much a village feeling.

Parkgate 🎷

Parkgate's story is one of change, from the woods and grassland of a deer park, though a century of fame as a port and as a resort for sea bathing, to years of decline as a fishing village. Its fortunes revived when it began to be a residential area, and it now relies on its power to attract both residents and visitors. A part of this power is its unusual story.

Parkgate's name derives from Neston Park, which was enclosed in about 1250 and served as a deer park for 350 years. The river shore by Neston Park was recorded as one of several anchorages where ships would unload their goods if they were too large to reach Chester. In 1610 a sailor was arrested for smuggling calfskins, which were being exported without the necessary licence, from Chester to Parkgate – the first use of this name so far discovered.

The village was firmly established by 1720, and throughout that century Parkgate was renowned as the terminal for packet ships which carried passengers to Dublin. Travellers of all types, from the Lord Lieutenant of Ireland to Irish labourers, would wait here for a favourable wind.

The improvement of roads to Holyhead, where the sea journey was half the distance, caused the Parkgate packet service to die in about 1810. Before then the village had become a seaside resort, and it continued to prosper from visitors until the 1830s. Parkgate then had to struggle to survive as a fishing village.

Peckforton 🌿

Peckforton is four miles south of Tarporley, on the eastern side of the sandstone ridge that runs across the Cheshire Plain.

The village, which has only a village room, a telephone box and a finger post to indicate its centre, sprawls out along three lanes leading to Beeston, Spurstow and Bulkeley. Once a busy village of 56 dwellings with 331 inhabitants in 1831, it has dwindled to 38 houses with a population of about 80. The oldest houses are black and white, square timber-framed on sandstone plinths. They were originally thatched; all but two have been reroofed with slates or clay tiles. Some of the cottages are named according to their purpose or position – hence Parkgate, Laundry Cottage, Smithy Cottage and Garden Cottage. Fountain Cottages are called after a pub of that name demolished long ago. On the other hand, Elephant and Castle is not called after a pub, but takes its name from the sculpture in its front garden, (near to and clearly visible from the road), thought to be the work of one of the stone carvers who embellished Peckforton Castle and, later, Manchester Town Hall.

In 1840 the estate was bought by John Tollemache, who already owned much land in the district. Almost immediately he started to build Peckforton Castle on the end of a sandstone ridge facing Beeston Castle. Designed by Anthony Salvin, it is described by Pevsner as 'the facsimile of a very grand 13th century castle, correct and substantial enough to deceive anyone'. It was finished by 1851 at a cost of £67,847 9s 7½d. It is said that John Tollemache, sailing up the Mersey to Liverpool on his return from America, could see his new home rising up on the Peckforton Hills.

He was created Baron Tollemache of Helmingham in 1876 in recognition of his services to agriculture. He had rebuilt or renovated the farmhouses and cottages, equipping each of the latter with a pigsty – in some cases very close to the back door! It was at this time that Peckforton buildings acquired their distinctive cast-iron diamond-paned windows and large chimneys.

During all this time the cottages in the village were occupied by people who were employed at the castle or on the farms. The school was held in the room over the arch of the castle lodge and church services were held in the castle chapel.

The Tollemache family lived in the castle until 1939. During the Second World War, it was used as a hostel for physically handicapped

180

children evacuated from London. After the war, the castle was guarded by a caretaker until the contents were auctioned in 1953. Following several lettings, the castle and lodge were sold by the family in 1988.

Penketh ✍

Penketh is essentially still a village, although it has spread its wings somewhat and now sits uneasily in the shadow of the formidable Fiddler's Ferry power station. Residents born and bred in Penketh still go 'up the village' to where the heart continues to beat.

Its main arteries in the past were the first canal to be cut in England and the highway used by the Liverpool to London stage coach. As the spring tidal waters from the river Mersey were exceptionally strong when they reached Sankey brook, a minor tributary, its flow was diverted and used to fill the historic Sankey – St Helen's Canal. It was a common sight, long ago, to see the barges or 'flats' lining the canal for more than a mile, waiting for the tide. Tradition tells of one lock keeper, old Robert Naylor, whose stentorian tones, they say, can still be heard on a quiet night calling 'Flood tide' to warn sailors to beware the rush of water.

On the banks of the river Mersey at Fiddler's Ferry, stands the Ferry Inn dated 1762. The name Fiddler's Ferry is derived from the name of the landowner, Adam le Vicleur, which through common usage became Violer, player of the viol or fiddle, thence 'Fiddler'.

More recently, a yacht haven has been opened alongside the Ferry Inn and the sleek modern vessels moored there are a far cry from the first concrete ship that was built on the same site, which promptly sank when launched!

For such a small village, the local industries were quite diverse. They included tanners, brewers, toolmakers, cabinet makers and a family of shoemakers called Gandy. Cobbler's Square was a hive of industry. Bounded by tiny cottages all housing members of the Gandy family, it was the centre of a unique and enterprising business venture, even exporting large shipping orders to America, through the Liverpool merchants. Sadly, only one of the Cobbler's Cottages still remains.

The old Quaker meeting house, built in 1681, sympathetically modernised and extended, is still the centre of local activities. The old gravestones still surround the lawns where the play-group children romp on sunny mornings.

It seems strange to think that the major employer in the village, the

181

local tannery, once provided almost every aspect of a worker's life. The siren sounded to rouse him from his bed and again to tell him that he should be on his way. The canteen provided his lunch, to the sounds of 'Workers Playtime' and the bowling green, swimming baths, cricket and football pitches provided his leisure activities. He could even take his wife to a dance in the company dance hall, from his company owned house, all within a few yards radius of his place of employment. Although not well paid, he had a sense of loyalty and security not always present today.

The Red Lion Inn still sits by the roadside for the benefit of travellers, although looking somewhat different today, and a very modern St Paul's church provides Sunday praise and prayer, as the old St Mary's mission did long ago.

Each year Penketh continues to expand, but anyone passing through 'The Village' can soon conjure up the smell of Routledge's bakery or the sound of Tom Webb in his smithy. Old Penketh is not quite buried by the new.

Pickmere

Pickmere as a village evolved slowly over the centuries. It lacked the large deposits of salt which attracted the Romans to the neighbouring areas of Marston and Wincham, and so there are no Roman settlements, but there are traces of a Roman road through one corner of the village. No village existed at Pickmere in 1086, as there is no mention in the Domesday Book, but in 1274 the mere was referred to as Pike Mere – and the pike are still there!

Until the end of the 19th century there was nothing more than a collection of a few scattered farms and some mainly thatched cottages gathered round communal wells. Thatch was at hand in the mere and bricks were made in the village from clay dug from deep pits behind Crown Farm and baked on the spot. Village names bear witness to this past. Spinks Lane was where the hazel 'spinks' were cut, which were used to pin down the thatching. Wellfield Close was the site of the village well. Frog Lane speaks for itself!

In the late 19th century, for those who wanted to visit Northwich market on a Friday, a local man did a round trip from the Red Lion, through Wincham to Northwich and back for 6d. His two-horse wagon trundled down the lanes between Pickmere and Wincham, avoiding a deep ditch on one side, picking up customers on the way. If another wagon came the other way, there was the greatest difficulty passing, as the road was so narrow, but that did not happen very often. However, on at least one occasion, when the driver had had perhaps a little too much ale whilst waiting for customers, the wagon overturned into the ditch.

In the early part of the 20th century, Pickmere Lake became enormously popular as a holiday centre. There were boats for hire on the mere for fishing and sailing and a funfair on the shore with a helter skelter, roundabouts and other amusements. Over 300 wooden chalets sprang up around the lake. Holidaymakers and day trippers poured into the area at weekends. The day trippers from Manchester arrived in huge four-horse wagons which pulled up at the Red Lion. The pub had stabling then for a dozen or so horses. Others came by train and on a fine summer's day a stream of people walked from Lostock station and over the footpaths to Pickmere. Then there were the cyclists, men and women, in their plus-fours who found that Pickmere made a pleasant day's outing and who refreshed themselves on lemonade and tea and cakes served by many of the local farms and cottages.

Pickmere school was built by public subscription on land donated by the Tabley estate, but by about 1910 it had closed down and the children had to walk the several miles every day to Tabley or Great Budworth schools. The building fell into disrepair for many years, but has now been repaired and is used as the village hall.

Beyond the village hall at the end of the village, and built right onto the road stands the old toll house, Cob Lodge. There are those in the village who avoid walking past here on a dark night as it is said to be guarded by an extremely fierce and savage looking ghost, in the shape of a dog which lies in the road, and frightens away all unwary passers by!

Plumley 🌿

Plumley, just off the A556, is at first sight an unremarkable village, quiet (apart from the peak times when Plumley Moor Road becomes a very busy thoroughfare) and modest.

It is still rural. Although the farms are gradually being sold for private homes, eight still remain worked by dedicated family farmers. There were 24 in 1834.

Most villages do keep to one modern spelling. Not so Plumley. In the 18th century it was decided that Plumbley was preferable. The 'b' was dropped in the 19th century but reappeared in official documents and signposts until finally banned by the Parish Council in 1944. One signpost still stands in the village today in memory of this confusion.

An area of ancient forest, Holford Moss (moss meaning the land is solid peat) is being reclaimed and replanted with a varied selection of trees. Holford estate once owned all the peat and let each tenant cut a plot twice a year for fuel. The resulting holes can still be seen today, the depth varying with the enthusiasm of the digger.

ICI now owns the wood together with the adjacent stretch of moorland, which unploughed for decades attracts plovers, curlews, hares and foxes. This is the Holford Moss brinefield and has many boreholes reaching down into the underground salt deposits. The brine is taken away in tanker lorries.

Nearby is the nature reserve leased by ICI. Here just before the First World War the Ammonia Soda Co Ltd came into being for the production of ammonium nitrate for making TNT. A row of houses built for the workers was called appropriately Ascol Drive (using the firm's initials). After the war when the factory was demolished, the houses became privately owned and now appear 'out on a limb' away from the village centre. The ruined buildings and foundations remain and the old lime beds have become the home of rare wild orchids – hence the protection of the nature reserve.

Nearby is Holford Hall, a half-timbered Elizabethan manor house. The present building was constructed in 1600 replacing one built three centuries earlier.

Holford Mill further down the river was built in 1340 and demolished in 1950. The mill pool and mill race remain and provide a good swimming place for children. One miller, George Dodson was so impressed by the exhortations of John Wesley to the masses to adopt a new 'Methodical View of the Bible', he bought land in the village and in 1827 built the original Plumley Methodist chapel.

Plumley is traversed by the Peover Eye. It is stocked with trout by the fishing clubs and visited by herons. The banks provide homes for water voles, mallards, moorhens and kingfishers. Although gently flowing and delightfully meandering it has claimed three lives during the past 30 years.

The railway arrived in 1863. There are two inns, The Smoker named after a racehorse belonging to a former Lord de Tabley and built in Elizabeth I's reign, and the more recent Golden Pheasant. A well stocked village shop and post office complete the amenities making Plumley a very pleasant place.

Poole 🐚

This is a tiny hamlet covering 745 acres, and was divided into three manors, Barratt-Poole, War-Poole and White-Poole.

Albert Neilson Hornby, the famous Lancashire cricketer and county captain for 15 years in the late 1800s, lived at Poole Hall for a time. Each year he arranged a two day match between the Lancashire X1 and Nantwich locals and paid each working man in the Nantwich team £5 for loss of earnings. He captained England in the famous Oval test match of 1882, the first time Australia beat England at cricket (by seven runs). A mock tribute appeared in a sporting magazine which ran something like this. 'In affectionate memory of English cricket which died at the Oval on 29th August 1882. The body will be cremated and *the ashes* sent to Australia'. A. N. Hornby is buried at Acton church, near Nantwich.

John Wesley visited Poole four times between 1749 and 1757. He preached in the kitchen at Gate Farm, which is just on the parish boundary of Poole and Cholmondeston. Poole Methodist chapel was built in 1834 and is still used for worship. There are several old farmhouses and a recently renovated and rethatched black and white cottage, Badger Point.

Poole Methodist Church

Dairy farming is predominant. There is a garden centre, a small agricultural engineering factory and a knitting machine agency. There is also a small biological supplies unit.

Pott Shrigley 🎐

What a curious name! How often this comment is repeated when Pott Shrigley is mentioned. As with so many village names, its origins are uncertain and there is doubt as to whether the landowning families brought their names with them to the settlement or took them from the locality. A popular theory seems to be that 'Pott' comes from an old word denoting a pool (the land is still low lying and marshy to the north-west of the church) and that 'Shrigley' denotes a clearing in the woodland.

Whatever the origin of the name, Pott Shrigley remains today, much as it has been throughout the centuries, a scattered, upland village on the western edge of the Pennines.

The Shrigleys were the earliest landowners of note. In 1313 their estates passed by marriage to the Downes of Taxal, Worth and Sutton and for the next five centuries this family acted as local squires of this small outpost on the outskirts of east Cheshire.

Members of the Downes family are assumed to have been responsible for building the church over a period of time in the 14th and 15th centuries. At first a private chapel, this later became the parish church of St Christopher.

Two of the present peal of six bells are of pre-Reformation date, and a third, perhaps the original 'Great Bell', is dated 1603 (when it was probably re-cast). The remainder have been recently added. There is a dedicated team of ringers. Nonconformity in religion gained strength during the late 18th century. In 1861 Green Close Methodist church was built.

It is likely that education in some form has been carried out in Pott Shrigley throughout the past 500 years. The endowments of various benefactors made this possible until the state system took over. At the present time the building housing the church primary school is owned by the Village Hall Trust, a system of shared facilities that makes sound economic sense.

Agriculture, coal mining, stone quarrying, brick making and estate work, both outdoor and domestic, have provided employment for villagers over the years. Farming and a variety of small-scale light industries on the site of the former brickworks are the modern day equivalent, although many residents commute.

The population has remained remarkably constant at around 350, with the exception of the mid-19th century when it peaked at 467. New housing is strictly limited, Pott Shrigley being in the Peak District National Park.

Poynton 🐝

Poynton is a thriving commuter village, straddling the A523 and nestling in the foothills of the Pennines. It is still a village, with a Parish Council, a brass band and its own agricultural and horticultural show and sports club, originally sponsored by the then Lord Vernon over 100 years ago.

Poynton Park and Pool are among the beauty spots of the village, being the place in which The Towers, the manor house of the Vernon family, was situated. Sadly, when the estate was split up and sold, The Towers, a grand stone building, was pulled down and the Vernons took up residence at Sudbury Hall, which now belongs to the National Trust.

The sportswear firm of Bukta started with a factory set in the lovely woods of Poynton and provided employment for numbers of girls leaving Lord Vernon's school. This continued until the early 1970s when the firm moved to larger premises in Stockport. Meanwhile new schools had been built and Lord Vernon's school was turned into a social centre.

Industry is now, in the main, contained in two purpose-built industrial estates which house a wide range of firms.

Until the 1930s Poynton was a coal mining village with the mines, the land and most of the property belonging to Lord Vernon. The majority of the menfolk were employed in the mines or on his estate. Nature and man together have removed all traces of the mines from the village and newcomers often find it hard to believe that Poynton was so recently a mining village.

The Groundwork Trust have done a magnificent job in developing the old gig railway inclines and the Macclesfield/Marple railway lines into pretty, wooded walkways known as the Middlewood Way. The towpaths of the canal have also been restored.

An exciting project is the Anson Museum, being developed by Mr Leslie Cawley, which will be a record of Poynton's history. It already houses a fine collection of gas engines.

Poynton is a mixture of the old and the new and the old cottages built to house the miners (sometimes with a family of up to 13 children) are much sought after. Some of these gabled stone cottages were built with the same warm stone that was used for Poynton church. There is a long row of 25 brick-built houses in Park Lane, and in Anson Clough a row of whitewashed stone cottages with a little stream meandering through their gardens.

There were many characters living in the village then, including one particular woman who could work charms. She could cure warts, coughs, boils and bed-wetting, and of course she was in great demand! People spoke in a different way, using the local dialect, which the Poynton Local History Society is trying to record before it disappears forever.

St George's church is at the hub of the village in Fountain Place, with the fountain standard which was placed at the crossroads to commemorate Queen Victoria's Jubilee. St George's and the Methodist, Baptist, Catholic and Pentecostal churches all form part of the social and spiritual life and well-being of the village.

Prestbury 🌿

The picturesque village of Prestbury stands on the river Bollin, three miles from Macclesfield. Before the 13th century there was a monastic settlement, from which the parish derives its name, Preost-Burgh, Priest's Town.

The parish was very extensive, the church at one time exercising ecclesiastical jurisdiction over 35 townships. It was the mother church, the only one licensed for marriages until 1878, and called locally 'The Joiner's Shop', the brides waiting their turn in the Unicorn Inn, now Peter Dominic's off-licence.

The present church, dedicated to St Peter, was built about 1220, and the tower with its eight pinnacles about 1480. One pinnacle which fell has been replaced by present day masons.

In the churchyard are two old yew trees said to be over 600 years old, and many old gravestones, some recalling sad episodes. One particular epitaph is to Maria Rathbone of Henbury, aged eight, who lost her way in the snow whilst returning from an errand for her father, and who was found dead many miles away near Northwich. Another records that one family lost seven children in eight years.

Legend has it that Bonnie Prince Charlie's route from Manchester to Derby lay through Prestbury. In December 1745 the bells were rung joyfully when the Duke of Cumberland marched through Prestbury in pursuit of the Jacobite rebels whose army he eventually overtook and defeated at Culloden.

In previous centuries Prestbury wakes began on a Sunday in July. In April and October cattle fairs were held in the main street, the last just before the First World War. There were many inns for refreshment, some of which remain to this day.

After the fasts of Lent, Easter Monday was for relaxing, known as Lifting Day. A chair was placed in the middle of the street, and any woman seen outdoors was placed in the chair and lifted up and down the street until she paid for drinks for those carrying her. She was then free to go on her way.

The Priest's House, built in the 15th century opposite the church, has been during its history, two dwelling houses, an antiques shop, vicarage and is now the National Westminster Bank.

Some 18th century houses still in use had three storeys, the top floor being used to house weavers' hand-looms for the Macclesfield silk industry. The homeworkers walked to Macclesfield to collect the silk yarn, then after weaving, they would return with the finished material, this journeying was known as 'padding'.

In the past the villagers have been farmers, joiners, tanners, smiths or weavers, and some farms exist today, but the majority of residents now commute to Manchester or surrounding areas. In 1988 the population had increased to 3,451, from 373 in 1851.

Like most villages the church was always the heart of the village, and there is still a strong community spirit. The bells are rung for services, the Sanctus or Pudden Bell is still used and on Shrove Tuesday it signals the frying of the pancakes.

Preston Brook 🦜

Preston on the Hill, or Preston juxta Dutton as it was formerly known, is the township containing the village of Preston Brook. After the Norman Conquest it was in the possession of the Duttons of Dutton Hall, the most powerful family in Cheshire at that time. In 1941 Sir Gilbert Greenall (later Lord Daresbury) sold the estate to his tenants.

The tunnel from Dutton, about a mile long, joined the Trent and

Mersey Canal. On the canal banks are the 'leggers' houses, where the men lived who lay on their backs on top of the barges, and pushed them through the tunnel by 'walking' their feet along the top of the tunnel. The horses were taken over the top.

About 1840 Lord Francis Egerton, a landowner and descendant of the Duke of Bridgewater, had a barge converted into a church, and the Rev Charles Dodgson, incumbent of Daresbury and father of Lewis Carroll, held services for the barge community at midday. It was, before 1860, lifted on land and became known as the Waterman's Church. A similar barge lay beside it and was used as a school. These were now maintained by Lord Ellesmere, who also supported a scripture reader for the large number of clerks, boatmen etc employed by him.

In 1851 there was a post office, tanner, wheelwright, tailor, schoolmaster, blacksmith, rope and twine makers, two boot and shoe makers, two shopkeepers, a butcher, corn miller, seven farmers, one victualler at the Red Lion, a stationmaster and several agents and carriers for the canal company. In 1841 there were 100 houses and 607 inhabitants. The windmill and miller's house were situated in Mill Lane – there was a miller there in 1851 but no records after that. The A56 now passes over the direct spot where the windmill stood. Today there is one shop and post office and the Red Lion. A marina for pleasure boats is the only activity on the canal.

In 1781 and 1783 John Wesley visited Preston on the Hill and the Primitive Methodist chapel was built on the site in 1882. The Wesleyans had a chapel in 1851 on the border with Aston-by-Sutton parish in Aston Lane. This was demolished along with several houses in about 1971 to make way for the Whitehouse industrial estate – part of Runcorn New Town.

St Faith's mission church, a daughter church of All Saints' Daresbury, in which parish Preston Brook is, was built by Sir Gilbert Greenall in 1888 as a mission room. It was later dedicated to St Faith as a mission church and services are held regularly.

The tannery is now closed and the Whitehouse industrial estate built around it – the Bass Charrington Brewery social club being on the actual site of the old tannery.

A new housing estate on the edge of the village was built in 1971 with a new village hall. Several acres of good farm land was also taken for the building of Runcorn New Town.

Puddington 🌿

Puddington lies on the southern edge of the Wirral peninsula, with a population of about 350, and overlooks the Dee estuary. Known as Potitone in the Domesday Book, the village is in the parish of Burton, with which it has been linked from the earliest times. The village consists of a cluster of cottages lining the road, a few modern houses, some outlying farms and a large ancient house known as Puddington Old Hall. This is about 600 years old and was a moated manor in medieval times. Parts of the moat can still be seen.

The village's most famous family, who lived in this house, were the Masseys. It has been said that the first member of this ancient family was granted the lands around Puddington by William the Conqueror. After the Reformation the Masseys remained Catholic and suffered social ostracism as 'Popish recusants'. Their schoolmaster, John Plessington, who was an ordained priest, was arrested in 1679 and nine weeks later was hung, drawn and quartered at Boughton Cross, Chester. His remains were brought back to Puddington Old Hall for display to deter further 'traitors'. His head was displayed on a pole at Chester.

Another large house, the Mansion, as it was called, was built in one of the fields nearby, but this was destroyed by a fire in the 1830s. Part of the chapel still exists, together with an old doorway. Another old building still stands in the Home Farm yard, just as it did years ago. This is the old pigeon house, or columbarium, as it is called. It was a source of fresh meat in the days when there was only salt meat in the winter.

The village today is a little oasis of quiet in Wirral, which is fast becoming one large dormitory for people who work in Chester, Merseyside and even Manchester.

Puddington children still attend the Burton school, endowed by Bishop Wilson in 1724 'for the free education of Burton boys and girls and four from Puddington'. The present Bishop Wilson Church of England primary school in Puddington Lane houses many more children than the original building could possibly have managed. This light and airy modern building was built with money raised by local residents.

The old walled garden of the Old Hall is now a nursery garden, one of the big houses is a nursing home and there is a thriving pig farm run as Wirral Farm Products on the outskirts of the village.

Pulford 🦢

It is possible that there was a Roman farmstead here as two coins of the Constantine period were dug up in Pulford.

In medieval times Pulford's position on the border of Wales meant that a castle was built here, made of wood, but replaced by a stone one later in the 13th century, when the first church was built as a chapel beside it. There is only a mound left now, in the field next to the churchyard.

The second Duke of Westminster rebuilt the church in cruciform shape, with a tower and spire and ring of six bells, still rung today. There is now no Hall, but the stable and saddleroom were converted in 1914 into two cottages, which are still inhabited to this day. The shrubbery, old yew tree and a ha-ha which surrounded the original Hall are still visible on the site.

During the 17th century, when Warburtons owned land here, four farmhouses and the Talbot Inn, with distinctive metal-framed windows, were built and still stand. Later distinctive houses, farms, and cottages were built by the second Duke of Westminster. Their characteristic hand-made bricks, Dutch gables, or black and white gables with spiral chimneys stand firmly today.

Poulton is part of the manor of Pulford, and was an abbey in medieval times, until the monks were transferred to Staffordshire. There is a Chapel House Farm there which possibly gained its name from the abbey.

During the Civil War when Chester was besieged by the Roundheads for five months, the people of the Pulford area were reported by an officer to be smuggling food to starving Chester, sometimes through Doddleston, sometimes via Eaton and the river.

The Grosvenor Arms (Talbot Inn) was the first 'post receiving station'. It then moved to the smithy built opposite, which has now disappeared, and later transferred to part of a 17th century farmhouse, Greve Farm, in the centre of the village. The farmhouse was divided into three residences and the old pump stands outside the middle cottage. This post office was a real village centre, medicine was left there to be picked up, notices put up, papers and news exchanged. The present post office is a separate building next door to the last one.

In the 20th century council houses have been built, and since the school closed down, the building has been turned into three residences and a further ten terraced houses built on the lovely grounds. Some small detached houses have been built on Fair Meadow off Old Lane.

In 1850 a gazetteer of Cheshire records that Pulford had a brickmaker, schoolmaster, blacksmith, shoemaker, parish clerk, victualler and post office receiver, a rector, schoolmistress and ten farmers. Today there are still the farmers and a postmaster, but there are also garage mechanics, a scrap-metal yard owner, and many people who commute to work.

Rainow 🖋

On the border of the Peak National Park, the village of Rainow is situated three miles to the east of Macclesfield on the Chapel-en-le-Frith road. Bounded by Kerridge Ridge on one side and the Buxton Road on the other it runs towards the moors and Pennines. The hills and stone buildings are a sharp contrast to the old brick and softer countryside of the Cheshire Plain.

Although stretching over many miles, the present village does have a centre where the church, school, post office/shop and village institute are all within easy reach of each other.

Outside the institute stand the stocks. It is thought that they were originally constructed in the 13th century but there are no records to confirm this.

The first Saturday in June is Rainow fete day. Organised by the church it is supported and enjoyed by the whole community, young and old alike. A procession passes through the village carrying the newly appointed 'mayor' to the fete field where together with the vicar and chairman of the Parish Council he opens the event. Traditionally he should ride backwards on a donkey but nowadays an alternative conveyance is provided!

James Mellor, born 1796, lived most of his life at Hough Hole House. A Methodist, farmer and stonemason, he became a reader of Emmanuel Swendenborg, a Swedish scientist and engineer, who claimed to have received revelations from God. He created the garden at Hough Hole House with flagged paths, stone steps and a pond with a weir. He also built a chapel in the grounds, created a burial ground and cut and inscribed his own tombstone. The present owners have restored the house, and the Mellor Gardens, which tell the story of Bunyan's *Pilgrim's Progress*, are open to the public on occasional Sundays during the summer.

White Nancy stands on the end of Kerridge Ridge. Resembling a whitewashed sugar loaf it was built in remembrance of the battle of Waterloo by the Gaskell family of Ingersley Hall. At one time it was possible to sit inside but due to vandalism the entrance has now been bricked up.

With the Industrial Revolution came the building of cotton mills and the sinking of coal mines. Stone had been quarried on the west side of Kerridge for hundreds of years but during this period demand increased and several new quarries were opened and the old ones extended. At the same time came the enclosure of common land. Many of the smallhold-ings were tenanted by builders, quarrymen and miners who could supple-ment their income with produce from the land. During this period Rainow was a thriving community and the population increased to 1,595 in 1810.

When the Macclesfield canal and the railway both bypassed Rainow and cheaper coal became available from Staffordshire, industry in the village declined and consequently the population decreased as people moved away to find work.

The only mill still standing today is at Gin Clough. Stone is still quarried on a small scale and the last coal to be mined was in 1926.

GREENWOOD '89

The Robin Hood Inn, Rainow

194

The parish, one of the largest in the country, includes Saltersford, now sparsely populated but once a thriving community in its own right. Saltersford Hall was built in 1595 by the Stopford family of Macclesfield. The Hall, a listed building, has been empty for many years (as have many of the farms nearby).

There is no longer any industry in Rainow and although there are several working farms, many of the smallholdings have been converted and the land used for horses. Many of the old houses have been renovated and this together with the building of a small housing development in the 1970s has brought new blood into the village. A strong community spirit exists in the village and this is reflected in the success of the many organisations and activities available.

Ringway & Hale Barns

The recent history of Ringway and of Hale Barns is to a large extent the history of communications. To many people in Cheshire, Greater Manchester and beyond, Ringway was synonymous with what later became called Manchester International Airport. As the airport grew in size and importance so did Hale Barns become even more an outrunner of suburbia, sprawling out from the Greater Manchester conurbation, and yet retaining its own character as a village.

Manchester boasted the first municipal airport in the United Kingdom. The opening day of 'Ringway' was 25th June 1938. During the Second World War military aircraft used its facilities, and eventually 1969 onwards saw a large expansion scheme.

Ringway was a truly rural area until the advent of the airport, which swallowed up many farms. There was no school nor any shops. Ringway has been known under many names but one used on many earlier documents was Ringey, and a chapel of that name had been erected there by the start of the 16th century. This was taken over by the non-conformists in Cromwellian times. Later when the chapel reverted to the Church of England a dissenting meeting house was erected in Hale Barns in 1723. This building still provides the village of Hale Barns with one of its most attractive old buildings.

The chapel at Ringway was dedicated to All Saints, and eventually, the village of Hale Barns having grown at a considerable rate, a church of that name was built there.

In 1964 the Catholic church of Holy Angels was erected a very short distance away from it. Over a period of time ecumenical links between these two churches have grown but one of the earliest of these concerned a church organ. The organ from the old Ringway church was given to Holy Angels and it was moved there piece by piece one stormy evening on which lightning struck the Bull's Head public house just across the road.

This public house and the nearby Unicorn are two of the oldest in the area, both being named in the earliest licensing register of 1812, though both are of earlier origin than that. The publicans at one time were also farmers.

Another building with a long history is a school; in fact, schools have long been associated with Hale Barns. The most detailed early record is of a day school, founded and endowed by Silas Sidebottom, the Unitarian minister of Hale chapel in 1740.

Hale as a name for the area appears in the Domesday survey, and it is unusual in being the same form of the name still used today. The tithe barn which gave Hale Barns its name was recorded in 1662, but it is believed to have been much older than that. It is shown in a later map as standing where All Saints' church hall now is.

Bagshaw's Directory, produced in about 1855, showed more farmers in Ringway and Hale Barns than any other occupations. Others included market gardeners, publicans, clergy, those connected with schools and also those who were just denoted as 'gentlemen'. The 1841 census showed that well over two thirds of the men named in it were engaged in farming. In addition, a wheelwright's shop and two smithies were important features of Hale Barns. The area of Ringway and Hale Barns does still have farmers among its population, but many of the newer residents are far more transitory.

Rudheath

Rudheath today has a quiet air of respectability. It is therefore difficult to envisage that at one time a lawless breed of men once roamed here. Rudheath was one of three 'criminal sanctuaries' established in Cheshire by the Norman Earls of Chester. The large tracts of heathland and forest once covering Rudheath's now fertile farmlands were the ideal haunts for outlaws and highwaymen who preyed on unsuspecting travellers.

In the late 1770s with the advent of the Trent and Mersey Canal, a wharf and warehouse were built at Broken Cross and Rudheath was used to store goods shipped from Staffordshire via the canal. The goods were off-loaded from the barges and subsequently transferred by horse-drawn transport to the river Weaver at Northwich. The Old Broken Cross public house nearby had stabling for the horses which drew the barges. This wharf was not profitable however and it was closed.

A few yards further along the canal stands a smithy and cottage, the smithy is still in use doing mainly small engineering work. Both the public house and the smithy are over 200 years old. The stables now form part of the public house and pleasure craft now use the moorings previously used by the barges.

In 1835 a chapel of ease was built in King Street not far from the Broken Cross and canal. This chapel became known as Rudheath church and in 1912 a chancel was added to the building.

In 1921 Northwich Rural District Council began erecting council houses in Rudheath, and the population increased dramatically; the census figure in 1851 was 435 and the census figure in 1961 was 3,264. Few houses were built after 1961, but in 1988 private housebuilding started and looks like continuing for some time.

For many years Charles Griffiths & Son of Broken Cross House were makers of cheese but a few years ago they ceased trading. Employment was also provided during the First World War by a munitions factory at Gadbrook, where all the workers were women. After the war Messrs Broadhursts, confectioners, also opened a factory at Gadbrook and traded there for many years. Robert's Bakeries have their bakery in Gadbrook and employ many local people, and recently a Business Park has been opened.

Within the parish is the Vale Royal leisure centre where one can take part in many sports and other activities and within the centre is the village hall.

Saighton 🐾

The quiet rural village of Saighton, set in the heart of the Cheshire countryside, comprises 1,719 acres of land and is located four miles from Chester just off the A41 Whitchurch road.

Although sparsely populated, Saighton is perhaps best known locally as one of the villages on the Eaton estate, with most of the cottages dating back to the second Marquis of Westminster and the first Duke of Westminster. Most of the cottages were built by John Douglas. Saighton Lane Farm is of particular interest with its twisted chimneys and its big half-timbered gable and brickwork, a good example of a farm designed by Douglas and Fordham.

Perhaps the most outstanding building in Saighton is that of Saighton Grange, now Abbey Gate College. This building stands back from the road and is rich in history. Centuries ago Saighton Grange used to be the principal country house of the Abbot of Chester. Little of the original building except the great 15th century gateway remains. On the west side of the gateway is a carving of a wolf's head marked with the initials of the builder.

Next to Saighton Grange on the top of the hill is a 19th century castellated water tower, ornately designed on Countess Grosvenor's instructions.

The Presbyterians had a place of worship in the chapel until 1923, and today it has been transformed into the village hall and a meeting place for the villagers.

The occupations of today's inhabitants include farmers, a nursery, a firm of architects, a cattery, a firm which tests safety devices and a local shop/post office. The latter, dating back to 1882, was originally built as a bakery-village shop.

Saighton's neighbouring village, Bruera, some five miles south-east of Chester, comprises 129 acres of land. The main feature of the village is the church of St Mary the Virgin. Although the present building is essentially Norman, there is evidence that some original Saxon stone-work was used in the Norman rebuilding of the 12th century.

The rare long-eared bats housed in the church cause quite a stir!

Bruera today contains only a few houses and dairy farms. The principal landowners are the Duke of Westminister and the Davies-Colleys of Newbold.

Saughall 🦡

When Chester was an important seaport, Saughall was a small settlement to the north-west where the villagers made a living by fishing. Constant silting up of the estuary and the later channelling of the river has meant that Saughall now looks out from the old Dee banks over the flat reclaimed area known as Sealand and is two miles from the river. Today ponies from the nearby riding stables graze the banks upon which the fishermen must have dried their nets centuries ago.

Saughall's history is closely associated with that of Shotwick as it was part of the parish of Shotwick until 1896 when it got its own church, All Saints. Even after that time people must still have had loyalties to Shotwick. Within living memory couples walked over the old footpaths to be married at St Michael's church, Shotwick. People also carried coffins over the fields for burial in the churchyard there.

When Saughall church was built, the first young woman to be married in the church, being consumptive, was tragically the first to be buried. There used to be a bier, which belonged to the village and could be used by any local family to take the coffin to the church.

Until Shotwick House was built in the 19th century, the present vicarage was the local manor house. The Vernon family who acquired the estate in 1906 gave the village its public hall and their name is remembered in its title, the Vernon Institute.

Saughall today is a large village with a population of over 3,500, with several shops and modern housing estates grouped around the original core of village buildings, some of which are quite ancient – the Charity House is 16th century and partly built with stones from Shotwick Castle. Just below the Greyhound pub is a black and white timbered farmhouse dating from about 1560. The tithe barn at Shotwick Lodge Farm is 15th century and its massive roof beams are hewn from oak from Shotwick Park. There is still a small area of woodland – a remnant of the once enclosed royal park.

The crossroads between Seahill Road, Church Road, Hermitage Road and the road to Shotwick House is the natural centre of the village. On the four corners stand the Greyhound pub, the vicarage where in June the annual ceremony of crowning the Rose Queen takes place in the lovely old walled garden, the Vernon Institute and the former 'Swinging Gate Inn' which dates back to 1490 but sadly relinquished its licence in the 1960s and became a private residence. The iron double manacle which used to be fastened to an oak beam in the bar parlour was used to hold prisoners by the wrists before they were taken off to Chester. This interesting relic is now housed in the Vernon Institute.

In the 17th century a woman of Saughall achieved a strange sort of fame. Mary Davies was known as 'The Horned Woman of Cheshire'. She grew horns at the sides of her head and she was taken to London and exhibited. She shed these horns from time to time and these were reputed to have been preserved at the British Museum. She lived in a farm where the Vernon Institute now stands.

Shavington

The village is reputedly the 'Santune' of the Domesday Book, which was recorded as being held by Godwin and Dot as two manors. These two manors are still in existence several centuries later, and one came by marriage to the Woodnoth family (sometimes written as 'Woolnoth' or even 'Woodnut' in old documents), in the 18th century. The site of their manor house was on or near the present Shavington Hall.

This house was rebuilt in 1661, and was leased in the late 19th century to the Earl of Shrewsbury as a hunting lodge. He and his Countess became very popular with the inhabitants of Shavington, allowing them to hold fetes in the grounds of the Hall, and distributing charity to the poorer villagers. Around Christmas time 1890, the Earl and Countess took communion at the new mission church in the village. This angered the Bishop of Chester, who forbade them the sacrament in the future, as it was against Church law, one of them being divorced. According to a newspaper report of the time ... 'On Sunday, a large portion of the congregation trooped out of the church on the vicar presenting himself at the evening service'.

In 1886, the Church of England built a wooden mission church. This was burned down in 1892; it is said that the stove, standing in the centre, became very hot and set the building alight. A corrugated iron church and hall were then built and opened on 11th April 1894, at a cost of £210, and this building is still used today.

Electricity was first introduced in 1928. The old electricity company reported that 'much canvassing had to be done before a sufficient number of consumers could be found, to warrant the expense that would be incurred'. Gas was not introduced until 1985, although application was made as far back as 1903.

About 1920, half a dozen men got together and decided that some form of social club would be an asset to the village. A sum of money was borrowed and the old mill was purchased from a Mr Warner. The club flourished and by 1936, the money borrowed had been repaid, the premises extended and a bowling green added. It still flourishes today.

At various times during the Second World War, bombs were dropped here. It is said that the first bombs to be dropped in the North of England, fell near the New Cheshire Cheese Inn, damaging a wall and several cottages.

Shotwick 🦢

This little hamlet, with a population of just 28 people, is half a mile off the busy Birkenhead to Queensferry road and looks really set apart from modern life. In the unreal quietness of the place, as you look upon the ancient church and the venerable manor house, Shotwick Hall, and the old cottages and farms, the feel of history will enter your bones.

The village has no shop, no school, no post office, nor buses to grind up and down its narrow lanes. Electricity only arrived in the mid 1950s. The hamlet is dominated by St Michael's church, which stands guard facing out across the Dee. It is not known exactly how long there has been a church in Shotwick, but a church has stood here certainly since Domesday times and possibly another 100 years before that. Shotwick is the only church in Wirral with a three-decker pulpit, something quite rare in the country.

The church attracts a congregation from beyond the village boundaries, and holds a place in the affection of people far afield. In 1971 an appeal was launched to save the church from wet and dry rot and to arrest the deterioration of the stonework. The response was so great that there was enough money to restore the organ as well!

The manor house was built in 1662 by Joseph Hockenhull, and is of picturesque red brick, a gabled house typical of the period. It stands at the end of Shotwick's other lane leading to Puddington village.

There was a period in the 17th century when Shotwick might have become a serious rival to the notorious Gretna Green for irregular runaway marriages. In 1674 Ralph Heath, clerk, curate and school-master, was presented in the Bishop's court for marrying two people from other parishes in a Shotwick alehouse without banns or licence. Whatever his punishment, if any, it did not prevent his carrying on his illegal but lucrative side-line for many years.

Many years ago Shotwick was a port, and even now in the south-west corner of the churchyard wall, you will find an iron ring where boats used to be tied up.

201

Smallwood 🪶

Smallwood is one of those villages which have changed very little. Its borders are the same, its road system is unchanged (except for the crossroads and outer lanes at Moss End) and its farms and population have been pretty constant. In 1831 it had 97 houses and 554 people; in 1841 it had 112 houses and 606 people and in 1851 it had 126 houses and 619 people. Today it has roughly the same number of inhabitants but rather more houses.

In 1831 there were 296 males and 258 females in the village. A third of the men were engaged in agriculture either as farmers or as labourers. Of the other men, 25 were employed in the retail trade or made things for shops (shop, mill, smithy), seven were labourers employed in jobs other than agriculture, four were personal servants and two were professional men. All we know of the women is that 22 of them were servants.

Smallwood has been for two centuries the garden of the Potteries. The market is there if you have good produce, arrive early enough and charge the right prices. Smallholders and farmers used to set off at 3.30 to 4 am any day of the week except Sunday, their block carts laden with potatoes, cabbage, carrots, beetroot, cauliflower, peas, beans, fruit and bunches of flowers. Some fortunate men in the late 19th and 20th centuries got contracts with the great Burslem Co-op, which kept 100 horses for pulling bread and fruit vans about. Such a man would go laden with potatoes, hand them in, and come back with his cart full of manure from the Co-op stables. By the time his cart trundled home it would be 6 pm. If trade was bad and a lost milk contract made a farmer take 40 lb cheeses and a great quantity of butter to sell off, it would be later than that.

In 1841 Edwin Foden, founder of the famous engineering firm, was born in Smallwood, where his family had lived since 1780. When a child he made steam engines out of old tins in the cubby hole under the stairs at the family house at Four Lanes Ends. He left school at an early age and began his working life as the village postboy. The first Foden traction engine was given public trials in 1887. His machine won a competition run by the Royal Agricultural Society and orders poured in. Very soon Foden's was one of the really important traction engine firms.

The pleasant little stone church of St John the Baptist was erected in 1845 with stone brought down in horse and cart from Mow Cop. The church lost its independence in 1955, having its vicarage sold and becoming a united parish with Astbury.

Spurstow

Spurstow, adjoining Haughton, is mentioned in the Domesday Book as having 180 acres cleared. In the 13th century it was held by William de Spurstowe and continued under the same family until 1685, when the estate was sold to the Crewe family.

Lower Spurstow, in the 15th century passed to the Aldersey family and in 1594 Thomas Aldersey, Citizen and Haberdasher of London, founded the free grammar school in Bunbury. The home of the Alderseys was at Lower Spurstow, a timber building in the shape of a half H, which stood until around 1891 when a new farmhouse was erected nearby. A short distance from here, there still stands a beautiful timbered house, said at one time to have been an inn.

Bath Wood, in the midst of Cheshire hunting country, lies in Spurstow, and here there was a spa, 'Spurstow White Water'. This gained a considerable reputation for its curative powers. A signpost is said to have read:

> 'If you are troubled with sore of flaw,
> This is the way to Spurstow spa.
> If all your sores you've left in the lurch,
> This is the way to Bunbury church.'

Another building of note is the school, erected in 1873 by Lord Crewe. This is a fine sample of Gothic architecture with tower, turret and clock. Unfortunately the school closed in 1983 due to dwindling numbers of children. The district also lost its post office and shop in the 1970s.

Stoak & Stanney

The adjacent villages of Stoak and Little Stanney have always been linked together and referred to as 'Stoak and Stanney'. This could possibly be because for centuries they have shared the church, the school and the local inn.

The name of Stoak is believed to have come from 'the stockade' and was an outpost of the Roman camp at Cestria. It is thought to have been part of land given to Hugh Lupus by William I, passing to the Thornton family in 1350, then by marriage to the Bunburys who became a well known local family and in whose possession it remained until 1750.

The church of St Lawrence dates from the Norman period and restoration took place in 1827. The three bells in the tower are thought to be the oldest in Wirral, dated 1615, 1631 and 1642 respectively. The Victorian stained glass window was damaged by bombs in the Second World War and has been replaced by plain glass.

The inn, called the Bunbury Arms, stands opposite the church. It is only in recent years that the Church Commissioners have allowed it to open on Sundays. Popular landlords for many years were a Mr and Mrs Bishop, whose descendants still live locally.

There are now only two working farms in Stoak but a few newer, privately built properties have sprung up over the past 20 years or so, as well as a small estate of houses erected by the council. The old vicarage still stands in its own grounds but is presently used as offices. The present population of Stoak is 170.

Little Stanney, with a population today of 200, was mentioned in the Domesday Book and was the home of some of the Bunbury family who lived at Stanney Old Hall, which until 1724 was Wirral's finest medieval house. This was pulled down in 1820 and replaced by the farmhouse which stands there today and is known as Old Hall Farm. Rake Hall, now an hotel, was also lived in by the Bunburys and much of its original interior still remains.

Shop Farm was once the village inn and the landlords brewed their own beer in the cellar. The building is about 300 years old and the remains of the old Roman road to Stoak lie beneath it. In front of this stands a modern petrol station. The old smithy building still stands but now forms part of a private residence.

Villagers tell a story of the ghost of the Stanney Duck. This bird haunted the lanes and so upset and frightened the natives that a band of men went out together, lay in wait for the duck and, having caught it, cut off its head and buried the body at the top of Stoak Lane. So, should you chance to meet the Stanney Duck nowadays, it will be hurrying by without a head!

The old wooden village hall, which was built with funds raised by the villagers of Stoak and Stanney, some 60 years ago, is still put to good use by the two Women's Institutes and the Stoak and Stanney Community Association. The small farm shop at Lime Tree Farm supplies locals with their immediate needs but Stoak and Stanney villagers do their main shopping either in Ellesmere Port or Chester. The family of Mr Ewart Price, who runs the shop, have lived at the farm for generations.

The old Stanney Mill with its water-wheel which used to grind grain for the local inhabitants, is now within the boundary of the Shell refinery. For many years the Shotwick to Helsby bypass has cut through the centre of Little Stanney but this has never divided the villagers. They are also well used to the sight of the Shell refinery standing on what were once green fields and Shell's oil-burning flame is today quite a well known landmark.

Stretton ✤

Stretton is a small village south of Warrington with a population of around 500. The busy crossroads, A49 London road, Hatton Lane and Stretton Road bisect it. Lights were installed to help control the traffic in 1975. Stretton is solely agricultural, dairy and arable farms, some with pedigree Friesian cattle.

Central to the village is St Matthew's church, built of sandstone in 1827. This has a Perpendicular western square tower built in 1870. From the top of the tower seven counties can be seen on a clear day. The six bells are rung each Sunday and at weddings. The church clock face was renewed in 1963 and reads on one side 'Time is not all' and on the other 'Forget not God'. The church hall was a horse stable in Colonel Lyon's day, used by parishioners attending divine worship at the church.

The Beehive Stores and post office, built of local sandstone, started business in the Mounfield family in 1885. There are two public houses – one, the Cat and Lion, built of local sandstone. The sign built in a ring over the front door reads 'The Lion is strong, The Cat is Vicious – My ale is good and so is my liquor'. Richard Braithwaite, self-styled drunken Barnaby, called here in 1636 on his journey to Lancashire. The Ring O'Bells is in Lower Stretton, now the other side of the M56. These pubs had a tontine club, used chiefly by the Irish who came to work on the farms.

There are two hotels, The Old Vicarage and the Hollow Tree. The latter was formerly Walls Pit House, owned for years by the Whitley family. The White House, owned by the Partons, is now a private hospital, opened in 1987. Stretton Hall, a listed building, is an old mansion built in 1650, once the seat of the Starky family. Traces of a Roman road could be seen before the A49 was widened. The road was of cobbled stones and hard to walk on.

There are a number of listed buildings in Stretton, including Tanyard farm built in the late 17th century. A chain still hangs in the chimney that was used to cook the roast. The local smithy and wheelwright's in Common Lane, Lower Stretton, built in 1860 and owned by the Savage family, closed a few years ago after being sold to a developer for housing.

Styal 🖋️

Styal has two different faces. One is of cottages standing just as they did in Elizabethan days, thatch and all, one up, one down, while the other is of new two-garaged houses with lions on gateposts and colourful gardens. The older section of the village has visitors by the hundred gazing at the thatched cottages threaded between the long rows of brick and slate.

Apprentice House, home for those who worked in the cotton mill founded by several generations of the Greg family, stands white, reminding one of those younger workers. And there's another face, for those very Gregs built a school and two chapels as well as the cobbled streets and, indeed, the village itself. Down in the valley, washed and worked by the river Bollin, stands the mill, once a deep green of ivy, now with bare walls and the water-wheel. The mill is still working and much of its produce is sold in the mill shop.

Styal Cottage Homes were quite a landmark for a long time. They provided shelter for orphans and unwanted children. There were house mothers, a band and bandmaster and, overall, an excellent record for their protégés in later life. Visitors come now and again and ask about people they knew when they had shelter in the Homes.

It is said the name 'Styal' meant 'the secret place' because when the taxmen of long ago came to check how many hectares of barley or wheat were being grown, the village was suspiciously silent and vacant. There is no proof of this, but it *is* a good story!

Villagers have a shop and post office under one roof, a railway with trains in each direction every half hour, for Manchester is but ten miles or so away, a garden centre, an inn called the Ship (once a shippon), a war memorial which comes into its own once a year, and an old Co-op shop, long-locked, with a window of old-fashioned Fry's Cocoa tins and a bowl of brown eggs and other such groceries your Grannie will remember. Yes, and there is a village green with grey squirrels, two football teams and one white-clad cricket team. All this and never a traffic light!

Sutton 🦚

The parish of Sutton lies about three miles south of Macclesfield and falls naturally into three areas – Langley, Sutton Lane Ends and Lyme Green.

The Macclesfield Canal runs through Lane Ends and Lyme Green. It was opened for traffic on 10th November 1831 and connects the Trent and Mersey Canal, near Kidsgrove, with the Peak Forest Canal near Marple. At the opening ceremony two processions of boats passed along the canal, 52 vessels from the north and 25 from the south. Coal, salt, lime and stone were the usual cargoes. Now the canal provides pleasure for walkers and boaters alike and an important habitat for varied wild life.

The canal has a special significance in Sutton for it was here that James Brindley, of canal building fame, served as an apprentice to Abraham Bennett from 1733 to 1740. Brindley had a childhood interest in engineering principles and this natural talent was developed during his apprenticeship. The turning point in his career came when the Duke of Bridgewater appointed him chief engineer for the construction of his canal from Worsley to Manchester.

C. F. Tunnicliffe, OBE, RA, the country and bird life artist, was born in 1901 in Langley where his father, William, was a shoemaker. By the time Charles was two years old the family had moved to a farm in Sutton Lane Ends. Stories are told of his early childhood drawings being found on fences and shippon walls. His early education was at the church school in the village before he went to the Macclesfield School of Art and to the Royal College in London.

Early in the 19th century the silk industry was started in Langley by William Smith. By the later years of the century the business had passed, through marriage, to the Whiston family. The fame of this company spread worldwide and it was acknowledged to be the largest hand-block printing, dyeing and finishing company in the world. Sadly, with changes in the textile world, 1964 saw the closure of the works and a change of identity in the village. However, a few years later, hand-block printing returned on a smaller scale in the hands of a new company.

The Lyme Green area provides a link with the road to Staffordshire. The old toll house of stage coach days can still be seen. The Hall is now a nursing home and its grounds provide the setting for a paraplegic settlement.

The face of Sutton changed during the late 1960s when a new housing estate was built. The influx of new families necessitated the building of a new school to serve the three areas of the parish. Old and new residents have combined amicably over the years, as is evident in the many thriving groups and activities which cater for all ages.

Sutton Weaver 🦢

On the A56 between Warrington and Frodsham a few miles from the mouth of the river Weaver, lies Sutton Weaver. It is a friendly village, with no public house or church.

It was originally a farming community but only three dairy farms and one arable farm with stables still remain. The village is skirted by the main Liverpool to London, and Manchester to Chester railway lines. There was in the past a station on each line, and when these were closed only one was redeveloped into a house. There is only one cottage with a thatched roof, which was originally a bakery, and another cottage named 'The Smithy' speaks for itself. These occupations are sadly no longer with us but the village boasts a large veterinary teaching practice on the site which was formerly a sweet shop.

To the south of the village the Weaver Canal winds its way through the Cheshire countryside, bridged by a swing bridge built by 'Parkes Steel Works' in 1926. Large ships from many parts of the world can still be seen holding up the traffic on the A56, carrying varied cargoes from timber to talcum powder.

A tunnel was constructed through Cloughwood when the railway was built, which is the centre of the legend of 'Tunnel Top'. The story goes that a train load of people were returning from Chester Races when the low-powered locomotive pulling the train broke down in the tunnel. Help was sent for in the form of a larger engine, which then ploughed into the back of the first engine, causing a tragic loss of life. Many years later when repairs were being carried out on the tunnel a few gold coins were found, and the story continued by saying that the coins could have been the winnings of the punters from the races.

There is still one 15th century listed building in the shape of Sutton Hall, which is a fine late medieval timber-framed house. Its notable first floor chamber has a magnificent open timber roof.

The hub of the village community is now the village post office, which was started in the garage of a past postmaster's house. There is also a church hall.

Swettenham 🦢

Swettenham is a tiny village lying on the north bank of the river Dane, between Congleton and Holmes Chapel. It consists of a 13th century church and a pub, and a handful of houses, surrounded by rich agricultural land and farms.

Swettenham Hall, an old manor house with its own chapel, is said to have a ghost, a lady dressed in black who appears to members of the Swettenham family as an omen of bad times. Another Swettenham ghost, a nun who was murdered because she broke her vows, used to be seen at the rectory. She has not been sighted since absolution was recited each night for two weeks earlier this century.

The 17th century mill was owned and run until fairly recently by Wilfred Lancaster. It is set in a secluded valley now known far and wide as Daffodil Dell due to the thousands of lovely flowers which appear each spring, most of which were planted by the Lancaster family. Following the death of Wilfred, the mill was sold.

The social life of the village community is carried on at the Swettenham Club. Consisting originally of an old army hut, it opened as a men's club just after the First World War, with a bowling green alongside created out of what was once an orchard. In the early years women and children were not allowed into the club. In the late 1970s however a new one-storey building replaced the old hut and it has become more of a village club.

In this part of south-east Cheshire annual gooseberry shows are held in several villages. Swettenham has two such shows, both of which are held at the club. On the last Saturday in July the village show admits only gooseberries grown in the parish of Swettenham. A week later on the first Saturday in August an open show is held when anyone from in or out of the parish may enter.

The village school, sited just up the road from the church, was built in 1840. It served the village well until its closure in 1969. Several other village schools were closed at the same time and a very modern big new primary school was built in Marton village to serve the surrounding villages.

In the 1850s the village of Swettenham had its own blacksmith, a tailor, two shoemakers and a shopkeeper. There has not been a shop here now for over 30 years. The post office has had a varied career, most recently having been sited in the little cottage which stood beside the deep ford, where pedestrians crossed the brook by a little wooden bridge to keep their feet dry.

It is not possible to drive straight through Swettenham village. It is approached by a narrow winding road which is also the only way out. Set in lovely countryside it has not greatly changed in the many hundreds of years of its existence. Some of the families who live in the Swettenham area have been there for many generations and would not want to live anywhere else. They, and more recent newcomers, think themselves lucky to do so.

Tarporley 🐿

The Anglican church, the manor house and the Swan Hotel are at the three points of a triangle and were the focal points of village life. There was probably once a village green in front of all three, but sadly a row of shops was built, blocking out the view of the beautiful church, the south side of which commands a magnificent view of the castles and hills.

There are records of the church from the 13th century, the failing structure being restored in early Victorian times. The old families of the Dones and the Earls of Haddington were generous benefactors. Indeed the parish hall, a listed building, is called the Done Room.

The Earl of Haddington founded the Tarporley Fire Brigade in 1869, when most fire brigades belonged to insurance companies. It was the first voluntary fire brigade in the country, and it still functions round the clock, manned by men who are in full-time work, and who provide cover at all times with modern equipment and the expertise of regular brigades – a great achievement.

The Swan Hotel is the headquarters of the Tarporley Hunt, meetings being held in the famous Hunt Room which can be observed from the street, the large windows of the room being over what was once the market hall and site for the ancient Cabbage Fair. The courtyard was wide enough to accommodate coaches and was a staging post on the Chester to London route.

The late 18th century, being an era of prosperity, meant that many of the timber-framed buildings were replaced with brick, as seen in front of the optician's where a brick is preserved dated '1796 S.S.', the S.S. being marked by fingers on wet clay. It was during this period that the front of the Swan Hotel was replaced by the present Georgian facade, although some of the older building still remains.

No doubt the oldest building of note is the manor house, rebuilt on the site of an older house dated 1585, as can be seen on the beam across the front. The house was placed at the left hand corner of the village triangle, the church being the apex, and it would appear that the village ended there, the later road swinging round the corner.

Apart from these main buildings, Tarporley was a self-sufficient village, catering for all needs, with a blacksmith, saddler, shoemaker, bakers, tailor, dressmakers, drapers, grocers, butchers, builders and schools.

The old craftsmen have disappeared and the High Street has taken a new look in keeping with the new age, and yet without destroying the character and heritage of the village. There are no more of the old characters, and, as every available plot of land is used for building, Tarporley has become a most desirable place for commuters – indeed two golf clubs are about to be built.

Tarvin 🐚

A battlemented church tower in mellow sandstone, cottages whose visible foundations are red rock, elegant Georgian residences, half-timbered houses, a centuries-old building originally the grammar school and brick dwellings of the 19th century – this is Tarvin, to which have been added many fine modern developments.

The village stands where the Nantwich and Manchester roads meet, five miles east of Chester and close to old Watling Street, which must have echoed to the tramp of Roman legions in the first centuries of the Christian era. Nowadays, two bypasses enable the hurrying traffic to avoid the village centre.

Five years ago, the Trinity and Zion chapels were closed, and a fine new Methodist chapel replaced them. St Andrew's, a lovely old parish church, incorporates a 14th century south aisle with its original roof, a 15th century tower and various additions from succeeding centuries.

The manor house opposite the church suggests a link with the days when the Bishop of Lichfield was lord of the manor. Tarvin Hall, facing into the broad end of High Street, was rebuilt in brick in the Georgian style. Holme Street Hall, now a farm, at 300 years is one of the oldest houses in Tarvin.

In 1752, a disastrous fire destroyed many of the timber-framed cottages, hence the Georgian rebuilding still evident in the village centre. At about that time the street market died out, but still observed to this day is the custom of ringing the Pancake Bell each Shrove Tuesday at 11 am.

Until the 1920s, there was a Tarvin souling play performed annually on All Souls' Eve. This comprised the usual exchanges between Saint, or King, George and his adversary, known in some areas as the Black Prince, but in Tarvin as the Cheshire Champion. Opening with the traditional souling song, one verse was exclusive to Tarvin, and was quoted in 1891 as:-

'Your lanes they are dirty, and your meadows grow cold,
And if you are willing with us you may go,
We will bring you safe back again, you have no need fear,
And it's all that we are souling for is your ale and strong beer.'

Over 250 years ago, Tarvin mourned the death of its schoolmaster, John Thomasen, a truly remarkable character for such a small village. Besides teaching for 30 years in the grammar school, founded in 1600, he was a skilled penman, known to have received money from Queen Anne for his copying of the *Ikon Basilike* of her grandfather, King Charles I. Thomasen used a skill he had been taught by a former Bishop of Chester to produce wonderful copies of the works of the Greek and Latin poets.

In the 19th century, Dr Brindley ran a boarding school for boys in Tarvin Hall. There was also a small school for girls in the Georgian house known as The Flaggs. Tarvin National school, first opened in 1859, was superseded in 1968 by Tarvin County primary school on Heath Drive.

Farming has always figured strongly in Tarvin's economy. Many of the ancient field boundaries, water courses and mills are still to be found. The village is moving with the times though. A veterinary centre now occupies Manor Court, the British United Turkey Company is based at Hockenhull Hall and an engineering company trades at the former mill. The old forge is now a centre for financial advice and people travel many miles to buy tropical fish at the former public hall. However, Northern Dairies, with their regional headquarters in Lower High Street, are the principal employers in Tarvin.

Present day leisure activities include football, bowls and tennis. Tarvin has three public houses. The George and Dragon and the Red Lion are both old coaching inns in the centre of the village. The Village Green, formerly the Ramblers Cafe, is now a popular rendezvous. The community centre, opened 1974 and the scout and guide headquarters, opened 1978, were built through the fund raising efforts of the villagers. Many organisations, too numerous to name individually, flourish here. Tarvin is a busy and friendly village, proud of its historic roots and its energetic present.

Tattenhall ﷯

Tattenhall lies approximately eight miles south-east of Chester on a slight rise in the ground between the river Gowy, which flows into the Mersey, and the Golbourne brook, which flows into the Dee. Roman coins were found in the 1970s when the new Park School was being built.

Throughout the centuries several churches have stood successively on the same site and it is possible that there was a pagan shrine here. A skeleton was dug up near the north wall of the present church of St Alban, of a tall man who had a coin under his head, perhaps to pay his fare across the 'river of death'.

During the 19th century the churchyard was used by robbers who lived in caves in the nearby Peckforton Hills, from where they terrorised the villagers. They are reputed to have hidden their ill-gotten gains in the graves, which they also plundered. Isabella Bird, the rector of the day's daughter, caught them at it and was offered a black silk dress as 'hush-money'. However, her morals too were questionable, as she both accepted the dress and then also 'split' on them. Dr Proudlove, the local doctor who also once surprised the villains, narrowly escaped being knocked on the head. Just in time he was recognised as the doctor who cared for the cave-dwelling families, so they left him unmolested.

John Wesley made several visits to the village and in the 1760s preached on Church Bank and in the tithe barn which has now disappeared, as has the cottage where William Dean, known as the Tattenhall wizard, lived in the 19th century. The local children feared having one of his spells cast upon them. Another thing to fear was the ghost of a headless woman who sat after dark by the Pool Head Field gate on the Chester Road. An old couplet runs:

'Coom thou yarly, coom thou leet
Be weer of the Buggin at the Poo Yed Geet.'

Latterly the Wakes festivities, which survived until the beginning of the 20th century, took place on the Flacca field where now the sports pavilion, war memorial, and the 1970s squash centre stand. During the 1920s an unusual kind of tug of war challenge event took place on the

213

Flacca field. Each team consisted of five large Shire horses with their riders holding the rope. Tattenhall team, who usually won, used to practise by pulling against a pear tree!

There are now approximately 3,000 people living here. In 1763 there were only 692 inhabitants living in 149 households, but then came the Shropshire Union Canal which brought jobs and small industries. Next came the railway. Tattenhall actually had two stations, one on the Crewe/Chester line and the other on the Whitchurch/Chester line. This meant that businessmen from as far away as Liverpool could live here and yet easily reach their offices. It is said that one 19th century stationmaster would not let the train depart if he heard a commuter's pony and trap hurrying along the road. Neither station exists now but the canal is much frequented by pleasure boats.

There are many old houses with strange names in and around Tattenhall, but one of the strangest to modern ears must be Russia Hall on the outskirts in Frog Lane. This originally moated house is now falling into disrepair but used to contain, in a room in the roof, a 7 ft long mangle, weighing 15 cwt and worked by a handle turning an enormous roller by means of a leather belt. However, the last tenant said that no maid had been asked to use it for at least four generations!

The majority of Tattenhall families now earn their living outside the village but Calypso soft drinks firm has a factory here, employing approximately 70 people. Some of the water comes from the factory's own well. There are also many small industries mushrooming in and around the village.

Thelwall ✤

'In the year AD 923 Edward the Elder founded a cyty and called it Thelwall'. So reads the legend on the gable end of the 17th century Pickering Arms. In fact, the Anglo-Saxon Chronicle records that he ordered the burh (a fort, mistranslated as cyty) at Thel Wael to be repaired and manned as a defence against the Danes.

Thelwall seems always to have been a crossing point of the Mersey – a Bronze Age hollow log boat was found in the area. Now thousands of vehicles cross on the M6 viaduct, a notorious hazard in foggy weather. However, you can still cross the water by the 'penny ferry' (a rowing boat). An Act of Parliament fixes the fare and compels the Manchester Ship Canal Company to maintain a daily ferry, once costing one old penny, then one new penny and now eleven pence, to take passengers across to Thelwall Eyes, once rich farmland but now the dumping grounds for the silt dredged from the Ship Canal and a wildlife reserve for many migratory birds.

Before the cutting of the Ship Canal and diversion of the Mersey the area was often flooded by high tides. The cry used to go up, 'River's rising get your water', and bread had to be delivered in a pig trough floated on the floodwater. Salmon were abundant in this part of the river for many centuries, the first recorded fishing rights being granted to the Abbot of Evesham for three shillings annually by Sir Geoffrey de Dutton in 1068. In 1749 a salmon weighing over 19 lbs was caught at Last Quay Bridge, now Laskey Lane. A 16th century salmon fisher's home and smokehouse still stands in Ferry Lane close by Thelwall Old Hall, built in 1618.

At the corner of Laskey Lane is a fine example of a half-timbered black and white Cheshire house, dated 1655, with an ice house in the garden. Inside is a handsome plaster frieze dated 1658 and above a door is a falcon's cage. When the falcons were returned from hunting trips they were put in the cage and from there had access to their roosts in the roof rafters.

The much enlarged Little Manor Hotel was once the 17th century Thelwall Cottage and a suit of armour was found there during restorations. Almost opposite, of the same period, is Rachel's Cottage which had a well beside the garden path. There were tales of a beautiful young maid haunting the place after an unhappy love affair but the only Rachel known to have lived there was a housekeeper who lived to a ripe old age.

John Stanton built Greenfield House in 1780. It is now part of Chaigley school and can be seen from Bell Lane. He had built a gunpowder mill on Thelwall Eyes in 1755 and made great profits from the American War of Independence and the Seven Years War. After exactly 100 years it was destroyed by fire.

On the other side of the Bridgewater Canal, now the haven of anglers and pleasure boats, the Rylands family occupied several fine houses still standing in Half-Acre Lane. Sir Peter and Lady Rylands lived at Massey Hall, now a residential school. He was a noted industrialist, head of Rylands Wireworks in Warrington and first President of the Federation of British Industries. The Rylands commemorative window in All Saints' church depicts a wire drawer at his bench. They were local benefactors as were the Naylors, timber merchants, whose home, Cuerdon Hall, was said to have one of the most beautiful wooden staircases in the country.

Locally it was known as Oyster Shell Hall because the front was covered with oyster shells. The church lychgate is a memorial to the Naylor family.

The church, built in 1843 on the site of an earlier chapel (inside there is a warden's staff dated 1757) was enlarged by the Stanton family in 1856. The artist Eric Gill designed two of the stained glass windows and the copy of the Anglo-Saxon Chronicle hanging on the wall.

Thelwall, with a population of 3,000, is entirely owner-occupied and although largely a dormitory for Warrington and surrounding towns it is still very much a village community. This is most clearly seen in the annual Rose Queen festival. Thelwall is a pleasant place to live and people who leave frequently return here.

Thornton Hough

Thornton Hough is situated in the middle of the Wirral peninsula, eleven miles north-west of Chester and three miles north-east of Parkgate, which was the principal port for the mail packets during the 18th century.

The village was called Torintone in the Domesday Book. In the reign of Edward II it was held by Roger de Thornton, whose only daughter became the wife of Richard del Hoghe, hence the name Thornton Hough. The village has been designated a conservation area.

Thornton Hough has chiefly evolved through the work of two enterprising men. Joseph Hirst, a Yorkshire woollen manufacturer from Wilshaw near Huddersfield, came here in the mid 1860s to retire, and built his home, Thornton House, All Saints' church and vicarage, and a village school which is now the church hall. Two years later he built the village stores and a row of stone cottages named Wilshaw Terrace, all located in one quadrant of the village. An unusual feature of the parish church tower is a fifth clock face high on the north aspect, so that Joseph Hirst could see it from his bedroom window.

The second person to complete the major part of this purpose-built village was William Hesketh, later the first Viscount Leverhulme, who came from Bolton in 1887 to set up a new soap factory in Port Sunlight. He bought Thornton Manor, later extending this Victorian house into what is now a neo-Elizabethan stately home. The lovely gardens of the manor are open to the public several times a year for the benefit of charities. He also built the post office and village club together with the

216

undenominational school which is still in use today as Thornton Hough primary school.

The village has a most attractive village green of some 14 acres surrounded by half-timbered black and white houses, all in different styles. Thornton Hough is a model estate village of character and charm, bringing many visitors. The modern sandstone church built by Lord Leverhulme in 1906 in the Norman style is said to be one of the finest examples in the Wirral. It is now the United Reformed church and a monthly service is held jointly with All Saints' church. There is also a smithy with a spreading chestnut tree!

Many residents living in the village are employed by the Leverhulme estate and some in agriculture. The public house known as The Seven Stars is situated in the centre of the village and has been there since 1859. A small modern estate set in a rural background on the outskirts of the village has enriched the local community. Before the arrival of motor cars for all and the frequent bus service through the village, there was a good community spirit with a flourishing brass band, regular whist drives and dances, concerts by the local school children and a drama and operatic society.

One mile away is the tiny village of Raby in the parish of Thornton Hough. A striking feature is the Wheatsheaf Inn dating from 1611, a half-timbered thatched building and a favourite haunt for Wirralians on summer evenings. There is no church or shop and the school closed many years ago. However, this small sandstone area will give you an impression of how the Wirral peninsula looked many generations ago. So near to suburban areas, one is surprised to come across such a relaxed, rural setting.

Thornton-le-Moors 🌿

The wind of change which has altered so many villages since the Second World War has left Thornton-le-Moors remarkably untouched. The church and the cluster of houses and farmhouses that constituted the centre of the old village are all still there at the centre of Thornton-le-Moors.

Bypassed by the railways in the 1850s and by the A5117 trunk road in the 1930s, it has become a backwater hidden from the view of the motorists who pass only a few hundred yards from the village centre.

Low, flat, and liable to flooding, much of the area was heathland until the Enclosure Acts, while some of the lower-lying areas, adjoining the river Gowy, were only drained during the Second World War. Thornton was a 'closed' village with two or three major landowners controlling building development and restricting the number of cottages to meet the requirements of the medieval agricultural economy. This situation only changed in the 1940s when the local authority built houses on a field called the Pigeon Croft. Even so, the roads were named after the lady of the manor, Clementina Churchill Park Yates, who died in 1935 in her 80s.

The ecclesiastical parish, until late in the 19th century, was made up of the five townships of Elton, Dunham Hill, Hapsford, Thornton and Wimbolds Trafford, with Thornton church as its parish church. The church's foundation is known to go back to Saxon times. Recently, by chance, part of an Anglo-Saxon cross was found by a knowledgeable visitor when repairs were being carried out outside the church walls. The Domesday Book entry for Thornton records the existence of a church and a priest.

In the churchyard is a fine carved tomb of the Morris family who farmed at Laurel Farm in Elton, and many Frodshams from Elton Hall lie buried within the church. There is also the grave of Ann Gerrard, related to Rev Gerrard Perryn, who lived at Wimbolds Trafford Hall and was lord of the manor and minister of Guilden Sutton. Moses Lanceley also lies here, who farmed Glebe Farm in the 1920s – and who was sexton, shopkeeper and carrier, and ran the post office.

Originally the school was a religious establishment attached, literally, to the east end of the church. By the 1780s the school was in such a bad state of repair that the building was taken down. As Rev Barker put it: 'The only remains of this school are certain holes made inside the church porch by the children, which testify to the national love of doing injury, and defacing buildings and inscriptions.' The 'new' school became a county school on 1st August 1961 and was closed the very same day.

The new M56 slices through the heath, passing south of Thornton Green, farmed in the early 19th century by Charles Gamon, corn merchant. In the Middle Ages the villagers would pasture their animals on the green.

Tilston 🌿

Tilston as a village dates from Saxon times and it comprises the four townships of Stretton, Carden, Horton and Grafton. Ormerod describes it as 'one of the most important and populous villages in the barony of Malpas'.

By 1346 the local landowner was John Leche who lived at Carden Hall. His son became leech or surgeon to Edward III from which time the family fortunes increased. Carden Hall, a beautiful timbered mansion, was burned down in 1912, after which the family moved to Stretton Hall.

In a cave in Carden Park lived a hermit who went around the villages preaching to anyone who would listen to him; while another old man lived in a shack near the village and the local people visited him to be cured of warts.

Tilston evidently harboured smugglers who were said to follow a smugglers' walk across the ford to the Stone House, which is one of the oldest houses in Tilston. Did the smugglers end up in the stocks, still in the centre of the village?

The church dating back to the 14th century was the centre of village life and the custom of rushbearing still continues; so does the annual Wakes where the ox-roast takes place, the first slice being auctioned and sold to the highest bidder.

Originally there were four public houses in Tilston: the Cape of Good Hope, the Fox and Hounds, the Butcher's Arms (now an antiques shop) and the Carden Arms. The Carden Arms was run at one time by Teddy Carlton, who put on music hall shows in Chester.

Tilston school was opened in 1872 on land given by Mr Leche; attendance was erratic, children being absent helping with the harvest, crow scaring, stone picking, fruit gathering, picking acorns and black-berries. A new extension to the school was built in 1976.

Tilston once had a local poet called Hopley and most of the Hopley tombstones have a line or two of verse carved on them, no doubt taken from his poems.

Most of the cottages and houses in Tilston stand on the sites of older buildings. In recent years two new estates have been built, increasing the population. Farming still continues to employ a certain number and recently a milk factory was opened at Stretton and milk and milk products are delivered daily to supermarkets all over the country.

Tilstone Fearnall 🐝

Tilstone Fearnall is a small hamlet on the busy A51 road, 13 miles from Chester, bounded on the west by Tarporley and on the east by Alpraham. It has neither a shop nor a public house. Agriculture is the main source of income.

A large number of the farms and cottages were owned by the Tollemache family until the 1950s when heavy death duties took their toll and part of the estate was sold.

The church, dedicated to St Jude, was built by the Tollemaches in 1836. It was originally built as a chapel of ease to Bunbury parish church and because the lord of the manor wished to walk through his own entrance gates and straight into the church it was built from north to south instead of the more conventional east to west.

The school was built in 1840, also by the Tollemache family, who for many years were largely responsible for its upkeep. It was handed over to the Cheshire Education Authority in 1905.

The Shropshire Union Canal and the river Gowy run through the southern part of the hamlet. The old lock house was demolished in the 1950s and pleasure craft are now a familiar sight along the canal, taking the place of the old coal and grain barges which were pulled along by horses in days gone by. During the 1940 blitz a land mine fell just beyond the London Midland and Scottish Railway line. The boundary was

Tilstone Fearnall Primary School

220

changed in the 1950s and this part of Tilstone Fearnall is now in Bunbury parish.

The mill, which ceased to operate in the 1930s, lay empty for several years, then it became a centre for Boy Scouts from Crewe and has now been made into a very desirable residence.

The Milk Marketing Board opened the Cattle Breeding Centre in 1948 and although the foot and mouth outbreak of 1967/68 eradicated a lot of cattle on the nearby farms, the bull stud was saved. The full story is told in *The Scourge of the Cheshire Plain*.

The original Tilstone Hall was demolished in 1736, the present one being built in about 1870. The ruins of an old priory stand adjacent to the two farm cottages which were built in the 1960s. A ghost, dressed as a monk and about 10 ft tall, is reputed to have been seen in the district many times. This is how the dip in the main road at the end of Rookery Lane became known as the 'Haunted Hollow'.

Timbersbrook 🐾

Timbersbrook, a sleepy little hamlet, nestles under Cloud Hill, which is an irregular mass of millstone grit rising to 1,190 ft above sea level. It is appropriate that Timbersbrook should derive its name from the brook in the wood, because its water is and always has been the life-force of the community, providing power and attracting industry to within its boundaries.

The view from the top of the Cloud has always been a great source of pleasure to climbers who reach its summit. From it, it is possible to see the Cheshire Plain almost to the Mersey. Today it is a National Trust area and its unspoilt beauty should be assured. Around this outstanding beauty spot there is a long standing tradition of the Good Friday walk, going back over 70 years. It probably originated when the workers from the surrounding mills and pits had a holiday but little money and no transport.

The water which feeds the brook comes from springs below Catstones, which is a local landmark surrounded by legend. It has been said they are called 'Catstones' because they were an ancient place of worship to the Cat Goddess 1,500 to 2,000 years ago. It is however far more likely that they are so called simply because they resemble a cat sprawling on the front of the larger stone, with its front paws tucked underneath and its back paws tensed ready to spring. This image is not man-made but is a result of cracks and fissures in the millstone-grit rock.

During the 19th century the main employment of the area was quarrying. Timbersbrook had three quarries. This together with farming employed most of the local labour. At the beginning of the 20th century the water from the brook was used to power the silk mill, which became the Silversprings Bleaching and Dyeing Company.

Not only was the Silversprings works the provider of employment and wealth for the community, it was also the landowner and centre of its social life. Timbersbrook even had its own show, which started during the First World War when local people were given pieces of land to cultivate to provide food for the war effort. To spur them on and create an interest a show was held in the institute and cups were presented for the best cow, horse and vegetable. At its height before the Second World War, the company employed 230 people.

The factory closed in 1961 and later the property, including the farms, was sold by auction. The premises of Silversprings was purchased by Congleton Borough Council in 1973, who demolished the buildings in order to create a recreational area. The mill pond is fished by the Buglawton Trout Club and it provides many hours of enjoyment for men from the outlying areas.

Today the character of Timbersbrook is very different from 50 years ago when it was a thriving industrial community. There is one small engineering works on the site of the dye works. The water treatment plant has fallen into disrepair because water now comes from the reservoir. The inhabitants who do not farm commute to their employment. The Methodist chapel has become a dwelling house.

Timbersbrook is again a reflection of what is happening in the country as a whole; at the present time it is concentrating on the leisure and service industry and moving away from traditional industry.

Tushingham 🦡

Tushingham is a rural village, three miles from Whitchurch on the Cheshire boundary, the main A41 Chester to Whitchurch road running through. Comprised mainly of good grassland for dairy farming, this is a scattered district of houses in 1,292 acres of land and a population of approximately 185.

Situated in a field in Old Chad Lane is a place known as the Saw Pits. At one time this field had many pits in it, dug out when it was the site of a steam saw-yard. In the 1920s and 1930s the hollows where the pits had been were still clearly visible.

The chapel of Old St Chad stands alone in a field surrounded by its churchyard, which is still a burial ground today. Special services are held there during the summer months, one of them being the annual Rush-bearing Service. The chapel was rebuilt in 1689, and is still licensed for baptisms.

Tushingham church is situated on the Main Road and was erected in 1860 to 1863. The six bells were hung there in 1898.

The Bluebell Inn, which is a black and white building dating from 1600, was for many years a coaching house. It was the scene of an unusual animal haunting. A duck lived there who grew from a small furry creature to a lusty animal, running around and pecking people's ankles. It became such a nuisance that eventually it was killed and buried beneath the bottom step of the cellar. However, the step kept coming loose and the duck haunted the inn, continuing its ankle pecking.

At last, in desperation, it is said it was decided to hold the rite of 'laying it down'. This consisted of twelve parsons standing in a circle, each holding a candle and praying until the bird's spirit was small enough to be placed into a bottle. The bottle was bricked up in a wall and was discovered when the Bluebell was renovated recently. It was of course firmly bricked up again.

Tushingham school was built in 1896. Tushingham was one of the last places to receive electric power, and even in 1965 the school had no flush toilets, no hot water and only coke stoves for heating.

Tushingham Hall lies in the fold of the hills. It was given a facelift at the beginning of the 19th century, but its venerability is apparent from the inside. A reference in 1650 speaks of it as an 'ancient manor house'.

Upton-by-Chester ᨏ

As its name implies, the village is not far from the delightful city of Chester and, because of that proximity, wages a continuing battle against encroaching suburbia.

But, despite progress, many of the features common to village life over the past generations still survive. The plague stone is resited in the wall of the 1830 sandstone church, the village school erected in 1885 is still going strong and the village hall, next to the school but 40 years younger, now sports a brand new roof.

Up to the time of the First World War, the village pump (almost opposite the Wheatsheaf) was in use and was found to be operative in 1939 when it was checked to ensure that it could be used in an emergency.

Sporting interests were possibly catered for further down the road where there is a tiny natural amphitheatre, at the bottom of which is a stone trough about 4 ft by 2 ft. Although known as 'The Cockpit', history is reticent as to whether cockfighting actually took place there and the only sporting presence one sees in this pleasant shady retreat nowadays is the odd small boy trying out his BMX bike!

The village does have one modern facility that is rapidly disappearing – our own railway station, which has been resited in a more convenient location about a quarter of a mile down the line – a great boon to those residents who commute to Liverpool, some 17 miles distant.

The baker's shop used to be attached to the mill. The mill itself has been rescued from dereliction and, renovated and sailless, has become a family house.

Most villages like to boast of a unique feature, but Upton-by-Chester must be outstanding in that it possesses a superb, internationally known zoo. In its struggling early years it was known simply as Upton Zoo, but as its size and status increased it became known as Chester Zoo.

In 1930 Mr George Mottershead bought a large house at the edge of the village with the intention of turning the grounds into a 'zoo without bars', an ambition born when, at the age of eight, he was taken to an (unidentified) zoo where the animals were housed in cramped, smelly cages and he found their situation appalling. His vision of animals being given space and dignity didn't at first go down too well with some of the local residents – a zoo without bars, they felt, was a recipe for disaster, but Mr Mottershead's dedication and determination paid off.

Local people now live quite happily with the sound of wild animals just down the road. There has been the occasional escape – a tree porcupine managed to get three miles away, a tapir was recovered from an adjacent farm's sludge pit (but not before he had pulled in one of the rescuers!) and an ambitious flamingo decided one day that the local canal offered more excitement than its pool.

224

Utkinton

High Billinge at 586 ft was a Bronze Age fort. It is a tree-covered focal point above Utkinton, overlooking the Cheshire Plain towards Wales.

Utkinton Hall, the most historic building in the village, was the home of the Done family from before the year 1200 until the 17th century. A feature of the hall was the magnificent staircase, which was moved to the old rectory at Tarporley. The Hall, now only a quarter of its original size, was supposedly built around an oak tree, which was shaped into an octagonal pillar to support the roof. The Royalists battered its walls and succeeding generations built them up, though the Hall is much diminished since former times and is now a farm. In the 1930s 17 people were employed on the land, using three pairs of working horses, but nowadays few people are needed.

Utkinton is situated in what was the forest of Mara and Mondrum (Delamere) stretching from the river Mersey to Nantwich. The Dones were the master foresters for centuries. A horn, in existence since 1123, symbolised the right to the forestership. This horn is still in the possession of the descendants of the Done family. In 1617 King James I, after hunting in the forest, knighted John Done for his services.

The village always had plenty of wells and springs which rarely ran dry, the most famous one being the Whistle Bitch or Newfound Well in the forest. A pamphlet written in 1600, now in the British Museum, reports that the spring had medicinal qualities.

Many people came to seek cures here, up to 2,000 a day from Cheshire and all surrounding shires. A small lake was formed so that more people could bathe in the water, as many as 200 persons at a time.

Visitors to Utkinton will find no pubs today, though fascinating names like the 'Glove and Billet', 'Hook and Mitten', and the 'Buggin in the Bush', also known as the 'Titty Fal Lal', were well known names of alehouses in the past, and well used when the sheep drovers were passing through the village. Cock fighting and bear baiting were additional amusements for them.

Utkinton's schoolroom is unusual in that it is also the church. The present building was built in 1893 to replace a school and church which was built opposite in 1847. Was there a population explosion? In the years between the World Wars the church and school had particularly good choirs, which competed in many competitions in Chester, Sandbach, and Winsford. Villagers of today remember when they were in the choir, and the church bell rang when a competition had been won.

Today the village still has the church and school on the hill, the chapel across from the shrine, and the very popular post office and general stores. The village cannot support many jobs since farming has become mechanised, and the craftsmen are to be found in local towns and cities. Utkinton however still thrives, as transport allows people to travel farther afield to their places of work. Nowadays, when distance is no object, people choose to live in Utkinton because they are attracted by its position and beauty.

Walton 🦡

The village of Walton is situated on the A56, two miles south of Warrington. The Bridgewater Canal runs through the village and the Manchester Ship Canal and river Mersey are to the north.

The village is recorded as early as the 12th century, but grew from the purchasing of the estate by the Greenalls, a local brewing family, when a Hall, church and school were built, along with many dwellings. The estate remained in the possession of the Greenall family until 1941, when part of the estate known as Walton Gardens, was sold to Warrington Corporation and is now a well known beauty spot.

The church of St John the Evangelist, likened to a small cathedral, was built at Sir Gilbert Greenall's expense, costing £10,000, and was consecrated in 1885. Decorated Gothic in style, it is built of Cheshire red sandstone. The spire forms a conspicuous feature of the landscape for some distance. The church contains some fine stained glass windows and a superb reredos of oak.

The churchyard contains graves of the Greenall family and their retainers. In an unmarked area lie the bodies of navvies and their families who died in the smallpox epidemic during the construction of the Manchester Ship Canal. To the right of the lychgate, estate cottages begun in 1912 are built of a smaller than usual brick, brought from Norfolk, but building was stopped during the First World War.

St John's Sunday school, formed in 1880, is still held in the parish room. The day school was built by Sir Gilbert and Lady Greenall for children of tenants of the estate. They paid the schoolmistress's salary, supplied milk to the students and provided food for the cookery lessons. The school has closed and is now a private residence.

Miss Parsons, the oldest inhabitant, recalls Walton as it was in her childhood at the beginning of the century. The village then consisted largely of estate workers and their families, including a shoemaker, coachbuilder, blacksmith and wheelwright. The blacksmith also rang the church bell and pumped the organ!

A granary was situated close to the Bridgewater Canal. This building contained the post office and the postmistress made deliveries on foot. The granary also sold provisions, horse fodder to the bargees and pig food. The pig food was supplied to the piggeries in Hough Lane to feed the famous Walton and Worseley herd; these large white pigs won numerous prizes nationwide and the strain was exported to countries as far apart as Lithuania, Mexico and South Africa. The piggeries were sold when the estate closed.

The local hostelry, the Walton Arms, was called the Bay Horse Inn until 1880. In 1892 a horse-drawn carriage service operated between the inn and Central Station, Warrington. The ale sold there was popular with locals, the carriage service and the horse-drawn packet boats, which stopped there.

In 1863 George Crosfield of Persil and Lever Bros fame, built himself a large country mansion in spacious grounds on Walton Lea. The house was demolished in mid 1920 but the remains of the garden can be found behind the Walton crematorium where the municipal plant nursery now stands.

Walton today retains an air of old world charm and is a popular area for recreation. The Gardens include a lake, greenhouses, bowling greens, crazy golf, pitch and putt, children's play area and a zoo. There is also a 70 acre municipal golf course and a pleasant circular walk around Walton reservoir.

Warmingham ꧁

Warmingham is a small village in the valley of the river Wheelock. The parish also contains the townships of Elton, Tetton and Moston.

The centre point of the village is the parish church, St Leonard's, with its 17th century steeple which remained unaltered when the present church was built – hence the local rhyme:

> 'Poor Warmingham, proud people,
> New church and old steeple.'

There had been a Norman church on this site, then a black and white

Tudor building, and in the churchyard there is a medieval cross dated 1298. Close to the cross is buried a famous inhabitant, John Kent, who lived at the Church House. He was known as 'Rebel Kent', having supported Bonnie Prince Charlie at the 1745 rebellion.

Some modernisation in the village has naturally taken place over the years – new private houses built, some council houses and elderly person's bungalows; the local inn The Bears Paw has been modernised and the old rectory is now a country club and leisure centre. However, the village school and school house, dating from 1839, still stand outwardly unchanged.

The old mill in the centre of the village is now an attractive and interesting craft centre. Formerly an old corn-grinding mill, it was later used to grind coconut shells for the modern plastics industry. The weir on the river Wheelock still flows, making a pretty picture below the churchyard.

There is a very old legend pertaining to the village and the surrounding hamlets, telling of how in Norman times a fierce dragon roamed the area, killing and eating small children. It was finally slain by Baron Venables of Kinderton in nearby Middlewich. The Venables Brass can be seen in Middlewich parish church, and one of the lanes passing by Warmingham is still known as Dragon's Lane to this day.

One remaining link with the past is the Warmingham Wakes festival which takes place on the first Saturday in May and involves the whole village. No longer does bear-baiting and cock-fighting take place as it did at the Wakes in the old days, but we now enjoy maypole dancing, tug-of-war, the crowning of the May Queen and a spectacular 'duck race' along the river Wheelock. In spite of many changes over the years, Warmingham is still a thriving and close-knit village, closely connected with farming and agriculture, although now many people living in the village work in such modern industries as computing, nuclear power and engineering.

Waverton 🐿

Waverton, spelled Wavretone in the Domesday Book 1086, is situated four miles south-east of Chester. It was largely a farming community, there being 14 farms, of which only five now remain, the greater portion of the old village being part of the Eaton estate. In the early 1700s there

228

was an inn opposite the church called the Lyon, and also the Black Dog on the main Chester to Whitchurch Road. The Lyon later became the White Horse and was demolished in 1865. Another pub called the Brown Cow was sited at the corner of Eggbridge Lane and the A41, but its licence was revoked in 1897. The Black Dog Hotel remains to this day.

The foundation date of the church of St Peter is not known, but it is probable that a church was here in Saxon times, which may well have been a wooden structure. The church was built of red sandstone taken from the nearby quarry. The Tudor doorway at the west end is notable for its square frame with curved shields of the Duttons and Hattons in the spandrels. Both corners of the frame are decorated with two headless figures, probably angels. Legend says that Cromwell's soldiers beheaded these figures during their purge of images from churches.

An architect of local fame was John Douglas, who was responsible for various buildings in the village – the Church of England school (now the village hall), farms in Guy Lane and Saighton Lane, as well as Church House Farm and various cottages rebuilt for the Grosvenor estate for the first Duke of Westminster.

In 1662 Jonathan Barker left £2 10s, while in 1702 Elizabeth Dutton left 'to the Poor of Waverton' the interest of £30 'to be paid on New Year's Day for ever'. In 1706 Richard Ralphson left the sum of £5, 'the Interest to be paid out in Bread to be distributed at Easter and Christmas yearly for ever'. The interest from these legacies, and the Sarah Bevan Charity, is still, to this day, distributed to the needy in Waverton.

The Ellesmere and Chester Canal built in the 18th century cuts across the village and is spanned by many bridges now listed as being of historic importance. The original Eggbridge was replaced in the 1930s because of the increase in traffic. The mill on the side of the canal is being converted into living accommodation and was formerly a very busy spot. The barges or 'flats' as they were called, were used to carry corn from the farms along the canal to the mill, where it was ground. The mill later became a trading centre and later still a marina and caravan centre.

Built in 1840, the railway provided better transport and easier movement of goods into the district and of farm produce to the towns. Sadly, on 2nd July 1971, Waverton was to experience a tragedy when a special train conveying school parties returning from North Wales was derailed, resulting in the deaths of two children. Hot weather had caused the track to buckle.

Waverton today has organisations which cater for everyone, from children from under three years old to the over sixties. There is an active

Women's Institute founded in 1925 and there is also a Men's Institute. There are modern shops and a new village green, a doctor's surgery and community centre.

Weaverham 🥀

Signs of a probable Roman road have been dug up over the years through the middle of Weaverham. The ancient road of Peytefynsty follows the route of the A49 to the west of the village. This road divided the forests of Mara and Mondrum, now known as Delamere.

Evidence of an Anglo-Saxon village can be seen in front of Hefferston Grange, a Georgian brick house, formerly a grange of Vale Royal Abbey, and where a Georgian ice house can still be found. During the Civil War Parliamentarians plundered Weaverham. Excavations in the churchyard in the 1930s found about 50 human skeletons, each having a large hole in the forehead. It was thought that these bodies might have been a mass execution from the Civil War. The last battle of this war took place at Winnington Bridge on the borders of Weaverham.

Weaverham grammar school, a low sandstone building, founded in 1638, was reputed to have previously been used as the court house of the abbot of Vale Royal, and from it an old lane led to the prison near the High Street.

The beautiful 15th century tower of St Mary's parish church can be seen from all points of the village, and from it a splendid peal of bells rings out each Sunday. The church was mentioned in the Domesday Book (as were the Salt House Meadows and possible salt workings).

A carved stone slab, found in the churchyard, is thought to be of pagan origin. This is now mounted and can be seen in a side chapel. In the late 19th century a Virgin's Club met yearly in the old thatched cottage in West Road. The members wore white and marched to a service in the church, followed by a meal in the Star Inn.

Weaverham Wakes was held in the spring. Fig pie was eaten Sunday, furmenty on Monday and pancakes on Tuesday.

The square in the centre of the village, between two pubs, was known as 'Parliament', where people met to gossip, and a few yards up the street a double maypole marked the market place.

Weaverham people are known as Russets, (named after a local apple), as in the old ryme 'Weaverham Russets, Crowton Crabs, Norley Gawbys, Acton Good Lads'.

One village character was Captain Hatton, who was responsible for the law on hanging being changed. The old law stated that a man should be hanged for one hour and his body given to his friends. Captain Hatton was arrested and hanged for piracy at the beginning of the 19th century. But he inserted a silver tube into his throat and survived. The law was then reworded that 'a man shall be hanged by the neck until he be dead'.

Poplar Cottage, a 17th century thatched cottage in the centre of the village, has a room on the ground floor called the 'Birth Chamber', where village mothers could enter by an outside door to give birth to their children. This followed an old superstition, that to rise in the world a newborn child must first be carried upstairs.

It is interesting to note that Weaverham well was an open spring which never ran dry. It was the only source of water for some houses well into the 20th century, and was credited with healing powers. It was believed that any visitor who drank the water, was bound to return.

Whitegate & Marton 🍃

The villages of Whitegate and Marton have, since 1988, been combined officially by the Boundaries Commission. Both villages grew by providing for the needs of their biggest houses, Vale Royal on the site of the largest Cistercian abbey in England, Cassia Lodge, Daleford Manor, Abbotts Moss and Marton Hall, formerly Marton Grange.

By 1881, so the census tells us, there were farm labourers and salt boilers, there were blacksmiths, joiners, bricklayers, shoemakers, a basket maker and even a couple of grocers. There were eleven children between the ages of one and 18 years living with their parents in Bark House, one of the larger farmhouses. Such large families were not rare and created a need for schooling, the boys using part of the Church Mews and the girls a small building nearby.

Robert Nixon, a 15th century prophet, was born in Whitegate and foretold many happenings, some of which apparently came true, as did his own predicted death 'in poverty surrounded by plenty', when he was locked in a closet at the Royal Court and forgotten.

At Beauty Bank is the Plough Inn, but gone are the Black Dog and the Rifleman, where in 1870 the Dowager Lady Delamere saw such unseemly goings-on she forced its closure!

The church of St Mary dates back to the 16th century. It stood opposite a white gate which led up to Vale Royal and which gave its name to the village. A Methodist chapel was opened in 1878 and a Sunday school room was added seven years later. In 1895 the Parish Council decided to hold its meetings there and has done so ever since.

The village green hosts an annual fete when the maypole dancers weave their intricate patterns and when visitors and residents past and present gather together in a scene of timeless beauty. The Church Mews and the recreation room by a clump of trees known as the Beeches are places where village functions are held.

Today farming is still an important part of village life, though with modern methods fewer people are employed. ICI is a major industry in the area and some of their employees live in the parish. The village itself has a flourishing agricultural machinery business, a dealer in fine antiques, a firm of builders and a garage which evolved out of a blacksmith's shop. At the top of Cinder Hill is the post office and store, opposite which is a seat presented to the village by the Women's Institute in 1967.

The Forestry Commission has an extensive tree nursery where the staff will talk lightly of planting six million trees in the spring. Sand extraction has left Marton with three new lakes, one for fishing and one for water skiing, but all three attracting large numbers of ducks, geese and other birds. In a few years young trees will have grown and the sand workings will be just a memory. Lakes long established are New Pool by the church, Rookery Pool and Pettypool, which is designated as a Site of Special Scientific Interest.

Whitley 🦢

At various times known as Over and Nether Whitley, Whitley Superior and Inferior, and now as Higher and Lower Whitley, the village name stems from the Anglo-Saxon lea or meadow, and white, probably from blossom or the bark of silver birches. Just off the busy A49 between Northwich and Warrington, and without one obvious centre, Whitley has houses clustered round the pond or Town Pit, the three pubs, the village church and Methodist chapel, and it retains its rural character.

The church of St Luke is an ancient foundation of uncertain age, but is thought to have been rebuilt on an earlier site in the 16th century by a member of the Touchet family, who were local squires up to the end of the following century. It has a particularly fine roof with richly carved oak hammer beams, the origins of which are a fruitful source of discussion and argument – at the moment public opinion favours a Continental

232

origin. The Methodist chapel dates from 1802, and is built on land purchased for two shillings! It is believed to be the oldest Methodist chapel in regular and uninterrupted use in Cheshire, and is unusual in having terraced seating.

A further religious link is the Quaker burial ground, separated from the meeting house at Frandley by several miles. The land is thought to have been given by a local family named Starkey (the oldest recorded burial is that of John Starkey in 1657), because at that time Quakers were refused burial in consecrated ground.

Whitley was affected by the events of the Civil War with both factions either passing through or camping for nearby battles. Cromwell is reputed to have watered his horses at a pool on a farm, known today as Crimwell Pool. Likewise the Chetwode family, who followed the Touchets as landowners, are commemorated in a local landmark, the Chetwode Arms. Now a draw for both locals and visitors as a pub, the building has been in existence for at least 300 years, and is conveniently near the church for the old custom of 'roping' to take place there. After a wedding, the way of the happy couple was barred by a rope, released only on payment of the price of a good drink. A photograph exists of this ceremony as recently as 1968.

Despite the gradual disappearance after the Second World War of the small shops and post offices, the smithies and wheelwright, the mill and other signs of self-sufficiency, Whitley retains its primary school (after a battle), and is still essentially an agricultural village with many farms and agricultural contractors, and even a herbalist. Just as the farms have diversified over recent years with fewer dairy herds, less hay, but more silage, intensive stock rearing and oil seed rape, so have the occupations of the inhabitants grown more varied. With a decreasing farm workforce and the easier access of modern roads, many residents travel to nearby towns and even as far afield as Manchester and Liverpool.

Wildboarclough ✏️

The 24th May 1989 is a day that will never be forgotten by the villagers of Wildboarclough, when vast devastation was caused by a flash flood sweeping through the valley. The early afternoon turned black as night as a tremendous thunderstorm approached. Torrential rain completely overloaded the Clough brook. The raging waters rose high up the bank across the road, uprooting trees, sweeping away stone walls, destroying bridges, and carrying cattle miles along the valley. Trout and frogs were strewn across the road when the floods subsided and a dead lamb was discovered mangled in a tree. The postman arriving to collect the late afternoon mail was unable to do so as the post-box had completely disappeared and has yet to be found! Not since 1930 has such a storm devastated the village, causing more than a million pounds worth of damage. There are earlier records of such deluges, suggesting that Wildboarclough is aptly named 'the wild stream in the valley'.

Unlike most Cheshire villages Wildboarclough, remotely situated on the Pennine foothills, has deep sheltered valleys and bleak upland moorlands. In the 15th century the land was owned by the Stanley family (later Earls of Derby) and was only gradually brought into occupation, with the farmsteads remaining few and scattered. With the coming of the textile revolution in the 18th century and the need for water power, the Clough brook in a narrow section of the valley attracted George Palfreyman over the border from Staffordshire. Around 1800 he established the Crag Works for calico printing. Crag Hall for his own residence, and several cottages for the workers.

The advent of steam-power inevitably led to the decline of water-powered rural industry and the closure of the works about 1860 brought about a dramatic fall in the population of the settlement. Cottages stood empty and many smallholdings, whose owners had relied upon taking in lodgers to supplement their incomes, were abandoned. When the Earl of Derby visited this eerily silent and neglected outpost of his estates he decided upon considerable renovations. Crag Hall was refurnished for use as his occasional residence, farms were reorganised into viable holdings, cottages rebuilt and the works repaired and used as a workshop, store-house and office for the estate. He also erected St Saviour's church in thanksgiving for the safe return of his five sons who had served in the Boer War.

Most of the works buildings were demolished in the 1950s, leaving few reminders of the industrial past, but one three-storeyed wing continued in use as the village post office until 1979 – reputedly the largest village post office in England. This building is now a private residence but outside, happily, the old red telephone box remains, one of the few preserved in East Cheshire.

Pubs in old Stanley estates tend to be called 'Stanley Arms', 'Derby Arms', or 'Eagle and Child'. One of the last (no longer licensed) stands in Wildboarclough overlooking the Dane near Gradbach. The emblem refers to a legend that an ancestor was found as a child in an eagle's nest

– in one version have been placed there to trick a wife into adopting her husband's bastard.

There are thin seams of poor quality coal under the hills, some only about two feet thick. These were last worked about 50 years ago by miners lying on their sides to attack the face. The earlier workings, by 'the Old Man', are unmapped, but even the charted portions show that the seemingly solid hills are tunnelled like cheese. A ventilation chimney is still a prominent landmark on the Congleton-Buxton road.

Today sheep farming is the main industry in Wildboarclough, and a sheep sale is held in the village every autumn.

> There once was a man from the Clough
> Who said: 'I have had quite enough!
> From Wincle to Sutton
> There's nothing but mutton,
> And I'm heartily sick of the stuff!'

Willaston 🌿

English villages have always been known for performing strange rites, but Willaston's is amongst the strangest. In mid summer they go a-worm charming! It is quite a recent pastime and only dates back to the 1970s.

In June each year the gates of the primary school are thrown open for the village fete and, armed with garden forks, 100 villagers, each accompanied by a 'gillie', vibrate the ground for worms. The arena is roped off into metre square patches and during half an hour of frenzied activity worms are charmed. They may not be dug up for they have to be persuaded that it is raining, yet water may not be used. Indeed there are strict rules, and just in case anyone at the World Worm Charming Championships cannot read English, these rules are available in 31 languages.

One aspect of worm charming is that it has universal appeal. People simply cannot resist coming to watch and hence the success of Willaston's Summer Fete. The money raising skill of a small group of people has led to a very successful Community Association. There is a village magazine and money from the fete is used to fund many projects. Plays are performed, bonfire night is celebrated, and at Christmas an outdoor carol concert takes place.

Much of the fabric of the village dates back over 100 years to the advent of the railway in Crewe. In 1882 Frank Webb insisted that his men should live no more than two and a half miles from the railway works. The present Community Association has supplied money towards renovating the public amenities from this period. The bowling green has been reclaimed from a wilderness and the Methodist church hall is being refurbished.

Much of what happens in Willaston is down to 'Willie Worm'. He has a logo that appears on mugs and T shirts. At the end of an afternoon's charming, two trophies for the most worms and the heaviest worm are awarded. That night a small ceremony takes place. After the birds have gone to roost, the worms are returned to the ground ready for next year.

Willastonians in the past had an identity crisis. Indeed for hundreds of years the name of the village was uncertain, being variously known as Wigstanton, Wisterson and Wilavestune. Additionally the hamlet was not even technically a village at all until 1965 when St Luke's church was dedicated. However, now the people are quite sure who they are – worm charmers extraordinaire!

Willaston-in-Wirral 🪲

This village in the heart of Wirral was first mentioned by name in 1230. Although not recorded as a settlement in the Domesday Book, it gave its name to the Hundred of Wilaveston, or Wirral. When the hundred comprised both the peninsula and the townships right up to the city of Chester, the hundred court was held here.

The substantial farmhouses built around the village green in the 17th and 18th centuries are of brick, with stone dressings, some incorporating older parts in half-timbering or stone. The most imposing is Wallaston Old Hall, with an Elizabethan-style façade, and still a much-loved home. The beautiful gardens are opened to the public in summer in aid of charity. The other farmhouses continued in use as such until after the Second World War, but today not one is a working farm. They are homes or businesses, and now the outbuildings too are being converted into dwellings.

The green forms a focus of village life, and was secured for future generations by registration in 1983. One picturesque event held there until recently was the Boxing Day meet of the Royal Rock Beagles, the oldest pack in England. The adjacent Memorial Hall is home to many local organisations.

Willaston was one of seven townships of the parish of Neston, until its own church was built in 1855. It became independent in 1865, with its own parish registers. The first burial entry was for Charity Taylor, a gypsy girl who died when camping nearby. For many years afterwards, her family ceremonially visited her grave.

Of the families from the large houses on the fringes of the village who provided generously for the church, and later the school and the village institute, the foremost was a Liverpool merchant, Duncan Graham of the Lydiate, who also paid for piped water to be laid on for the village. In 1980 his mansion was opened by the Home Farm Trust as a home for a number of mentally handicapped adults. They take a keen interest in local events, and their fund-raising activities are always well supported by the other villagers.

The windmill, the tallest in Wirral, which was built in 1800, once provided employment for up to 40 people, but has not worked since 1930. During the Second World War, it was a lookout post for the Home Guard. Now without sails, and converted into a private home, it is still the principal landmark of the village, and is the motif on the school badge, and on the guide posts of the village walks.

The first great change was the coming of the railway in 1866. Although only a single track between Hooton and West Kirby, it gave the farmers swift access to Liverpool and Chester, as well as the rest of Wirral. Milk could be sold directly, rather than as cheese, though the farms retained their cheese presses for the summer glut of milk. The line has now been converted into the Wirral Country Park, known as the Wirral Way, a twelve mile walk and bridleway. Hadlow Road station has been preserved exactly as it was in 1956 when the line closed.

Willaston has continued to expand as a commuter village, though not wholly dependent upon the car, as Hooton station is only a mile away. This new reason for the village's existence has caused a six-fold increase in population to over 3,000 over the last hundred years, and pressure for building land continues.

Wimboldsley

Wimboldsley is best described as a small Cheshire hamlet rather than a village, and is situated two miles south of Middlewich on the A530.

Formerly known as the Plough Inn, Wimboldsley's only public house was in 1881 run by a well known local character called Abigale Broad.

She was a kind hearted soul who was reputed to have one day taken pity on a poacher fleeing from the police. The police searched the pub, but to no avail, for throughout the search Abigale remained firmly seated on a large blanket chest and after the police departed, needless to say empty handed, Abigale arose and the poacher gratefully departed with his freedom.

The Wimboldsley estate purchased by the Verdin family incorporated the Plough Inn and after purchase the pub was modernised and renamed The Verdin Arms, a name which it has retained into present times. The five farms which made up the estate were all dairy farms and each and every weekday morning milk from the farms was delivered by horse and lorry in twelve gallon churns to Nestles, the Anglo-Swiss condensed milk company. On Sundays the farmers either made cheese or sent the milk by rail from the local station to Liverpool.

The local station, then known as Minshull Vernon station, was located on the Crewe to Liverpool line and the railway company built six cottages for their workers. The cottages were occupied by signalmen, pointsmen, plate layers and brakesmen, not to mention the station-master. The local policeman and schoolmistress resided as boarders in the cottages. All these dwellings are now privately owned and the station has been closed since 1946. The last passengers to depart from the station were the evacuees returning home to Liverpool after the war.

Several of the Wimboldsley farms are now privately owned, except a few which were bought by ICI and are used as experimental farms. The farms on the east side were originally owned by the Roylance Court family from the manor, the family having won the estate in a cock fight. A painting of the fighting cock was hung in a position of honour in the manor's hallway, as were the original 'silver spurs' worn by the victorious bird; these items remained on display until the death of Mrs Roylance Court in 1933.

A feature of the locality was the toll bar situated on the road from Middlewich; the charge for salt taken away from Middlewich if it was a 'wain' drawn by four horses or more was 4d, but if drawn by two oxen the fee was only 2d. Mr Yoxall was the toll keeper and lived in a house right up to the road at 'Bells Smithy'. His descendants are still farming in the area up to the present time.

No discussion of Wimboldsley would be complete without mention being made of the 'New Cut', as the locals call it. The Shropshire Union Canal joining Chester and Ellesmere to the Trent and Mersey was completed on 1st September 1883, 50 years after reaching Wardle. This passes through most of the farms and was cut mainly by Irish navvies. A

238

feature of the canal is the aqueduct where it passes over the A530, although regrettably this now fails to cater for the height and flow of modern day traffic.

The canal has seen a dramatic change in use. Now no longer the arterial route for the transportation of goods, it is undergoing major renovation and redirection in the leisure industry, with pleasure craft and converted barges abounding. The canal's main traffic is now in 'people' not 'goods' – the 'New Cut' has a 'new face', as does the quiet hamlet of Wimboldsley.

Wincle 🐟

Surrounded by the hills of the Pennines and on the outer fringe of the Peak District National Park, the village of Wincle nestles on the banks of the Dane valley. From the church and school down to the Ship Inn, houses and farms straggle along the main road or are dotted about on the nearby hillsides or on the wooded slopes down to the river Dane.

There was a church on the site of the present one in about the 11th century, when it was a chapel of ease. The present church was reconstructed in the mid 1600s, later modified by the Victorians in the 1880s. The school and the vicarage were built at the same time from the local sandy gritstone.

Wincle Grange, now a farmhouse, has close links with the church, as in the 14th century it was a Cistercian priory with, it is said, an underground passageway to the chapel of ease.

When Bonnie Prince Charlie rode out of Macclesfield with his army of faithful followers on his way south to capture the throne of England, he travelled through Wincle. He is said to have stopped at the Ship Inn, leaving behind his gun and other items. There is supposed to be a headless horseman who rides through the village and down the Dane valley on misty nights. Perhaps he was a lost supporter of Bonnie Prince Charlie, returning home after the defeat of the last battle.

The population of Wincle has dwindled over the years, being at present around 200 inhabitants. As the little watermills down by the river fell into disuse, the village's prosperity died, with little or no employment except on the farms. Today work is still to be found on the farms, well stocked with herds of milking cows and sheep brought down from the moors for lambing in the spring.

Winsford 🌿

Winsford has no mention in the Domesday book, but the parishes of Over and Wharton were listed. Much of its history and growth is rooted in the salt mining industry. Salt mining still flourishes today with the only working rock salt mine in the UK. Winsford Flashes is a local beauty spot, arising from land subsidence through mine workings and subsequent flooding by the River Weaver. Today the Flashes are used for marine sports.

Although parts of old Winsford have disappeared, there are still buildings of historical value remaining. One of the oldest houses in Winsford is Dawk House dated 1711, with the oldest house being Littler Grange Farm, part of which dates from the sixteenth century. Other buildings of interest are Brunner Guildhall, Verdin School, the old Free Library building and Church House Farm, formerly the medieval Blue Bell Inn.

Perhaps the most famous son is John Bradbury who was born in Winsford in 1872 and lived in the town until the age of 15. After moving away his career took him to the position of Chief Cashier at the Bank of England which he held when the very first issue of the old ten shilling and one pound notes was made. Both bore his signature, and consequently became nicknamed 'Bradburies'. John Bradbury never forgot the town of his birth as on elevation to the peerage he chose the name 'Lord Bradbury of Winsford'.

A local custom up until the 1960s was that of giving each child in the town a present of a bat and ball on Good Friday. The origins of this custom are unknown – other nearby towns and villages had never had such a custom.

Winsford today has grown up into a town which has expanded and taken on the new, but it still retains many links with its village past.

Winwick 🌿

In ancient times, to travel north through the bogs, mosslands and forests of the Mersey valley, it was necessary to ford the tidal river Mersey at Warrington and follow the trail through Winwick. Being of such strategic importance, it is not surprising to find within the parish a 3,000 year old Bronze Age burial barrow, a Roman road, one of the earliest

St Oswald's Church, Winwick

Christian burial grounds circa AD 700 and, of course, the beautiful church of St Oswald.

'Can you tell me where I can find the Winwick pig?' This question has been asked times without number of the residents. The Winwick pig, now looking very worn and weighed down by a heavy bell round its neck, is carved on the west wall of the tower, the oldest part of the church, next to statues of St Anthony and St Oswald. Legend has it that the church was to be built at the foot of the hill but, each night, a pig moved the stones to the top. This was seen to be an omen of such portent that the church was built at the top of the hill.

Dominating the village, its spire visible for miles around, stands this ancient church of St Oswald. The first church on the site was mentioned in the Domesday Book of 1086, but the first Christian monument was a Saxon preaching cross, the arm of which is displayed in the church.

St Oswald, King of Northumbria, was killed in the battle of Maserfield on 5th August AD 642. As he lay dying, it is said that, in his agony, he

241

scratched the soil. Where his fingers had touched, water appeared and, at the spot, a well was formed. It was discovered that the water of the well had miraculous properties curing people of illness and disease. In 1988 people of the village joined in a procession to the well, where a short open-air service was held under the surprised gaze of nearby cows and sheep.

During both World Wars, the large psychiatric hospital, where many villagers have worked, opened its doors to wounded soldiers, brought back from horrific conditions, to a more restful haven.

In those far-off days, there were whitewashed cottages, where afternoon tea in the garden was a speciality. A villager recalls, with nostalgia, the aroma of home-baked bread and floury scones mingling with the scent of roses and the cottage garden flowers.

Whilst 1870 marked the introduction of the first Education Act, there had been schools in existence for many years in Winwick. As early as 1547 there was a grammar school, which closed its doors in 1890 due to lack of pupils. On the corner of Newton Road and Green Lane stood the old school house. This house contained the girls charity school. The boys charity school was opened in 1815, housing the schoolmaster and his family as well as the schoolroom.

Today, most people travel to work outside the village but are pleased to return to its peace and tranquillity. Winwick remains unspoiled, surrounded by fertile land tilled by generations of farmers. The village has remained a rural gem amongst the modernisation all around.

Woodford 🎍

When the Danes invaded this area in AD 800 and destroyed the Roman city of Manchester, an earthwork was built along the Wydeford or Woodford border, in an effort to keep the invaders from going further inland. By AD 900 the Danes had been routed, and Woodford had played its part.

By the Middle Ages, Woodford was a prosperous agricultural area with large estates and many farms. These were eventually sold in the 20th century, many of the farms being purchased by the tenants. During these later centuries Woodford had been a peaceful rural community, with little interruption, save when during the Civil War the area was plundered by both Royalists and Roundheads. During the Jacobite Rebellion of 1745, the Highland army passed through Woodford en route to

Derby, and the inhabitants of Woodford lined the lanes to cheer as the Prince and his men passed by. However, Cumberland's men forced the retreat, and the area suffered much from the English looting, plundering and even murder.

The late 1780s saw the rise of silk weaving in Macclesfield, and Woodford's close proximity meant that outworkers were recruited from the area. It is said that 'weavers lived well on such things as porridge, thick-tol-lols, lob scone, barm balls, cheese broth, flour dip, fried onions, bacon and clear tea'. But the trade declined and was known locally as 'poverty-knocking'.

Not until 1873 did Woodford become a parish in its own right. By that date Christ church, built in 1841 by public subscription, had been erected on waste land formerly used for bear and bull baiting.

The 1920s and 1930s brought many changes to Woodford. New Hall Farm, dated 1630, was purchased by A. V. Roe for development as an airfield, in 1925. From small beginnings the factory, now owned by British Aerospace, presently employs 3,000 people, the majority living outside the area. Light aircraft, the famous Lancaster bombers, Shackletons, Vulcans, 748s and Nimrods have been extensively tested in the skies above. Currently the ATP and 146 airliners are being assembled.

The introduction of more modern amenities, electricity, street lighting, mains drainage and road widening made life easier and more houses were built. A bus service started at this time linking the area with neighbouring villages and towns. Around 500 dwellings stand today, a pleasing mixture of pre-war and the very old, enjoying unrivalled views of the countryside and the Derbyshire hills.

Woolston ✣

There were once two public houses in the village, the Horse and Jockey and the Rope and Anchor. Adjoining the latter was a wheelwright and joiner's workshop. Amongst other things he had farm carts and also repaired cart wheels. Children loved to see the red hot iron rim being fixed onto the wooden wheel and then being doused in water to shrink it to a perfect fit. How the completed wheel hissed and steamed! There was an annual visit of gypsies who stayed on the land across from the Rope and Anchor and they made use of the wheelwright to repair their caravan wheels.

Cooper's Pit and Longbarn Pit proved not to be bottomless and are now both filled in and built upon, but Spittle brook is still there with its sticklebacks and even kingfishers. It no longer passes through fields but through a very pleasant park. Bonfires are now organised by the Parish Council or the Park Rangers and they are much safer than they used to be. Farms are fast disappearing but on the eastern side of the village the mossland still grows some of the finest lettuce and celery to be produced anywhere.

The old schools have been replaced by new. St Peter's has been demolished and the C of E school is now the church hall of the church of the Ascension.

The walk down to the Ship Canal is still enjoyable enough but it is a rare sight to see a ship pass by. For an interesting hour or two the boys and girls of the village used to go down by the weir on the river Mersey and cross the footbridge to the Ship Canal. There they would watch the endless flotillas of ocean-going ships heading for Manchester, or downstream to the Mersey estuary. Many of them tasted their first oranges or bananas that were thrown to them from the ships by foreign sailors. The other bonus of going to the Ship Canal was to see Tom Wareing's wonderful display of cacti. Tom Wareing was the weir keeper on the river Mersey.

The Horse and Jockey was knocked down to make way for the slip road to the M6 motorway and the old Rope and Anchor has been replaced by a modern building. There are more houses, more shops, a clinic, a library, a comprehensive school, a leafy industrial estate attracted to the area by the proximity of the motorway, playing fields, a leisure centre and a swimming pool.

Although no longer a small tightly-knit village community, Woolston is still a splendid place in which children can grow up.

Worleston ✍

Worleston (two miles north of Nantwich) covers just over 1,000 acres. Roman remains and evidence of a Roman road were found near Reaseheath Old Hall in 1920.

Rookery Hall was built in the early 19th century (probably on the site of an older house) by William Hilton Cooke who owned a sugar plantation in Jamaica. It was sold in 1868 to Baron Wilhelm von Schroeder, son of the founder of Schroeder Wagg Merchant Bankers, whose subsequent alterations to the hall gave it the appearance of a

The Royal Oak Hotel, Worleston

German 'schloss'. Rookery Hall is now a luxury hotel. The Royal Oak dates back to c1730 and was a coaching inn.

Reaseheath Hall, once owned by the Wilbraham family, later by the Tomkinsons and subsequently passing to the Cotton family, became the Cheshire School of Agriculture in 1919. It is now the Cheshire College of Agriculture.

St Oswald's church was built in 1872 on land given by the Tomkinson family. There is a stained glass window at the east end in memory of George Edward Lynch Cotton, Bishop of Calcutta, who was drowned in the Ganges. His widow came back to live at Reaseheath Hall and worshipped at the church. All the brass in the church was given in memory of Rev Walter Hilyard, the first vicar. St Oswald's primary school was built in 1888. Centenary celebrations were held in 1988 when three old pupils (average age 90 years) planted a tree.

In the centre of the village is Hulse's shop, established in 1878, incorporating grocery, post office and village bakery. Dairy farming is still dominant. A stud farm and racing stables have recently been built.

245

Wrenbury 🦢

The earliest recorded mention of Wrenbury is in the Domesday Book of 1086. At that time, like much of south Cheshire, it was part of the lands held by William de Malbanc, who had come over with the Conqueror. A church is first mentioned in the early part of the 12th century, and in those early days it was in the charge of the monks who had settled at Combermere Abbey, some four miles away. The present building was erected about 1500 with stone from the nearby Bickerton hills. After the Dissolution of the Monasteries, which closed down Combermere Abbey, Wrenbury became one of the several daughter churches of the parish of Acton.

It is a typical Cheshire country church, though of course no two are alike. It was not built just as we see it now, though. Every generation has left its mark on the building somewhere. It still has 17th century box pews. The crests on the pew doors are not those of the people who sat there, but of the landlords. From an old seating plan it appears that a seat in the church went with the tenancy of a particular farm, so that if a family moved to a different farm in the parish they had to move to a different pew as well!

One unusual feature is the Whipper's Pew just by the door. It was the seat of the dog whipper, who was not there to keep dogs out, but to keep in order those that were in! For this he was paid five shillings per year, and received a coat and hat from the parish too.

All this time Wrenbury was a remote country village, and the people lived as country people had always done, rarely moving out of the parish except to go to the markets in Nantwich and Whitchurch. The centre of village life was the village green, which is still there. It was used for sports, the occasional visit of the dancing bear, even dancing to celebrate great events such as the battle of Waterloo.

At the end of the 18th century, the Ellesmere canal was built through Wrenbury. Until then everything had to go on rough wagons over atrocious roads. Every parish was meant to keep up its own roads, but this was rarely done efficiently. The canal made it much easier to trade with Chester, North Wales and the Midlands.

The railways came soon after, in the 1860s, when the line was built from Shrewsbury to the new railway town of Crewe. Now the village was much less isolated than before, and for the first time some of the villagers became 'commuters' to jobs in Crewe or Nantwich.

After the Second World War, the village doubled in size as more houses were built. As a result the village still has a school, a post office, petrol pumps, two shops and a hairdresser, as well as a pub and a restaurant, an occasional bus and a railway station! Recently, too, a pavilion has been built by the bowls green, tennis courts, football field and children's playground.

In the past Wrenbury was well served by a smithy, a butcher who slaughtered on the premises, a tailor 'who made the best breeches in Cheshire', a post office which at various times was sited in several of the cottages, two water-powered mills, and all the country trades without which no village could function. There were also two pubs in what are now houses by the green.

The canal, no longer used by commercial traffic as its builders intended, has a brisk trade in holiday craft every summer, when the village looks a bit like a holiday resort! Since farming is now so mechanised, almost all of those of working age have jobs elsewhere to which they commute, though there is a cheese factory and a cattle feed business nearby, as well as some newly built small factory buildings.

Wybunbury ༄ྀ

Wybunbury is in South Cheshire, roughly four miles south of Crewe and three miles south-east of Nantwich. It was a settlement established before the Norman Conquest and on early maps is shown as one of the most important places in Cheshire. The most common form of pronunciation nowadays seems to be 'Winbury'.

The church is dedicated to St Chad, first Bishop of Mercia who was canonised after his death in AD 672. Unfortunately, the site on which Wybunbury churches have stood is unstable due to the action of running sand, salt and springs. Five churches have been built on the site, only to be demolished as they become unsafe. Of the 15th century church only the magnificent tower remains – 96 ft tall and a landmark for miles around. While its solid construction has enabled it to survive, the tower has nevertheless required attention over the years to correct a tendency to 'lean'. In the 18th century 'as crooked as Wimberie steeple' was a saying throughout the county.

In 1833 James Trubshaw of Staffordshire built a new church and straightened the tower, by then nearly 6 ft out of true. The 'wonderful machinery' and 'secret inventions' he employed were actually no more

247

than digging into the foundations and lowering the subsoil. Half a century later the church was pronounced too dangerous for public worship and closed. Around 1893 another church was built. At the consecration a remark was made that 'Nothing but an earthquake will ever move Wybunbury church again'. Sadly, this confidence was misplaced – the church, the last on the site, was demolished in 1976.

A few years before, in 1968 the church was the scene of an amazing discovery when an iron chest, untouched for years in the tower, was opened. Inside were silver items dating from the 16th and 17th centuries: two chalices, a lidded tankard, tazzo, spoon, flagon and a private communion set. The Charles II tankard was later sold and the £10,250 raised was put towards a new church. This was built on a new site further along the main road and consecrated in 1978. When the tower itself was threatened with demolition, villagers formed a Trust Fund to save it.

A school was established next to the church in 1707, but by the mid 19th century, several schools existed. Under the terms of the Delves charity, 20 boys dubbed the 'Blue Cap Boys' were given free education and a coat and blue cloth cap. At the National girls school 16 girls received a gown and bonnet. The original boys Delves school was extended and reopened as the village primary school in 1965. The girls school then became the parish rooms, now the village hall.

The annual custom of Wybunbury Wake was referred to as 'the season of idleness and drunkenness and dissipation'. An 1819 poster advertises races at Wybunbury Wake – a two mile race for 1lb of tobacco, a race for lads who had to grab a hat from a greasy pole, a donkey race etc. Fig pies were made and rolled down the church bank, although on one occasion they were hurled from the church tower. Much beer drinking went on. Eventually, like wakes elsewhere, rowdyism got worse. Men charged with crimes such as horse stealing would plead they had 'been at Wybunbury Wakes'. The Wakes' popularity declined after 1880 when a man was killed in a brawl at the neighbouring Boar's Head Inn.

Wybunbury was by then a large village with farms and tradespeople such as a brick and tile maker, bootmaker, bricklayer, joiner, saddler and grocer. There were three public houses, the Swan Inn, the Red Lion and the Black Horse, now a private dwelling. Former trades have gone but the village still has a post office/store, butcher, garage, dairy and grain merchant.

As well as the tower, Wybunbury is equally famous for the nature reserve located to the north of the village. Wybunbury Moss covers 26 acres. In the centre is a deep and rather dangerous hollow filled with water on which floats a 'raft' of peat covered in sphagnum moss. Pine and birch trees and other plants add to this unique habitat – the home of many rare species of plants and other wildlife.

Index